LAND ROVERS
In British Military Service
Coil sprung models 1970 to 2007

James Taylor and Geoff Fletcher

www.veloce.co.uk

First published in August 2018 by Veloce Publishing Limited, Veloce House, Parkway Farm Business Park, Middle Farm Way, Poundbury, Dorchester DT1 3AR, England. Tel +44 (0)1305 260068 / Fax 01305 250479 / e-mail info@veloce.co.uk / web www.veloce.co.uk or www.velocebooks.com. . ISBN: 978-1-787112-40-7 UPC: 6-36847-01240-3 © 2018 James Taylor and Veloce Publishing. All rights reserved. With the exception of quoting brief passages for the purpose of review, no part of this publication may be recorded, reproduced or transmitted by any means, including photocopying, without the written permission of Veloce Publishing Ltd. Throughout this book logos, model names and designations, etc, have been used for the purposes of identification, illustration and decoration. Such names are the property of the trademark holder as this is not an official publication. Readers with ideas for automotive books, or books on other transport or related hobby subjects, are invited to write to the editorial director of Veloce Publishing at the above address. British Library Cataloguing in Publication Data – A catalogue record for this book is available from the British Library. Typesetting, design and page make-up all by Veloce Publishing Ltd on Apple Mac. Printed in India by Repika Press.

LAND ROVERS
In British Military Service
Coil-sprung models 1970 to 2007

James Taylor and Geoff Fletcher

INTRODUCTION

After we had finished our book about the leaf-sprung Land Rovers in British Military Service,* it seemed only logical to carry on and produce a follow-up that would cover the coil-sprung models. So we did, and, nearly three years later, here it is.

We have deliberately followed the same format as before, with a chapter devoted to each major type. Within each chapter, we have a brief overview, descriptions of major variants, and then lists of all known examples, plus relevant technical specifications. We recognise that we may have omitted the odd vehicle purchased for trials or similar purposes. This time, we have put our explanations of serial numbers and chassis numbers into appendices for what we hope will be greater convenience.

This book starts with the first coil-sprung Land Rover product, which was the original Range Rover of 1970, and continues to the end of 2006. It covers the Land Rover Ninety, One-Ten and One-Two-Seven, their Defender successors, the first two generations of Land Rover Discovery, and the two experimental military Land Rover models that were developed in the same period – the Llama and the Challenger. It does not cover later Range Rovers or Discovery models, which all had air suspension rather than coil springs. We have also omitted the Freelander, as only a handful were purchased, and they were used in much the same way as the MoD uses many other commercial-specification saloons.

Although Defender production continued up to early 2016, we have deliberately not covered British military purchases of these vehicles in the last ten years. There are several reasons for this; not least being that many are still in service, and some are in use for sensitive projects. It is also true that many were standard civilian types with few, or no, interesting differences from ordinary showroom vehicles. Broadly speaking, then, our coverage ends with the demise of the Td5 diesel engine in 2006, so that the Defenders not covered are those with the 'humped' bonnet and Ford 2.4-litre or 2.2-litre engines.

It is worth adding a few further words of explanation here. We have included code names, where they are known, but have made a distinction between Land Rover's development code names (shown in standard type) and military code names (for which we have adopted the military practice of using all capitals). As for 'variants,' we have used the MoD asset codes as our guide. New asset code, therefore, equals new variant, although we are well aware that there were multiple other modifications, especially by the operating units themselves.

We are also well aware that the asset code definitions are not entirely consistent (so, 'litre' may be expressed as 'litre,' 'ltr,' or even 'L' for example). Rather than change them all to meet a theoretical standard, we have left them as they are in the records – although we have corrected a few obvious errors, such as 'T525' for Td5.

In cases where no dating information would otherwise be available – as, for example, with the 'unified' serials – we have included a date in the remarks columns of our tables wherever possible. These refer to the date a contract was placed or amended; delivery would have followed later. For local purchases, however, the only date available is the date into service, and this is what we have shown.

We have also used a few abbreviations for convenience. Two in particular deserve comment. One is LP, which stands for 'Local Purchase'. The other is N/K, which of course means 'Not Known'. When applied to chassis numbers, N/K means that the chassis number is not revealed in the MoD records we have been able to consult. So, a request for further details under the 'Freedom of Information Act' is unlikely to get any more information than we have already found!

We are pleased to acknowledge the help of many organisations and individuals in assembling the information that this book contains.

In particular, we are grateful to the following:

British Motor Industry Heritage Trust, Gaydon (BMIHT)
D&ES Policy Secretariat
The Dunsfold Collection, Dunsfold (DLR)
The Ex-Military Land Rover Association (EMLRA) and its members
Freelance Military Writers (FMW)
Jaguar Land Rover (LR)
The RAF Museum, Hendon
The REME Museum, Arborfield
The RLC Museum, Deepcut (RLC)
The Six Appeal Wheel Group
The Tank Museum, Bovington (TMB)

The Vehicle Specialist Museum (VSM)
Graham Archer
Andy Brend (AB)
John Carter
Roger Crathorne
Roger Conway (RC)
Ian Davies (ID)
Colin Dunford (CD)
Clive Elliott (CE)
Norman Hinchcliffe (NH)
Peter Hobson (PH)
Brian Mitchell (BM)Tim Neate (TN)
Tim Neate (TN)
David Payne (DP)
Carl Schulze (CS)
Richard Stickland (RS)
Robert Swan
Robin Taylor (RT)
Clive Westwood.

(Initials in brackets after a photograph caption can be decoded by reference to the list above; our own are represented by GF and JT respectively.)

Geoff Fletcher and James Taylor

An update on Volume One
Some extra pieces of information have arrived since the first volume was published and as a result the authors have produced an update. In addition there were one or two small errors which we have taken the opportunity to correct. You can view the update at: http://fmwuk.org/LRBMS_1.html

*British Military Land Rovers, Leaf-sprung Land Rovers in British Military Service, published by Herridge & Sons, 2015.

CONTENTS

1

RANGE ROVER

The Range Rover was developed in the second half of the 1960s to overcome the disadvantages of the Land Rover station wagon, combining its all-terrain ability with respectable road performance, and higher levels of passenger comfort. Its basic design was a five-seat station wagon, or estate car. Strong road performance came from the 3.5-litre, V8 petrol engine that Rover had bought from General Motors' Buick division in the mid-1960s. Improved ride comfort came from long-travel coil-spring suspension, while a permanent four-wheel-drive system allowed the use of lighter duty axles, which, in turn, improved ride quality. The vehicle had disc brakes all round, and a self-energising, ride-levelling system on the rear axle.

The Range Rover was introduced in June 1970 as a two-door model; however, customer demand had a major influence on its later development, and the vehicle gradually became a luxury car without losing its original dual-purpose nature. The model was gradually developed into a luxury car after 1981, and went through a number of changes. Those relevant to the military deliveries were the introduction of a four-door body in 1981, an automatic gearbox option in 1982 (the original three-speed was changed for a four-speed in 1986), a five-speed manual gearbox in 1983, fuel injection on top models in 1984, a 2.4-litre diesel engine in 1986 (2.5-litre from 1989) and a 3.9-litre petrol engine in 1989. From 1992, air suspension was available in place of coil springs. The last examples were built in early 1996, and the final year's production was badged as 'Range Rover Classic,' a name which is often wrongly used to describe the first-generation model in general.

More luxuriously equipped models were known from 1984 as Range Rover Vogue types.

Rover did some development testing of Range Rovers at the FVRDE trials ground in Chertsey, and one of the press launch vehicles (NXC 239H) was given an initial evaluation there by the military in the summer of 1970. There was further military evaluation of an unidentified early example in December 1970, probably at Solihull, but the first one to acquire a military serial number was 03 SP 51, which was purchased under WV8765 in summer 1971. The first official set of photos of the vehicle was not taken until 1973. It would seem that after arrival at MVEE, it was sent for evaluation with 22 SAS and did not return to Chertsey until 1973, when the first three production examples were delivered to that Regiment. Range Rovers were used in a variety of specialised roles by the UK armed forces.

Note: This chapter deals only with first-generation Range Rovers, which were coil-sprung (although air suspension was available on late models from 1992). It does not cover the second-generation or 38A models (1994-2001), the third-generation L322 models (2001-2012), or the fourth-generation L405 models (from 2012), all of which had air suspension.

Armoured

Armoured Range Rovers were used in Bosnia Herzegovina by senior military commanders and for VIP transport duties. The approved conversion on the standard-wheelbase model was by McNeilie of Wolverhampton, and it used heavier-duty Land Rover

NXC 239H was one of the press-launch vehicles, and as such, was really a pre-production example. It was given an early examination at FVRDE and used here during the visit of General (later Field Marshal) Michael Carver to MVEE in August 1970. (TMB)

Above: '19 RR 71' was mocked-up as a military radio vehicle for the Commercial Motor Show in 1970. (Land Rover)

Right: 03 SP 51 was probably the first Range Rover evaluated at FVRDE, and was supposedly examined with a 22 SAS order in prospect. (TMB)

One-Ten axles with plain steel disc wheels. The standard body specification incorporated twin side-hinged tail doors because the standard tailgate was too heavy to use when armoured; nevertheless, pictures exist showing supposedly armoured Range Rovers with the standard two-piece tailgate.

McNeillie also built an armoured Range Rover on the 110-inch wheelbase extended chassis, and examples of these were operated by the MoD Police for special duties (such as escorting nuclear weapons convoys) and carried blue lights and sirens. In the end-Chapter tables, SWB denotes an armoured Range Rover on the standard wheelbase, and LWB denotes one on the 110-inch wheelbase (and not the 108-inch wheelbase available on standard production models such as the Vogue LSE).

BRIXMIS

BRIXMIS was the British Commanders'-in-Chief Mission to the Soviet Forces in Germany. Under a 1946 agreement, there was a reciprocal exchange of liaison missions in order to foster good working relations between the military occupation authorities in the two zones of East (Soviet) and West (NATO) Germany. There were similar arrangements with the French and US authorities in West Germany. In practice, both sides used the monitoring 'tours' to spy on each other's military installations, and there were many uncomfortable confrontations when observers were caught away from their prescribed routes.

By the start of the 1970s, BRIXMIS teams were using Opel saloon cars for these tours, but later took delivery of some Vauxhall Senators (UK-built Opels) that had been modified in the

Bearing the serial number UK 37 22 (which should read UK 37 ZZ!), this is an armoured four-door Range Rover that was attached to IFOR, the NATO-led Implementation Force in Bosnia-Herzegovina in 1995-1996. It was used for the transport of senior commanders and other VIPs, and was later allocated the serial DU 35 AA. (RS)

UK with a 4x4 system made by FF Developments. These provided a greater degree of off-road ability, enabling the teams to get closer to some of their targets of interest. From 1975, BRIXMIS bought a quantity of Range Rovers which gave even better off-road ability than the converted saloons. The last of these were delivered in 1985, but the vehicles had proved fragile and expensive to maintain, so later deliveries were of Mercedes-Benz G-Wagens.

There were at least 28 BRIXMIS Range Rovers. One, 55 XB 88, is undated, and, although *Soldier* magazine linked it to the Trans-Americas expedition of 1971, this is probably an error. It is more likely that it had started life as the trials vehicle, 03 SP 51.

Four more were delivered in 1975, three in 1977, one in 1979, four in 1980, three in 1981, and four each in 1982, 1983 and 1985. One of the 1975 vehicles (56 XB 89) was converted by 14 Field Workshop REME to a state review vehicle for a visit by the Queen in May 1978. The last BRIXMIS Range Rovers were not struck off until 1992, although BRIXMIS itself ceased operations in 1990.

The vehicles had a number of special features, including reinforced roofs with an electrically-operated Webasto sunroof; this acted as an observation hatch, and the roof could be used as an observation platform. Some vehicles seem to have had a self-recovery winch mounted at the front at delivery (and others may have been so fitted after delivery). On early vehicles, this was a capstan-type, driven from the nose of the crankshaft. On later ones, a Warn 8000 electric winch was fitted. Some, and possibly all

This BRIXMIS Range Rover had just performed a spectacular 'yomp' for the camera. The picture shows the blacked out rear glass and the special roof with its observation hatch. All these vehicles were equipped with self-recovery winches. (Web source © unknown)

of the BRIXMIS Range Rovers had additional lights front and rear to enable the vehicle to simulate East German civilian cars. These could be used in place of the vehicle's standard lighting, and were intended to alter their lighting 'signature,' so that they were less recognisable in the dark as Range Rovers (which were otherwise almost never seen in East Germany).

Under the terms of the agreement with the Soviet forces, the vehicles had to be clearly identified, and crews had to wear military uniforms. However, these vehicles never wore their military serials but instead carried a special identifying plate with a union flag symbol and an identity number (such as 3 or 5).

Ex BRIXMIS vehicles

The 247 Provost Company Royal Military Police – attached to the Berlin Brigade – used ex-BRIXMIS Range Rovers. Those known include 56 XB 90, 56 XB 91 and 57 XB 46. Early examples were two-door models. These vehicles were normally painted white with a red stripe and Military Police identification markings.

Other units also received ex-BRIXMIS vehicles. They included 43 Transport & Movements Squadron, Royal Corps of Transport which, it is assumed, carried out training for BRIXMIS. 62 Transport & Movements Squadron, Royal Corps of Transport, also received some examples after their time with BRIXMIS and these were used for VIP Transport.

RAF vehicles

A number of Range Rovers joined the fleet of the RAF Provost & Security Service – the RAFs police. These typically carried an RAF police sign and a rotating blue beacon on the roof, and were painted white. Some had a red side stripe on each side and an RAF crest on the doors. There were both two-door (such as 40 AJ 89) and four-door (such as 84 KF 69) models.

57 XB 46 was delivered to BRIXMIS in 1977, but was pictured here in later years looking rather more standard and in use by the Berlin Military Police. (GF)

Left: 40 AJ 89 was a two-door model with the 1980 specification that was delivered to the RAF P&SS around 1979. (GF)

Right: 84 KF 69 was a 'Tri-Service' order, a four-door that also joined the RAF's P&SS fleet. (GF)

45 AJ 49 was one of two special review platforms for the RAF. (Huddersfield Land Rover Centre)

RAF review

The RAF Provost & Security Service also ran two Range Rovers as review vehicles. Both were delivered as review vehicles, which suggests that the bodies were built by a commercial company before delivery and not by RAF workshops. Both had the same body design, although 45 AJ 48 was painted in RAF Blue and 45 AJ 49 was painted gloss black.

RNAS ambulance

The 110-inch wheelbase version of the Range Rover chassis was developed in the early 1970s primarily to give enough length in the body for a stretcher to be carried. Among the companies that offered ambulance conversions was Wadham Stringer, of Waterlooville, in Hampshire. This company was awarded the contract for a quantity of Range Rover ambulances for the Royal Naval Air Service. The earliest examples seem to have been delivered in 1977, and the final ones in the 1980s, but these vehicles did not remain in service for very long and were withdrawn progressively from approximately the early 1980s. The bodies were constructed of GRP panels over a light alloy framework.

SAS

22 SAS acquired a number of Range Rovers from late 1972, primarily for use by the Regiment's counter-terrorist squadrons. Further batches were purchased right through until the end of first-generation Range Rover production in 1996, changing to four-door models from the mid-1980s approximately.

These Range Rovers had dual identities, and were allocated military serial numbers, but also had civilian plates, so that they would attract less attention on the roads. They retained standard civilian colours, and had modifications which allowed troopers to be carried on the outside of the vehicle during an assault on a building or hi-jacked aircraft; an assault platform with ladders could also be fitted to the roof to enable assault teams to gain access to a terrorist stronghold at high level if necessary.

The suspension was also uprated and some vehicles had a Roll-cage inside the body. Some allegedly had run-flat tyres, and a split-charge electrical system with a second battery used to power communications equipment. Some supposedly had lighting

Above: The second RAF review vehicle, 45 AJ 48, was painted dark blue.

Above: The black vehicle is seen here during its service life, with an RAF police identification board at the front and weatherproof cover over the back body. (GF)

RNAS

Pictures of the Lomas-bodied ambulances in Royal Navy service are rare, but this one shows 62 RN 46 in the yellow characteristic of the ambulances used at RNAS stations. (RT)

modifications to provide infra-red headlights when all other lights were extinguished, and some probably had secure weapons lockers in the rear or in the passenger cabin. Some examples were equipped as command and control variants for the operation commander.

TACR-2

Conversion specialists, Carmichael of Gloucester, developed a three-axle Range Rover chassis in the early 1970s as the basis of a fast-response fire tender. The trailing axle was undriven. The conversion had Land Rover approval, and was normally sold on the civilian market with Carmichael's own bodywork under the name of Carmichael Commando.

The MoD chose this chassis as the basis of an airfield crash-rescue tender, but ordered bodywork to its own design. The vehicles were known initially as TACR-2 types (the original TACR Land Rovers retrospectively became TACR-1 types), and three basic variants were delivered in the 1970s and 1980s. The first variant, delivered from 1977, was based on the two-door Range Rover body, and was converted to provide a four-door cab. The second variant, delivered from 1985, was based on the four-door body. The third variant, classified as a TACR-2A and delivered from 1988, had a number of differences, and had the injected derivative of the 3.5-litre V8 engine.

The specification called for a vehicle capable of carrying a four-man crew, with 200 gallons (900 litres) of pre-mix.

A four-door cab was required, and the vehicles had to have the standard RAF front crash bar for bursting through airfield crash gates. The initial development vehicle, built by Gloster Saro and delivered in 1974 or 1975, was later gifted to the RAF and became 31 AG 41. The four-door cab was created by fabricating new rear doors, and shortening the standard front doors. All doors had sliding glass rather than winding windows. The rear bodywork and roof were made of GRP. This was the 'Truck Fire-Fighting Airfield Crash Rescue, 2 Ton, 6x4 Mark 2, Range Rover.'

This prototype led to an order for 37 vehicles, and deliveries began in April 1977. All of these were also for the RAF, and carried serials 30 AG 92 to 31 AG 28. Most were delivered in IRR green (also known as NATO Satin Green) with a reflective yellow stripe, although many were later repainted in gloss red (Signal Red, BS381C, code 537). Two were allocated to the Queen's Flight, and were painted Royal Blue. Most TACR-2 models carried no spare wheel, because they rarely strayed far from unit workshops, but these two carried one on the roof due to the fact that they regularly saw road use whilst following the Queen's Flight detachment around the country. Ten more were ordered while these were in build, and were delivered in late 1978. Four went to the Royal Navy as 01 RN 00 to 01 RN 03, and the other six were delivered to the RAF with a winterised specification that had been developed on the prototype 31 AG 41. These were 31 AG 29 to 31 AG 34. The winterised specification brought blinds above each window; additional heating for the crew and rear compartments; thermal blankets for controls and the water system, and 240v AC heaters for the engine and pre-mix tank. Some vehicles also had a petrol heater to warm the engine when there was no 240-volt supply. It is possible but not proven that the RN vehicles were also winterised: such vehicles would have been needed for RN

The first TACR-2 models were built by Gloster Saro and were delivered in khaki drab with a yellow stripe for use by the RAF. (Gloster Saro)

Vehicles of the early RAF delivery in AG line up outside the premises of Gloster Saro. (Gloster Saro)

These are TACR-2 chassis awaiting bodywork. Visible on the bumper of the nearest one is a CC serial number, which was a temporary allocation. The picture was supposedly taken in a storage yard used by Carmichael & Sons, who did the chassis conversion. (Six Appeal Wheel Group)

helicopter operations in support of the Royal Marines in Norway.

Gloster Saro was unable to accommodate a third order in late 1981 or early 1982, and so the business went to HCB-Angus. One evaluation prototype was built (94 AM 37), and this was followed by an order for 17 more, which were delivered as 31 AG 52 to 31 AG 61 and 51 AG 46 to 51 AG 52. Because of a change in numbering policy, the second batch was to have been numbered 51 AJ 46 to 51 AJ 52.

Later deliveries had bodywork as well as chassis by Carmichael. This is 03 AY 51, based on a four-door Range Rover and painted in the gloss red that gradually replaced the earlier livery. The ladders had not been fitted to the roof when this picture was taken at the manufacturer's premises. (Carmichael & Sons)

TACR-2

Another special feature of the MoD six-wheel crash tenders was the recess in the rear of each body side that carried the foam branches for rapid access. (JT)

Land Rover offered a four-door Range Rover from mid-1981, and subsequent TACR-2 deliveries were based on this. The full designation changed to 'Truck, Fire-Fighting, Airfield Crash Rescue, 2 Tonne, 6x4, 4-Dr, Mark 2, Range Rover', but this second version of the crash-rescue tender retained the TACR-2 designation. There were 52 of these in all. The first 14 were built by Gloster Saro, but thereafter production was transferred to Carmichael's.

Ten of the Gloster Saro vehicles were for the Royal Navy, and gained serials 93 RN 15 to 93 RN 22 and 95 RN 01 to 95 RN 02, the latter pair possibly winterised. Four more were definitely winterised examples, attracting serials 01 AY 67 and 01 AY 68 (delivered August 1985) and two more which have not been identified.

Of the 38 Carmichael-built vehicles, 26 were for the RAF (03 AY 39 to 03 AY 62 and 04 AY 46 and 04 AY 47, the latter two winterised). The 12 Royal Navy deliveries were 34 RN 50 to 34 RN

09 AY 71 was a TACR-2 built entirely by Carmichael & Sons. The commercial-pattern crash bar was unique to these later vehicles. It was attached to RAF Benson when pictured in the early 1990s. (IT)

Above: 31 AG 60 was one of the early Gloster Saro deliveries, and here shows the Niphan trickle-charge socket (painted red) that was a feature of these vehicles. (IT)

60 and 01 RN 04, the last one a replacement for 93 RN 18 which was written off in 1987, possibly after a rollover accident. The first dozen Carmichael builds were delivered in May 1985, and two of them went to the Queen's Flight. All the Carmichael vehicles were delivered in red, but some were later repainted to suit local requirements.

The third iteration of this vehicle type was the TACR-2A, or 'Truck, Fire-Fighting, Airfield Crash Rescue, 2 Tonne, 6x4, 4-Dr, Mark 2A, Range Rover'. All of these were built by Carmichael, and they incorporated a number of modifications suggested by the builder that were intended to reduce production costs. The most obvious were a commercial-type bull bar in place of

the RAF-pattern crash bar (the repeater lamps were relocated in the grille), a one-piece headlining in the cab, and side hose-stowage lockers that were moulded as part of rear body, and not separate items.

The RAF took 78 examples of this type, numbered as 09 AY 39 to 10 AY 16, and all delivered between September 1988 and August 1989. The Royal Navy may also have taken a pair as 95 RN 01 and 95 RN 02, so making the total up to 80, although it is possible that these serials may have been allocated to second-variant vehicles and were not examples of the third type.

ASSET CODES

The Asset Codes (in use from 1972 to around 1993) are:

1038-0782	Ambulance, 2 stretcher, 4x4, Range Rover
1126-9107	Car, saloon, Armoured, LHD, LWB, Range Rover
1154-4100	Car, Utility, 3/4 ton, Special Forces, 4x4, 3.5-litre V8 petrol, Range Rover Vogue
1154-4101	Car, Utility, Special Forces, 4x4, Automatic, 3.9 litre V8 petrol, Range Rover Vogue
1154-4102	Car, Utility, Special Forces, 4x4, 3.9-litre, V8 petrol, Range Rover Vogue
1163-0782	Car, Utility, 4x4, Range Rover
1163-4100	Car, Utility, 4x4, 4-Dr, Range Rover
1163-4101	Car, Utility, 4x4, 4-Dr, Range Rover (3.5 EFi) Automatic
1163-4102	Car, Utility, 4x4, V8 3.9-litre petrol, Range Rover Vogue
1163-5782	Car, Utility, 4x4, LHD, Range Rover
1163-6782	Car, Utility, 4x4, w/winch, LHD, Range Rover
1163-9100	Car, Utility, 4x4, 4-Dr, LHD, Range Rover
1163-9101	Car, Utility, 4x4, 4-Dr, LHD, Range Rover
1164-4100	Car, Utility, SAAS, 4x4, 4-Dr, Range Rover
1164-4101	Car, Utility, SAAS, 4x4, Range Rover Vogue (3.5-litre petrol)
1164-5782	Car, Utility, SAAS, 4x4, LHD, Range Rover
1164-5786	Car, Utility, SAAS, 4x4, LHD, Range Rover
1164-6782	Car, Utility, SAAS, 4x4, w/winch, LHD, Range Rover
1164-8100	Car, Utility, SAAS, 4x4, LHD, Range Rover Vogue (2.4-litre Turbo-diesel)
1164-9100	Car, Utility, SAAS, 4x4, 4-Dr, LHD, Range Rover
1164-9102	Car, Utility, SAAS, 4x4, LHD, Range Rover Turbo-diesel
1164-9103	Car, Utility, SAAS, 4x4, LHD, Range Rover Vogue (3.5-litre petrol)
1164-9104	Car, Utility, SAAS, 4x4, LHD, Range Rover Standard (3.5-litre petrol)
1166-0001	Car, ceremonial, VIP, 4x4, Range Rover
1168-0782	Car, Utility, Police Special, 4x4, Range Rover
1168-4100	Car, Utility, Police Special, 4x4, 4-Dr, Range Rover

1168-5782	Car, Utility, Police Special, 4x4, LHD, Range Rover
1168-9100	Car, Utility, Police Special, 4x4, Police Range Rover LHD
1168-9102	Car, Utility, Police Special, 4x4, 4-Dr, LHD, Range Rover
1963-0782	Truck, Firefighting, Airfield Crash Rescue, 4-Dr, 2 ton, 6x4, Range Rover Mk 2
1963-4100	Truck, Firefighting, Airfield Crash Rescue, 4-Dr, 2 ton, 3x4, Range Rover Mk
1963-4101	Truck, Firefighting, Airfield Crash Rescue, 4-Dr, 2 ton, 6x4, Range Rover Mk 2A
1964-0782	Truck, Firefighting, Airfield Crash Rescue, (winterised), 2 ton, 6x4, 4-Dr, Range Rover Mk 2
1964-4100	Truck, Firefighting, Airfield Crash Rescue, (winterised), 2 ton, 6x4, 4-Dr, Range Rover Mk 2
1964-4101	Truck, Firefighting, Airfield Crash Rescue, (winterised), 2 ton, 6x4, 4-Dr, Range Rover Mk 2A

The later Asset Codes (from around 1993) are:

NB1126-9105	Car, saloon, Armoured, LHD, Range Rover Vogue
NB1126-9106	Car, saloon, Armoured, LHD, SWB, Range Rover
NB1126-9107	Car, saloon, Armoured, LHD, LWB, Range Rover
NB1154-4102	Car, Utility, Special Forces, 4x4, 3.9-litre V8 petrol, Range Rover Vogue
RB1963-4101	Truck, Firefighting, Airfield Crash Rescue, 4-Dr, 2 ton, 6x4, Range Rover Mk 2A
RB1964-4100	Truck, Firefighting, Airfield Crash Rescue, (winterised), 2 ton, 6x4, Range Rover Mk 2
WB1163-4102	Car, Utility, 4x4, V8, 3.9-litre petrol, Range Rover Vogue

SUMMARY OF RANGE ROVER DELIVERIES, 1972-1996

Note: The only vehicle discussed in this Chapter is the first generation Range Rover, which ceased production in February 1996. The second-generation model had meanwhile entered production in 1994. Late examples of the first-generation vehicle, from autumn 1994, were known and badged as Range Rover Classic.

ARMY

Serials	Contract	Chassis nos	Total	Remarks
04 FM 52 to 04 FM 54	WV8765 R2373	355-05329B to 355-05332B	3	RHD; for 22 SAS; 24 Nov 1972
06 GB 48	WV8765 R2510	355-08850C	1	RHD; for 22 SAS
07 GB 05	WV8765 R2510	355-08851C	1	RHD; for 22 SAS
08 GF 04	WV8765 R2736	355-09701C	1	RHD; for 22 SAS
33 GF 35 and 33 GF 36	WV8765 R2780	355-10536D and 355-11000D	2	RHD; for 22 SAS
06 GN 24	WV8765 R2962	358-29516D	1	LHD; for Services Attaché, Warsaw
07 GT 56 and 07 GT 57	WV8765 R3142	355-37893D and 355-37892D	2	RHD; 07 GT 56 for Bélize and 07 GT 57 for 22 SAS
25 GT 64 and 25 GT 65	FVE 22A/44R3163	355-39610F and 355-39610F	2	RHD; for 22 SAS
96 GT 18	FVE 22A/44 R3202	355-43589F	1	RHD; for 22 SAS
16 GX 15 to 16 GX 17	FVE 22A/44 R3258	355-49901F to 355-49908F	3	RHD; for 22 SAS
45 HF 22	FVE 22A/44 R3325	100488	1	LHD; for Services Attaché, Warsaw Feb 1980
03 SP 51	WV8765 R2101	355-01846A	1	RHD; trials vehicle at MVEE Chertsey, probably for 22 SAS
		Total	19	

Although top-specification models were not normally on the military agenda, this 1992 Range Rover Vogue SE was an exception. It was presented to the aircraft carrier HMS Invincible, where it was kept aboard and used for shore duties.

The picture shows its handover by Land Rover's Marketing Director to the carrier's Captain Tolhurst. As was the Royal Navy tradition with vehicles attached to vessels (and some shore-based institutions as well), the vehicle carries a large board with the name of its parent ship. (Land Rover)

O2 KC 31 was being used for two-star officer transport when pictured at the Headquarters of the British Forces in the Falkland Islands. It was an early four-door model. Note the twin radio aerials and the flagstaff on the bonnet. (RLC)

RAF

Serials	Contract	Chassis nos	Total	Remarks
30 AG 92 to 31 AG 28	WV8765 R2582	355-09547C to 355-10888D	36	TACR-2 RHD
31 AG 29 to 31 AG 34	WV8765 R2582	355-09159C to 355-34318D	6	TACR-2 winterised RHD
31 AG 41	Gifted	355-09066C	1	TACR-2 RHD; prototype
31 AG 52 to 31 AG 61	FVE 22A/44 R3451	113700 to 108872	10	TACR-2 RHD
51 AG 46 to 51 AG 52	FVE 22A/140 R3505	113701 to 355-48271F	7	TACR-2 RHD; intended to have serials 51 AJ 46 to 51 AJ 52
38 AJ 39	FVE 22A/44 R3327	358-52514F	1	LHD; later converted to police special
40 AJ 88 to 40 AJ 89	FVE 22A/44 R3349	100003 to 100004	2	Police Special RHD; for HQ P&SS
40 AJ 90 to 40 AJ 93	FVE 22A/44 R3349	100005 to 100022	4	Police Special LHD; for RAF police Rheindahlen
45 AJ 48 to 45 AJ 49	FVE 22A/140 R3522	N/K to N/K	2	Ceremonial RHD; for HQ&PSS
48 AJ 52	FVE 22A/44 R3452		1	Police Special LHD; for unknown unit
94 AM 37	FVE 22A/44 R3259		2	TACR-2 RHD
01 AY 67 and 01 AY 68	FVE 22A/140 LR3675	140650 and 140651	2	TACR-2 winterised RHD
03 AY 39 to 03 AY 62	FVE 22A/140 LR5214	155006 to 155356	24	TACR-2 RHD
04 AY 46 and 04 AY 47	FVE 22A/140 LR5214	155356 and 162623	2	TACR-2 winterised RHD
09 AY 39 to 10 AY 16	FVE 22B/925	333888 to 337089	78	TACR-2A RHD(09 AY 62 to 09 AY 66 were Winterised)
		Total	177	

RN

Serials	Contract	Chassis nos	Total	Remarks
01 RN 00 to 01 RN 03	N/K	N/K to N/K	4	TACR-2 RHD; Gloster-Saro
01 RN 04	N/K	N/K	–	TACR-2 RHD; Carmichael
01 RN 30 and 01 RN 31	67761	355-31585D and 355-31574D	2	Ambulance RHD
02 RN 40	FVE 22A/373 LR/BN13/014	485623	1	Vogue 3.9 Petrol RHD; for director SF; delivered 21 Feb 1991
34 RN 50 to 34 RN 60	FVE 22A/48LR5651	N/K to 169290	11	TACR-2 RHD; Carmichael; in service from Oct 1987
62 RN 41 to 62 RN 49	30741	35509845C to 355-09847C	9	Ambulance RHD
93 RN 15 to 93 RN 22	LR3683	140447 to 140545	8	TACR-2 RHD; Gloster Saro; in service from Mar 1985
95 RN 01 and 95 RN 02	N/K	N/K to N/K	2	TACR-2 RHD; Gloster-Saro
		Total	34	

TRI-SERVICE

Serials	Contract	Chassis nos	Total	Remarks
20 KA 27 to 20 KA 34	FVE 22A/140 LR3561	125524 to 125531	8	RHD; for 22 SAS
28 KB 09	LP	126277	1	LHD; for Defence Attaché, Abu Dhabi Oct 1982
49 KB 92	LP	133250	1	LHD; for Defence Attaché, Warsaw
80 KB 70	FVE 22A/140 LR3747	141092	1	4-Dr RHD; for BDLS India Oct 1983
99 KB 72	LP	137154	1	LHD; for Defence Attaché, Muscat Nov1983
02 KC 31	FVE 22A/140 LR3770	140652	1	RHD; for Falklands Islands
37 KC 61	LP	143640	1	4-Dr LHD; for MA Budapest
40 KC 17	LP	503816	1	4-Dr; for Defence Attaché, Canberra Apr 1984
00 KD 46	LP	145912	1	4-Dr LHD; for Defence Attaché, Khartoum Nov 1984
25 KD 40	FVE 22A/140 LR5251	155077	1	4-Dr LHD; for Belize; 16 Oct 1984

25 KD 41	LP	146786	1	4-Dr LHD; for Defence Attaché, Warsaw Oct 1984
25 KD 54	LP	145185	1	4-Dr LHD; for SAAS Oct 1984
47 KD 69 to 47 KD 71	FVE 22A/140 LR5251	146524 to 146685	3	4-Dr RHD; for 43 T&M Squadron RCT
48 KD 99	FVE 22A/140 LR5274	151491	1	4-Dr; for Services Attaché, Pakistan Nov 1984
05 KF 18	FVE 22A/248 LR5694	167631	1	4-Dr LHD; for Defence Attaché, Rabat Jun 1986
08 KF 61	LP	152230	1	4-Dr LHD; for SAAS Dec 1985
79 KF 73 to 79 KF 75	FVE 22A/248 A72	271034 to 271046	3	4-Dr RHD; all for service Adviser, New Delhi Apr 1987
84 KF 68 and 84 KF 69	FVE 22A/248 A108	277298 and 277304	2	Police Special RHD; for HQ P&SS
84 KF 70 to 84 KF 75	FVE 22A/248 A108	277335 to 277340	6	Police Special LHD; for RAF police in Germany
89 KF 01 to 89 KF 04	FVE 22A/248 A116	275383 to 276095	4	2-Dr RHD; for 22 SAS
90 KF 32	FVE 22A/248 A121	275511	1	4-Dr LHD; for services Adviser Nigeria Nov1986
90 KF 34	FVE 22A/248 A119	277313	1	4-Dr LHD; for Defence Attaché, Rangoon Jan 1987
91 KF 17	FVE 22A/248 A120	275515	1	4-Dr LHD; for Services Attaché, Manila in May 1987
99 KF 78	FVE 22A/248 A128	283486	1	4-Dr; for Services Attaché, Bangladesh Sept 1986
31 KG 18	FVE 22A/248 A118	288516	1	4-Dr LHD; for Services Attaché, Oslo in December 1987
64 KG 73	LP	163650	1	4-Dr LHD; for Services Attaché, Budapest Feb 1987
74 KG 00 and 74 KG 01	FVE 22A/248 A178	314450 to 314453	2	4-Dr RHD; 74 KG 00 for N Ireland and 74 KG 01 for Falklands Islands
79 KG 37	LP	294414	1	4-Dr LHD; for Service attaché, Dubai Sept 1987
81 KG 64 to 81 KG 68	FVE 22A/373 A491	324074 to 324098	5	4-Dr RHD; for 22 SAS
81 KG 99	LP	298239	1	4-Dr LHD; for Defence Attaché, Warsaw Dec 1987
87 KG 76 and 87 KG 77	FVE 22A/373 A449/045	334089 and 334092	2	4-Dr RHD; 87 KG 76 for 22 SAS, 87 KG 77 for Belize
96 KG 85	FVE 22A/373 A549/053	343892	1	4-Dr LHD; for Defence Attaché, Guatemala Dec 1987
36 KH 65	LP	331127	1	4-Dr LHD; for Defence Attaché, Prague Oct 1988
57 KH 61	LP	369735	1	2.4 Diesel RHD; for HQ RSME
60 KH 30	LP	351383	1	4-Dr LHD; for Services Attaché, Riyadh Dec 1987
73 KH 46	FVE 22A/373 BA5/067	404366	1	Turbo-Diesel LHD; for Defence Attaché, Madrid May 1989
73 KH 58	FVE 22A/373 A581/064	386907	1	4-Dr RHD; for Services Attaché, Colombo Jun 1989
91 KH 93	FVE 22A/373 BA13/069	406705	1	4-Dr RHD; for Services Adviser Nigeria Jun 1989
92 KH 10 to 92 KH 19	FVE 22A/373 A617/068	420995 to 421300	10	4-Dr 3.5 EFi Auto RHD; for 22 SAS; Jul 1989
35 KJ 09	LP	406400	1	4-Dr LHD; for Services Attaché, Budapest in Nov 1989
46 KJ 63	FVE 22A/373 LR/BA86/093	431835	1	Vogue 2.4 Turbo-Diesel LHD; for Defence Attaché, Algiers Nov 1989
46 KJ 70	LP	411277	1	4-Dr LHD; for Service Attaché, Budapest in Feb 1990
88 KJ 75	FVE 22A/373 LR/BA77/94	480390	1	Vogue LHD; for Services Attaché, Ankara in Aug 1990
89 KJ 56 to 89 KJ 60	FVE 22A/373 LR/BA44/099	600778 to 600777	5	4-Dr 3.5EFi Auto RHD; for N Ireland; 14 Aug 1990
89 KJ 61	FVE 22A/373 LR/BA78/102	477976	1	Vogue RHD; for Services Attaché, Islamabad in Aug 1990
89 KJ 74	LP	443683	1	Vogue LHD; for SAAS Aug 1990
21 KK 36	[ex 02 RN 40]	485623	1	RHD; for Dir SF 21 Sept 1990
41 KK 26	FVE 22A/373 LR/BA226/107	614250	1	Vogue 3.5L RHD; for 22 SAS Jul 1991

84 KK 43 to 84 KK 49	LV2A/153	617489 to 624261	7	Vogue 3.9L Auto RHD; for 22 SAS
51 KL 06 to 51 KL 10	LV2A/183	645734 to 645693	5	Vogue 3.9L Auto RHD; for 22 SAS; 25 Jan 1994
81 KL 02 to 81 KL 03	LV2A/123	658669 to 658872	2	Vogue 3.9L RHD; for 22 SAS; 19 Jan 1995
CG 52 AA to CG 55 AA	BA574/091	656463 to 656486	4	Vogue 3.9L RHD; for 23 Parachute Field Ambulance; possibly for Op Gabriel in Rwanda
DU 33 AA	LP	433065	1	LWB Armoured LHD; for IFOR in Bosnia and Herzegovina; 12 Mar 1995
DU 34 AA	LP	320667	1	SWB Armoured LHD; for IFOR in Bosnia and Herzegovina; 12 Mar 1995
DU 35 AA	LP	614603	1	Vogue Armoured LHD; for IFOR in Bosnia and Herzegovina; 12 Mar 1995. Initially carried serial UK 3722 (correctly UK 37 ZZ).
EV 69 AA to EV 75 AA	BA004/LV8012	662155 to 663158	7	Vogue 3.9L RHD; for 22 SAS; 10 Aug 1995
		Total	115	

BERLIN SENAT

Serials	Contract	Chassis nos	Total	Remarks
55 XB 88	–	N/K	1	LHD, with winch
56 XB 88 to 56 XB 91	–	358-13218D to 358-13399D	4	LHD; for BRIXMIS, Jun 1975
57 XB 44 to 57 XB 46	–	N/Kto 358-28851D	3	LHD, with winch; for BRIXMIS, Mar 1977
44 XB 89	–	358-52124F	1	LHD, with winch; for BRIXMIS, Jul 1979
45 XB 68 to 45 XB 70	–	109995 to N/K	3	LHD, with winch; for BRIXMIS, Jun 1981
46 XB 33 to 46 XB 36	–	120090 to 120091	4	LHD, 4-Dr; for BRIXMIS, Jul 1982
61 XB 46 to 61 XB 49	–	102033 to 102038	4	LHD, with winch; for BRIXMIS, Jun 1980
02 XK 08 to 02 XK 11	–	136137 to 136254	4	LHD, with winch; for BRIXMIS, Jul 1983
03 XK 74 to 03 XK 77	–	151865 to 151863	4	LHD, with winch; for BRIXMIS, Feb 1985
		Total	28	

NON-CENSUS

Serial	Contract	Chassis no	Total	Remarks
00 NC 06	Loan	355-06365B	1	Ceremonial Range Rover
		Total	1	

A Ceremonial Range Rover was loaned for a Royal Tour of Germany including the Queen's review of the fifteen BAOR-based Royal Artillery regiments at Napier Barracks, Dortmund on 23 May 1984. Photographs show that the vehicle was actually the 1975 State Review Range Rover that normally wears no number-plate. Its Non-Census military serial was probably allocated on a temporary basis to meet German regulations. (The NC series was used to designate loan vehicles that were not accountable assets.)

Technical specifications, Range Rover

Note: There were multiple changes in Range Rover specifications over the years, and a simplified breakdown appears below:

Engine (petrol)
3528cc V8 with carburettors and 125-132bhp, 1970-1985
3528cc V8 with injection and 165bhp, 1985-1989
3947cc V8 with injection and 180-188bhp, 1989-1996

Engine (diesel)
2393cc turbocharged four-cylinder with 112bhp, 1986-1989
2500cc turbocharged four-cylinder with 119bhp, 1989-1992
2495cc turbocharged four-cylinder with 111bhp,1992-1996

Transmission
Permanent four-wheel drive with lockable centre differential (automatic locking, 1989 on)
Four-speed manual gearbox (to 1983)
Five-speed manual gearbox (1983-1996)
Optional three-speed automatic (1982-1985)
Optional four-speed automatic, V8 only (1985-1996)
Two-speed transfer gearbox
Axle ratio: 3.54:1

Suspension, steering and brakes
Coil springs all round
Recirculating-ball steering; power assistance optional from 1974 and standard from 1979
Disc brakes on all four wheels; separate internal expanding drum-type parking brake, operating on transmission output shaft

Electrical system
12-volt with dynamo and negative earth

Dimensions
Overall length:	176in (4470mm)
Overall width:	70in (1780mm)
Overall height:	70in (1780mm)
Wheelbase:	100in (2540mm)
Track:	58.5in (1480mm)

Kerb weight
3800lb (1723kg) (early UK-market two-door model)
3942lb (1788kg) (early UK-market four-door model)
4308lb (1954kg) (late UK-market four-door model with injected V8 engine and four-speed automatic gearbox)
4429lb (2009kg) (typical UK-market four-door model with turbodiesel engine)

Performance
(3.5-litre carburettor petrol engine):
0-60mph:	14secs
Maximum:	95mph approx (153km/h)
Fuel consumption:	14mpg approx

(3.5-litre injected petrol engine):
0-60mph:	12secs
Maximum:	102mph approx (164km/h)
Fuel consumption:	18mpg approx

(2.4-litre diesel engine):
0-60mph:	16.5secs
Maximum:	92mph approx (148km/h)
Fuel consumption:	25mpg approx

ONE TEN 1983-90

In March 1983, at the Geneva Motor Show, Land Rover introduced the new One Ten model – a direct result of a £250 million Government investment in the business. It came just in time, because the company had found itself losing market share to Japanese 4x4 makers, particularly Toyota, but also, increasingly, Nissan and Mitsubishi. However, the design of the One Ten had actually been initiated in 1976 after the Ryder Report into British Leyland's financial troubles had recommended that Land Rover should be made into a standalone business unit and should benefit from substantial investment. At that stage, part of one of British Leyland's multiple divisions, Land Rover, became Land Rover Ltd during 1978.

Although these new, long-wheelbase models were recognisably derived from the Series III types that had preceded them, there were some fundamental differences. The most important of these was that the suspension now had coil springs all-round, instead of the leaf springs of earlier models. This was derived from the type pioneered on the Range Rover, and provided a more comfortable ride. Like Range Rovers, these new vehicles also had permanent four-wheel drive, rather than the selectable type of their leaf-sprung predecessors. A further innovation was disc brakes on the front wheels – although the rear wheels retained drum brakes.

As on the Stage 1 V8 derivatives of the Series III, the radiator grille was moved forwards to become flush with the wing fronts

so that there was adequate room for the large-capacity engine and its cooling system. A completely new black plastic grille was fitted, and its colour was matched by impact-resistant wheelarch 'eyebrows' that covered wider-track axles. The windscreen was not only taller than before, but also came as a single pane of glass.

From launch until the end of the 1990 model-year, the long-wheelbase models were known as Land Rover One Ten types, with the number spelled out in full in advertising, handbooks and manuals. Their badges above the front grille, however, displayed 'Land Rover 110'!

From summer 1989, and for one year only, the badge was simplified to read '110.' Note that the 1983-90 models were never called by the Defender name when they were new, even though Land Rover itself tends to refer to them as such now.

The engine options for the One Ten were four-cylinder petrol and diesel types, each with a 2286cc capacity, and five main bearings, as well as the 3.5-litre all-alloy petrol V8. From 1984, the diesel engine took on a longer stroke to become a 2.5-litre, and the petrol engine followed suit a year later. In 1986, a turbocharged version of the diesel engine (known as the Diesel Turbo type) was made available, but there were no military deliveries of this type.

The British military derivatives of the One Ten came with a number of special features not available on their civilian counterparts. The majority were delivered in full soft-top form; a body style that was not available in the civilian market, except in some overseas territories. The GS and FFR types (but not the civilian-specification CL models) all had 'pusher' bumpers, and, the majority had a NATO-pattern towing jaw at the rear. Although civilian models changed to one-piece doors with winding windows in 1984, British military models retained doors with sliding Perspex windows in removable door tops – which, of course, was of value when a vehicle was being stripped down for low-profile operations. In addition, British military models retained the traditional recessed outer door handles after civilian types changed to car-type handles in October 1986. GS and FFR models normally had a lidded compartment in the body side ahead of the rear axle, large enough to contain a jerry can.

The order date of the first 12 trials vehicles, in January 1983, makes clear that the Ministry of Defence was involved prior to the public launch of the new vehicle. This was only to be expected, as Land Rover depended heavily on British military

sales at the time. The vehicles were delivered to Ashchurch in June 1983, and were known as 'Stage 2 Validation Vehicles, 0.75 Tonne, Land Rover.' The 'Stage 2' designation was actually an internal one from Land Rover; the Stage 1 V8 models had been developed with funding provided by the first stage of a Government investment grant, and the much larger sum of money that followed it allowed development of the radically different coil-sprung or 'Stage 2' types.

Most of the trials vehicles went to MVEE, and were in use there until October 1986,

ONE TEN

The early demonstrator and trials vehicles had some differences from the 'production' models delivered to the MoD.

Below: This otherwise unidentified One Ten was pictured in May 1983, probably at the Land Rover factory in Solihull, and is almost certainly one of the validation batch that were delivered the following month. Note the unpainted, galvanised windscreen surround characteristic of these early examples. (LR)

although there were other trials users. These 12 vehicles – pre-production models to Land Rover, but prototypes to the MoD – included both General Service (GS) and Fitted For Radio (FFR) types with RHD and LHD. All had four-cylinder, 2.3-litre petrol engines, although ultimately, the One Ten fleet would be diesel-powered. Around five had a front-mounted winch, a fitment that was not carried over to production contracts. All were given serials in KB, and all were delivered with galvanised windscreen frames, a feature not pursued on the batch deliveries for the MoD.

A further contract for four RHD 'validation' models followed in March 1984, and these had the newly-introduced,

2.5-litre, diesel engine. They carried KC serials. Two were retained by RARDE (as MVEE had now become) and two were trialled by 10 Field Workshop, REME. These four vehicles presaged the big change that was to underlie the introduction of the One Ten model into British military service – the move to diesel fuel. This was in line with the emerging NATO single-fuel policy and foreshadowed other vehicles in the fleet moving to diesel.

The main exceptions to the all-diesel policy then, and for several years afterwards, were motorcycles and All-Terrain Vehicles (quads), which still relied on petrol (gasoline).

The vast majority of Land Rover One Tens delivered to the British armed forces were GS (General Service) soft-tops,

Below: Pictured here after withdrawal from service (the serial number was added hastily for the picture), 30 KB 68 was also one of the validation batch. Its military identity plate (left) describes it as a 'Land Rover Stage 2 12-volt LHD 3/4 tonne.' (JT)

30 KB 75 was another of the validation batch, this time in RHD with a 24-volt specification. It was pictured on exercise at Larkhill with 49 Field Regiment, Royal Artillery. The vehicle had been issued to REME Wing of the Royal School of Artillery for trials but seems to have been loaned to 49 Regiment. (GF)

with a civilian-type 12-volt electrical system, or FFR (Fitted For Radio) soft-tops with a military-only 24-volt system. There were also purchases of CL (civilian-specification) types, which, of course, had the 12-volt system. Some of the FFR vehicles were delivered in hardtop form, and there were also some Station Wagons and a few truck cab vehicles, plus hardtops with windows for the RAF. Most deliveries came with the 2.5-litre, four-cylinder, naturally-aspirated diesel engine, although a few vehicles for special purposes had the 3.5-litre, V8 petrol engine.

As explained below, there was also an interim purchase of more than 600 V8 models with various body configurations in 1989.

The initial contract for the GS, FFR and CL versions (FVE 22A/304) was dated November 1985, and consisted of RHD and LHD models with seven variants as follows: GS in Hard Top and Soft Top versions; FFR Hard Top; CL Hard Top; CL Truck Cab (mainly for the Royal Navy), and Station Wagon. This led to various 'items' on the contract numbering at least as far as 48, the last of which was ordered in August 1987.

It was not long after the One Ten was introduced into service that there were severe problems with the diesel engine. It is said that there was a problem in the way the pistons were manufactured, and this, together with a general practice amongst servicemen of overfilling the sump with oil, caused the engines to over-breathe and ingest the oil. This led, in some cases, to piston failure. Subsequently, a centrifugal separator was introduced into the breather system of military-specification engines in order to allow excess oil to drain back to the sump.

However, the problems were severe enough for an 'interim buy' of One Tens with V8 petrol engines to be made in 1989, and it has been said that the contract was on extremely advantageous terms to the Ministry of Defence. This may

well be true, as the Army was struggling with the Land Rover fleet, and would have needed a strong inducement to move back to petrol versions, and, worse still, a mixed fleet of petrol and diesel Land Rovers. This interim purchase of V8-engined Land Rovers was extremely popular with the troops, as the vehicles offered significantly more power and a higher top speed.

The last One Tens to reach the British armed forces were delivered in the first half of 1990. From the summer of that year, a major revision of the utility Land Rover range (which, by then consisted of three models – Ninety, One Ten and One Two Seven) was introduced, with the new name of Land Rover Defender, and there were, of course, military versions. The Defender 110

Right: 79 KE 04 is a One Ten Station Wagon for the SAAS. The forward setting of the grille and the black vent panels on the bulkhead indicate that it was fitted with air conditioning. (VSM)

Left: 80 KG 54 is a One Ten Station Wagon of the UK Mobile Air Movements Squadron RAF, pictured on display at IAT Fairford in July 1989. Later it served on Operation Granby – the liberation of Kuwait. Note the protection bar for the front suspension, underneath the bumper. (GF)

models in British military service are discussed in Chapters 6, 7 and 8.

One Ten variants
Electronic Warfare FFR
A special version of the FFR was used by Electronic Warfare squadrons of the Royal Corps of Signals.

Glover Webb APV
Oddly enough, the very first One Ten delivered for British Army service was a variant. It was the Armoured Patrol Vehicle for Northern Ireland made by Glover Webb, which entered service in June 1985.

There were no fewer than 63 of these vehicles, with serials 93 KC 72 to 94 KC 34. The body was made of armoured steel plate and the vehicle could carry two personnel in the cab and six troops in the rear. Power came from the V8 petrol engine, which was chosen because of the weight of the armour. Further purchases followed on the One Ten and later the Defender chassis (see Chapter 6).

Hard Top with windows
The Hard Top with Windows version was for the Royal Air Force, who had long favoured this body variant for their long-wheelbase Land Rovers, and was used largely as an airfield runabout carrying out a variety of tasks.

Below, and opposite page, bottom: The first deliveries were of this armoured Glover Webb variant, for use in Northern Ireland. 93 KC 82 represents the 'standard' configuration, while 93 KC 76 has been fitted with an experimental revolving turret for a rear observer. (TMB)

Helicopter support

The Helicopter Support variant had an up-rated power supply and a strengthened roof and safety rail to allow maintenance crew to work on the upper parts of helicopters. It was designed to allow helicopter maintenance in the field, and was used by RAF Helicopter squadrons intended for such deployments.

Linelayer

There is said to be photographic evidence of the Line-laying Kit (see Volume 1) being fitted to a One Ten, but by the late 1980s, such equipment was becoming obsolete and no details of its users are known.

Above: Glover-Webb APV 09 KF 21 was pictured at a vehicle depot shared with the Royal Ulster Constabulary, whose grey-painted armoured Land Rovers can be seen alongside. The faces of the crew have been deliberately obscured. (JT Collection)

SAS LRPV

Another early arrival was a One Ten with the V8 engine, 9.00 x 16 tyres (the standard size was 7.50 x 16) and the High Capacity Pick-Up (HCPU) body. This became 90 KB 62 and was trialled as a first stage in developing a replacement for the SAS 'Pink Panther' long-range desert patrol vehicles, which, by this stage, were over 15 years old. Interestingly, its military plate bears no vehicle description. Meanwhile, Glover Webb carried out a series of modifications to the basic design in order to meet the Regiment's requirements, and an order was placed, apparently independently of other British military orders (the SAS is able to by-pass the normal and rather cumbersome MoD procurement system). Land Rover knew these vehicles by the code name of Aardvark during the development phase.

In fact, the SAS One Tens were designed as dual-purpose vehicles, and

Left: 90 KB 61 was equipped as a patrol vehicle, and its configuration generally anticipated that of the later SAS long-range patrol vehicles. The back body is a High-Capacity Pick-Up type. (RLC)

Right: 90 KB 62 was trialled as part of the SAS patrol vehicle programme. It is seen here after withdrawal from service and onward sale. Note the High-Capacity Pick-Up body and the big 9.00 x 16 tyres. (JT)

Left: 24 KD 32 was one of the SAS long-range desert patrol vehicles, and was pictured here at the British Army Equipment Exhibition in June 1990. Most of the usual equipment is not on the vehicle, so the body configuration can be seen quite clearly. (GF)

TRUCK-UTILITY-SAS-4X4. LAND-ROVER-110-V8-HEAVY-DUTY.		
MANFR GLOVER-WEBB-LTD	TYPE	
SERIAL No SALLDHHV1BA232260	REG No 24-KD-33	
CON No FVE-22B/695	ITEM-NO.02	
CES No	CODE No 1725-3100	
N.S.N.		

Above: Although this identification plate is a reproduction, it is claimed to be a faithful copy of the original on an SAS One Ten. The vehicle type is "Truck-Utility-SAS-4x4. Land-Rover-110-V8-Heavy-Duty." Not surprisingly, it would have been removed for covert missions. (JT)

Right: Pictures of the SAS patrol vehicles in service are rare, but this one of two vehicles when nearly new shows that they were delivered in green, and were only later painted in the sand colour that most people associate with them. 24 KD 33 had already sustained minor damage to the front bumper. (Anonymous via Barry Pocock)

Left: An SAS example as delivered to Vehicle Depot Ashchurch. The 'grid' behind the passenger seat reveals it was receipted into the depot on 18 November 1985. (VS)

Left: Heavily laden with equipment as it would have been in service, this is 24 KD 33 after entering preservation. By this time, it was wearing the familiar sand colour. (JT)

Above: This close-up of 24 KD 33 shows the stowage arrangements for the large amounts of kit typically carried on a behind-the-lines mission. (JT)

much of their special equipment could be demounted so that they could be used as general-purpose load carriers, complete with a full-length canvas tilt. Whether this happened in practice is not clear.

A total of 33 vehicles were delivered in November 1985 and gained serials in KD. Although they arrived from Glover Webb in standard NATO green with full windscreens, it was not long before they lost those windscreens and were repainted in sand camouflage. Despite the beige colour, they were once again known familiarly as 'Pinkies' like their Series IIA predecessors.

The fact that the SAS could risk using vehicles with the notoriously thirsty V8 engine for long-range work behind enemy lines was explained by changes in resupply logistics since the original Pink Panthers had been built. Those had been fitted with huge fuel tanks that gave them a range of some 1200 miles. However, by the end of the 1970s, the SAS was using both helicopters and Mercedes-Benz Unimog 'mother ships' to deliver supplies to patrols in remote areas; therefore, the 200-mile range of a heavily-laden One Ten V8 relying on military-pattern twin underseat fuel tanks was not going to be a serious handicap – and the extra power of the V8 engine was certainly welcome.

The SAS One Tens were equipped in service with 9.00x16 tyres to give additional ground clearance. They were designed for a crew of three, and carried a forward-facing machine gun and post-mounted machine gun in the rear.

Safety considerations dictated a rollover bar behind the cab, and a vertical grille, or metal panel, behind; this was used to hang more equipment. The back body carried jerrycans as needed, ammunition boxes, additional weaponry for the operation in hand, and had a covered 'cupboard' for food and other supplies. There were two spare wheels: one on the bonnet and one mounted on the side behind the driving compartment.

There was a front-mounted winch for self-recovery (a UK-made Superwinch 8552 fitted within a specially-made bumper).

Pioneer tools, sand ladders and other paraphernalia were distributed around the flat surfaces of the body. All vehicles carried the then-new Magellan GPS equipment, plus a traditional sun compass mounted on the dashboard. Beyond that, what went on board was down to the crew. They knew what they needed for their mission, and they packed it into their bergens or stuffed it into bags slung from every hook or bracket fitted to the vehicle. Camo netting went across the

scuttle in the traditional way, and more would be slung across the rear or carried within the back body.

The One Ten SAS vehicles were most famously deployed during 1991 on Operation Granby, the operation to liberate Kuwait after the Iraqi invasion. The Regiment went on to take delivery of a further batch of similar vehicles immediately after the Gulf war in about 1991. These vehicles were Defender 110s, with the Tdi engine instead of a petrol V8. They are discussed in Chapter 6.

SB401

The original Shorland armoured car design had been developed into a range of armoured vehicles, and those based on the One Ten chassis became Mk 4 types. The Shorts SB401 was the Armoured Patrol Vehicle (APV) variant. Like the other models in the Mk 4 range, it had a V8 engine that necessitated moving the radiator and grille forward.

The British Army's SB401s were used by the US Marines Custodial Detachment at RAF St Mawgan, where B57 nuclear depth charges were kept. These were primarily for use by the RAF Nimrod aircraft under 'dual-key' arrangements, although US and Dutch P-3 Orion aircraft were also supported. There seem to have been only four RHD vehicles, although five LHD examples had been issued to RAF Germany in October 1983. In June 1992, the Defence Secretary announced that the nuclear depth charges would be returned to the USA.

Brand new One Tens are seen here being loaded for despatch by train at Vehicle Depot Ashchurch. In the foreground is 95 KE 78. (VSM)

Plain and unadorned, 87 KE 30 represents the typical GS Cargo vehicle. (GF)

13 KJ 43 has been painted in all-over white for use by a British UN contingent. Note the rollover bar installed behind the cab area, with a radio and radio aerial mounted on it. There are weapons mounts on the front bulkhead and on the tailgate. The vehicle was in use by 7 Regiment, Royal Horse Artillery. (GF)

38 KF 45 is another standard GS Soft Top model, in use by a Phoenix drone detachment, and carries a recruitment advertisement for the army on its right-hand rear panel. The bag on the rear panel carries the wings of the Phoenix drone. (DP)

38 KF 43 has been converted to a Phoenix drone recovery vehicle with a dedicated loading ramp and rack at the rear. (GF)

31 KG 49 is a civilian-specification hardtop. Note the gloss green paint, the plain front bumper (without tow hitch or quarter-bumper mountings), the one-piece doors with black plastic handles, and the civilian-specification lights. (FMW)

By contrast, 89 KE 32 has a military specification, despite its white paint, which was presumably applied for display and possibly recruitment use. The front bumper is a military type, and the lights are all FV-pattern items. The side locker is also a feature not found on civilian-pattern vehicles. (GF)

1710-3103	Truck, Utility, Medium, GS, Cargo, Soft Top, 12v, 4x4, Land Rover 110 Diesel
1710-4100	Truck, Utility, Medium, GS, Cargo, Soft Top, 12v, 4x4, w/uprated suspension & chassis, Land Rover 110 Diesel
1710-4101	Truck, Utility, Medium, GS, Cargo, Soft Top, 12v, 4x4, Land Rover 110 (V8 Petrol)
1710-8100	Truck, Utility, Medium, GS, Cargo, Soft Top, 12v, 4x4, LHD, Land Rover 110 Diesel
1710-9100	Truck, Utility, Medium, GS, Cargo, Soft Top, 12v, 4x4, LHD, Land Rover 110 (V8 Petrol)
1711-4101	Truck, Utility, Medium, CL, w cab, 12v, 4x4, Land Rover 110 (V8 Petrol)
1711-9100	Truck, Utility, Medium, CL, w cab, 12v, 4x4, LHD, Land Rover 110 (V8 Petrol)
1714-3101	Truck, Utility, Medium, CL, Cargo, 4x4, Hard Top, 12v, Land Rover 110
1714-4100	Truck, Utility, Medium, CL, 4x4, Hard Top w/windows, 12v Land Rover 110 (V8 Petrol)
1714-4101	Truck, Utility, Medium, CL, 4x4, Hard Top, 12v, Land Rover 110 (V8 Petrol)
1714-8100	Truck, Utility, Medium, CL, Hard Top, 12v, 4x4, LHD, Land Rover 110
1714-9101	Truck, Utility, Medium, CL, 4x4, Hard Top, 12v, LHD, Land Rover 110 (V8 Petrol)
1716-3100	Truck, Utility, Medium, CL, Hard Top, (Winterised), 4x4,12v, Land Rover 110 (Diesel)
1717-4100	Truck, Utility, Medium, GS, Hard Top, 12v, 4x4, Land Rover 110 (V8 Petrol)
1717-8100	Truck, Utility, Medium, GS, Plain Hard Top, 12v 4x4, LHD, Land Rover 110
1717-9101	Truck, Utility, Medium, GS, Hard Top, 12v, 4x4, LHD, Land Rover 110 (V8 Petrol)
1720-3100	Truck, Utility, Medium, FFR, Plain Hard Top, 12/24V, 4x4, Land Rover 110 (Diesel)
1720-8102	Truck, Utility, Medium, FFR, Plain Hard Top, 12/24V, 4x4, LHD, Land Rover 110
1721-3100	Truck, Utility, Medium, (Winterised), FFR, Plain Hard Top, 12/24v, 4x4, Land Rover 110 (Diesel)
1723-4100	Truck, Armoured Personnel Carrier, USMC, 3/4 Tonne, 4x4, RHD, Shorland
1722-4101	Truck, Armoured Patrol, 4x4, Land Rover 110 (V8), Heavy Duty, Prototype
1722-4102	Truck, Utility, Heavy Duty, Armoured Patrol, 4x4, Land Rover 110 (US) Version 1.5, Land Rover Chassis*
1722-4103	Truck, Utility, Heavy Duty, Armoured Patrol, 4x4, Land Rover 110 (US) Version 1.5, Courtaulds Chassis*
1723-9100	Truck, Armoured Personnel Carrier, 3/4 Tonne, 4x4, LHD, Shorland SB401
1723-9101	Truck, Armoured Personnel Carrier, 3/4 Tonne, 4x4, LHD, Land Rover 110 (V8) Heavy Duty
1725-3100	Truck, Utility, SAS, 4x4. Land Rover 110 V8 Heavy-Duty
1731-3100	Truck, Utility, Medium, FFR, Soft Top, 12/24v, 4x4, Land Rover 110 Diesel
1731-8100	Truck, Utility, Medium, FFR, Soft Top, 12/24v, 4x4, Land Rover 110 Diesel
1734-3100	Truck, Utility, Medium, GS, Mould, 4x4, 12v, Hard Top, Land Rover 110 Diesel
1734-3101	Truck, Utility, Medium, GS, Mould Repair, 4x4, 12v, Hard Top, Land Rover 110 Diesel
3623-4300	Equipment, Radar, RM1290 (Racal), Truck Mounted, Medium, 4x4, Land Rover 110

* Note: Version '1.5' may be a misreading for 'IS', ie: Internal Security.

SUMMARY OF ONE TEN DELIVERIES, 1983-1990
Tri-Service

Serials	Contract	Chassis nos	Total	Remarks
30 KB 67 to 30 KB 78	FVE 22A/203	192311 to 193498	12	Several variants, RHD and LHD petrol; stage 2 validation; for various trials units, 4 Jan 1983
90 KB 62	FVE 22A/208	212206	1	V8 HCPU trials vehicle
47 KC 24 to 47 KC 27	FVE 22A/203	213842 to 215963	4	GS RHD diesel; stage 2 validation; for various trials units, 23 Mar 1984
93 KC 72 to 94 KC 34	FVE 22A/241	222618 to 246039	63	Glover-Webb APV V8 RHD; for N.Ireland
24 KD 32 to 24 KD 72	FVE 22B/695	n/k to n/kN/K to N/K but including 232260	31	Glover Webb V8 HCPU RHD, for SAS
78 KE 27	FVE 22A/304	250758	1	Recovery RHD; 11 Nov 1985
78 KE 28 to 78 KE 55	FVE 22A/304	249434 to 254613	28	Station Wagon LHD; 11 Nov 1985
78 KE 56 to 78 KE 81	FVE 22A/304	249442 to 249588	26	Station Wagon RHD; 11 Nov 1985
78 KE 82 to 78 KE 90	FVE 22A/304	249951 to 253882	9	Station Wagon RHD; 11 Nov 1985
78 KE 91 to 79 KE 02	FVE 22A/304	252384 to	12	Station Wagon RHD; 11 Nov 1985
79 KE 03 and 79 KE 04	FVE 22A/304	249445 and 249449	2	Station Wagon V8 RHD; 11 Nov 1985; for SAAS
79 KE 05	FVE 22A/304	249441	1	Station Wagon V8 LHD; 11 Nov 1985; for SA Cairo
79 KE 06 to 79 KE 11	FVE 22A/304	250558 to 253074	6	GS Hard Top LHD; 11 Nov 1985
79 KE 12 to 79 KE 35	FVE 22A/304 Item 12	250552 to 253754	24	GS Hard Top RHD; 11 Nov 1985
79 KE 36 to 82 KE 06	FVE 22A/304 Item 12B	247915 to 251536	271	GS Soft Top LHD; 11 Nov 1985
82 KE 07 to 87 KE 46	FVE 22A/304 13B	247230 to 251881	540	GS Soft Top RHD; 11 Nov 1985
87 KE 47	FVE 22A/304	251559	1	GS Soft Top RHD; 11 Nov 1985
87 KE 48 to 87 KE 60	FVE 22A/304	251538 to 251559	13	GS Soft Top LHD; 11 Nov 1985
87 KE 61 to 87 KE 63	FVE 22A/304	251884 to 251887	3	GS Soft Top RHD; 11 Nov 1985
87 KE 64 to 87 KE 89	FVE 22A/304	248600 to 252841	26	CL RHD (Truck Cab) 11 Nov 1985
87 KE 90 to 88 KE 58	FVE 22A/304 Item 17	248898 to 252244	69	CL Hard Top RHD; 11 Nov 1985
88 KE 59 to 88 KE 86	FVE 22A/304	252810 to 252249	28	CL Hard Top RHD; 11 Nov 1985
88 KE 87 to 89 KE 06	FVE 22A/304	247971 to 254463	20	GS Hard Top LHD; 11 Nov 1985
89 KE 07 to 89 KE 86	FVE 22A/304 Item 19B	247940 to 254733	80	GS Hard Top RHD; 11 Nov 1985
89 KE 87 to 91 KE 09	FVE 22A/304 Item 20A	250367 to 253859	123	FFR Hard Top LHD; 11 Nov 1985
91 KE 10 to 94 KE 53	FVE 22A/304 20B	249413 to 253849	344	FFR Hard Top RHD; 11 Nov 1985
94 KE 54 to 96 KE 87	FVE 22A/304	252009 to 255666	234	GS Soft Top LHD; 11 Nov 1985
96 KE 98 to 01 KF 62	FVE 22A/304 23B	251888 to 255635	464	GS Soft Top RHD; 11 Nov 1985
01 KF 63 to 01 KF 72	FVE 22A/304	253858 to 255639	10	GS Hard Top LHD; 11 Nov 1985
01 KF 73 to 02 KF 02	FVE 22A/304	254762 to 255819	30	GS Hard Top RHD; 11 Nov 1985
02 KF 03 to 02 KF 97	FVE 22A/304 Item 28	254227 to 256709	95	CL RHD (Truck Cab); 11 Nov 1985
02 KF 98 to 03 KF 17	FVE 22A/304	254241 to 255067	20	CL Hard Top RHD; 11 Nov 1985
05 KF 15	FVE 22A/248 -	252914	1	Station Wagon LHD; 25 Sept 1985; for DA Accra
05 KF 16	FVE 22A/248 -	252935	1	Station Wagon V8 RHD; 25 Sept 1985; for DA Nairobi
05 KF 17	FVE 22A/248	253538	1	Station Wagon V8 LHD; 25 Sept 1985; for DA Lagos
08 KF 60	([ex -00 WA 83)	211802	1	Glover-Webb APV V8 RHD; for Northern Ireland
08 KF 62	[LP	245474	1	Station Wagon V8 LHD; 17 February 1986; for Berlin
08 KF 92 to 09 KF 36	FVE 22A/241	246168 to 248335	45	Glover-Webb APV V8 RHD; for Northern Ireland
10 KF 76 to 10 KF 84	FVE 22A/304 Item 26a	259791 to 259984	9	GS Hard Top LHD; 11 Nov 1985

10 KF 85 to 10 KF 87	FVE 22A/304 Item 26b	259661 to 259665	3	GS Hard Top RHD; 11 Nov 1985
10 KF 88 to 13 KF 34	FVE 22A/304 Item 27a	260205 to 264603	247	FFR Hard Top LHD; 11 Nov 1985
13 KF 35 to 16 KF 66	FVE 22A/304 Item 27b	259647 to 266957	332	FFR Hard Top RHD; 11 Nov 1985
35 KF 87 and 35 KF 88	FVE 22A/248	256883 and 256888	2	Station Wagon RHD (V8); 13 Jan 1986; for 33 EOD Regiment RE
35 KF 91 to 38 KF 70	FVE 22A/304	288018 to 319109	280	GS Soft Top LHD; 11 Nov 1985
38 KF 71 to 43 KF 04	FVE 22A/304 Item 30B	287888 to 291841	434	GS ST RHD; 11 Nov 1985
43 KF 05 to 43 KF 12	FVE 22A/304	300463 to 301951	8	GS Hard Top LHD; 11 Nov 1985
43 KF 13 to 43 KF 30	FVE 22A/304	287900 to 315881	18	GS Hard Top RHD; 11 Nov 1985
43 KF 31 to 43 KF 34	FVE 22A/304	304808 to 306459	4	GS Hard Top LHD; 11 Nov 1985
43 KF 35 to 43 KF 44	FVE 22A/304	310946 to 319745	10	GS Hard Top RHD; 11 Nov 1985
43 KF 45 to 45 KF 92	FVE 22A/304 Item 34A	288541 to 319081	48	FFR Hard Top LHD; 11 Nov 1985
45 KF 93 to 49 KF 78	FVE 22A/304 Item 34B	288547 to 319756	386	FFR Hard Top RHD; 11 Nov 1985
49 KF 79 to 50 KF 08	FVE 22A/304	290956 to 317302	30	CL Hard Top RHD; 11 Nov 1985
82 KF 61	[Local Purchase]	254814	1	Station Wagon V8 LHD; 19 May 1986; for DA Algiers
91 KF 24 to 91 KF 98	FVE 22A/304	272066 to 277348	75	FFR Hard Top LHD; 20 Jun 1986
91 KF 99 to 92 KF 73	FVE 22A/304 Item 27B	272075 to 276844	75	FFR Hard Top RHD; 20 Jun 1986
99 KF 58	FVE 22A/248	283641	1	Station Wagon V8 RHD; 23 Sept 1986; for SA Bangkok
31 KG 43 and 31 KG 44	FVE 22A/304	276453 and 276634	2	GS Soft Top RHD; 30 Apr 1986
31 KG 45 to 31 KG 53	FVE 22A/304	282227 to 282655	9	CL Hard Top RHD; 14 Nov 1986
31 KG 54	FVE 22A/304	282405	1	Station Wagon RHD; 14 Nov 1986; for RN
31 KG 55 to 33 KG 32	FVE 22A/304	281762 to 283084	178	GS Soft Top RHD; 14 Nov 1986
33 KG 33	FVE 22A/304	286107	1	GS Hard Top RHD; 14 Nov 1986; for RN
34 KG 57	FVE 22A/248	291388	1	Station Wagon V8 LHD; 27 May 1987; for SA Baghdad
34 KG 63 and 34 KG 64	FVE 22A/304	277491 and 277493	2	FFR Hard Top LHD; 14 Nov 1986
34 KG 65 to 34 KG 69	FVE 22A/304	277494 to 277757	5	FFR Hard Top RHD; 14 Nov 1986
34 KG 70	FVE 22A/304	277859	1	FFR Hard Top RHD; 14 Nov 1986; for RN
34 KG 71 to 34 KG 78	FVE 22A/304	290627 to 290947	8	CL Hard Top RHD; 14 Nov 1986
45 KG 89	FVE 22A/304	286462	1	GS Hard Top RHD; 14 Nov 1986
72 KG 67 to 72 KG 75	FVE 22A/304 Item 34a	319123 to 319764	9	FFR Hard Top LHD; 10 Jun 1987
75 KG 40	FVE 22A/248	318533	1	Station Wagon V8 LHD; 29 Jul 1987; for SA Riyadh
79 KG 42	[LP	298810	1	Station Wagon V8 LHD; 6 Oct 1987; for SA Warsaw
79 KG 43	LP	N/K	1	Station Wagon V8 LHD; 6 Oct 1987; for SA Warsaw (possibly cancelled)
80 KG 52 to 80 KG 78	FVE 22A/304 Item 48	322565 to 324882	27	Station Wagon RHD; 27 Aug 1987
80 KG 79	FVE 22A/304	323832	1	Station Wagon RHD (V8); 27 Aug 1987
88 KG 86 to 88 KG 91	FVE 22A/353	330674 to 331957	6	Glover-Webb APV V8 RHD; for Northern Ireland
92 KG 96	FVE 22A/373	343548	1	Station Wagon V8 LHD; for DA Algiers 9 Feb 1988
93 KG 19	FVE 22A/373	343298	1	Station Wagon V8 LHD; 22 Feb 1988; for SA Seoul
94 KG 45	FVE 22A/373	342628	1	Station Wagon V8 RHD; 18 Mar 1988; for SAAS
94 KG 50	LP	321465	1	GS Hard Top LHD; 23 Mar 1988; for GKN Warrior Trials Team
96 KG 84	FVE 22A/373	343046	1	Station Wagon V8 RHD; 18 Mar 1988; for SAAS
96 KG 86	FVE 22A/373	344782	1	Station Wagon V8 RHD; 17 Mar 1988; for DA Kampala
23 KH 61	LP	326453	1	Station Wagon V8 RHD; 14 Jul 1988; for SAAS

26 KH 94	LP	31856 (sic)	1	Station Wagon V8 LHD; 9 Oct 1988; for DA Warsaw
39 KH 26	LP	259885	1	GS fitted Compressor Prototype; 13 Dec 1988
54 KH 85	Loan – 6 months	571704	1	Details N/K; 18 Jan 1988; for Trials
11 KJ 77 to 12 KJ 09	LV2A/004 Item 1	422631 to 425408	33	Station Wagon RHD (V8)
12 KJ 10 to 14 KJ 54	LV2A/004 Item 3	415251 to 424619	245	GS Soft Top (V8) RHD
14 KJ 55 to 16 KJ 92	LV2A/004 Item 4	416634 to 424608	238	GS Soft Top (V8) LHD
16 KJ 93 to 17 KJ 07	LV2A/004 Item 5	415693 to 418662	15	CL (V8) RHD (Truck Cab)
17 KJ 08 to 17 KJ 17	LV2A/004 Item 6	422042 to 425511	10	CL (V8) LHD (Truck Cab)
17 KJ 18 to 17 KJ 72	LV2A/004 Item 7	415829 to 425024	55	CL (V8) Hard Top w/Windows RHD
17 KJ 73 to 17 KJ 77	LV2A/004 Item 8	415691 to 415749	5	CL (V8) Hard Top LHD

Right: 47 KC 27 was part of a further validation batch fitted with diesel engines, and was pictured here in later life whilst at Shrivenham wearing a hardtop body containing a perspex window in one side only. The purpose of this conversion is not clear. (GF)

Bomb Disposal

Below left and right: Both of these vehicles have the red-painted front wings that denote vehicles used by the ordnance disposal teams. However, 89 KE 22 is a hardtop model otherwise painted in standard drab, while 35 KF 87 is a civilian-pattern model painted in off-white. (FMW)

17 KJ 78 to 17 KJ 81	LV2A/004 Item 9	421542 to 422319	4	CL (V8) Hard Top RHD
17 KJ 82 to 17 KJ 90	LV2A/004 Item 10	416464 to 420635	9	GS Hard Top (V8) RHD
17 KJ 91 to 18 KJ 09	LV2A/004 Item 11	419990 to 423433	19	GS Hard Top (V8) LHD
18 KJ 25 to 18 KJ 34	LV2A/004 Item 4	424319 to 424782	10	GS Soft Top (V8) LHD;
34 KJ 34	FVE 22A/373	412392	1	GS RHD uprated chassis; 30 Sept 1989; possibly for NP Aerospace CAV Prototype
34 KJ 37 and 34 KJ 38	FVE 22A/373 Item 1	435694 and 435094	2	County V8 Petrol RHD; for BRIGNEPAL
34 KJ 39 to 34 KJ 42	FVE 22A/373 Item 1	435384 and 436694	4	Station Wagon V8 Petrol RHD; for BRIGNEPAL
34 KJ 81 to 34 KJ 85	ML22B/700	407380 to 413344	5	FFR RHD & LHD; for EASAM Ltd – ADCIS trials
40 KJ 36	FVE 22A/373	426718	1	Station Wagon (P) LHD; 20 Nov 1989; for SA Amman

RAF

Serials	Contract	Chassis nos	Total	Remarks
99 AO 01 to 99 AO 04	N/K	168475 to 168469	4	Shorts SB401; for USN at St Mawgan US Naval Weapons Facility in 1986
01 AY 37 to 01 AY 41	FVE 22B/622	180500 to 178939	5	Shorts SB401 for RAF Germany in Oct 1983
04 AY 67 to 04 AY 70	FVE 22A/248	247687 to 247699	4	Station Wagon RHD (V8)
06 AY 03	N/K	254355	1	Station Wagon RHD (V8)
17 AY 40	LV2A/138	N/K	1	Servicing Platform RHD

RN

Serials	Contract	Chassis Nos	Total	Remarks
63 RN 77 to 63 RN 80	FVE 22A/304 Item 50	N/K to N/K	4	Station Wagon, diesel, RHD; Feb 1988

Berlin Senät

All Berlin Brigade vehicles listed were procured under special contracts.

Serials	Contract	Chassis nos	Total	Remarks
06 XK 39 to 06 XK 71	–	257507 to 253798	33	FFR Hard Top LHD; May 1986
06 XK 72 to 06 XK 96	–	256195 to 256624	25	GS Hard Top LHD; Apr 1986
07 XK 78	–	270614	1	GS Hard Top LHD; Apr 1987
07 XK 79	–	277716	1	FFR Hard Top LHD; Apr 1987
07 XK 80 and 07 XK 81	–	273837 and 278172	2	GS Hard Top LHD; Jan 1987
07 XK 82	–	273836	1	GS Soft Top LHD; Feb 1987
07 XK 83 and 07 XK 84	–	275017 and 273835	2	FFR Hard Top LHD; Feb 1987
07 XK 92 to 08 XK 03	–	277714 to 277714!	12	GS Hard Top LHD; Mar 1987
08 XK 04 to 08 XK 18	–	278237 to 280995	15	FFR Hard Top LHD; Mar 1987
08 XK 19	–	278413	1	GS Hard Top LHD; Jan 1987
08 XK 20 to 08 XK 22	–	276424 to 276432	3	GS Soft Top LHD; Feb 1987
08 XK 23	–	275000	1	FFR Hard Top LHD; Jan 1987
		Total	97	

Non-Census

Serials	Contract	Chassis nos	Total	Remarks
00 NC 04 and 00 NC 05	Loan	212837 to 212948	2	110 Stage 2 Validation 2.5L Diesel RHD; Apr 1984
00 NC 07 and 00 NC 08	Loan	215986 and 215983	2	110 Stage 2 Validation 2.5L Diesel RHD; Jun 1984
		Total	4	

Land Rover loaned four diesel-engined One Tens to the Military Vehicles and Engineering Establishment (MVEE) as Stage 2 validation vehicles. These were in addition to the four registered in KC and listed above. Their purpose was probably to demonstrate the new 2.5-litre diesel engine that had replaced the earlier 2.3-litre type on production in February 1984. As they were not accountable assets but loan vehicles, they were given temporary serials in the NC (Non-Census) series. The vehicles were presumably returned to Land Rover after evaluation.

The RAF still favoured a hardtop with windows configuration, as seen here on 00 KF 82. (GF)

Even after the introduction of tri-service serials, vehicles in RAF use remained distinctive thanks to their yellow markings, intended to improve their visibility on airfields. 99 KE 44 is a standard GS cargo vehicle. (FMW)

A and (opposite page,) B: Not all RAF Mountain Rescue vehicles were the same. 31 KG 45 is a hardtop with the full military specification, but 11 KJ 95 (pictured in preservation), is a Station Wagon that appears to have a civilian specification. Both carry the same type of heavy-duty roof rack. As a late One Ten, the KJ vehicle also carries the '110' grille badge (see inset, opposite page) used only on 1989-1990 deliveries. A: (JT) B: (FMW)

In this case, an RAF V8 Station Wagon was doing duty as a Mountain Rescue ambulance, and carried appropriate markings. (GF)

OO NC 05 was one of four vehicles loaned by Land Rover for Stage 2 validation trials in 1984. It was pictured at Chertsey. These Non-Census vehicles were presumably returned to the company afterwards. (TMB)

Technical specifications, One Ten models

Petrol engines
2286cc four-cylinder with single carburettor and 74bhp
2495cc four-cylinder with single carburettor and 83bhp
3528cc V8-cylinder with two Zenith-Stromberg carburettors and 114bhp (to 1986) or 134bhp (1987 model-year and later)

Diesel engines
2286cc four-cylinder with indirect injection and 67bhp
2495cc four-cylinder with indirect injection and 67bhp

Transmission
Permanent four-wheel drive with lockable centre differential

Main gearbox
(a) With four-cylinder engines: Five-speed manual
(b) 1983-1985 model-years, with V8 engine: Four-speed manual
(c) 1986-1990 model-years, with V8 engine: Five-speed manual
Two-speed transfer gearbox, integral with main gearbox on four speed V8 models

Axle ratio
3.54:1

Suspension, steering and brakes
Coil springs all round
Worm and roller steering
Disc brakes on the front wheels and drum brakes at the rear; dual hydraulic circuits; servo assistance; separate drum-type transmission parking brake

Electrical system:
12-volt with alternator or (FFR models) 24-volt with 90-amp alternator; negative earth

Dimensions:
Overall length: 175in (4445mm) for truck cab and Soft Top
                     180.3in (4580mm) for Station Wagon
                     184in (4674mm) for HCPU
Wheelbase: 110in (2794mm)
Overall width: 70.5in (1791mm)
Unladen height: 80.1in (2034mm)
Track: 58.5in (1486mm)

Unladen weights:
3743lb (1698kg) minimum with V8 petrol engine
3799lb (1723kg) minimum with four-cylinder petrol engine
3840lb (1742kg) minimum with diesel engine

Performance:
(Four-cylinder diesel engine)
0-60mph   25secs approximately
Maximum: 70mph (112km/h)
Fuel consumption: 23mpg approximately (V8 petrol engine):
0-60mph: 15secs approximately
Maximum: 80mph (128km/h)
Fuel consumption: 13-15mpg

ONE TWO SEVEN, 1984-1990

Land Rover developed an extended-wheelbase derivative of the One Ten by cutting the chassis in two, and adding a centre section that increased the wheelbase to 127 inches. The first production examples were built at the end of 1983, and were marketed as One Ten Crew Cab types. Early vehicles were converted from One Tens and carried One Ten chassis numbers, but, from mid-1985, the extended-wheelbase Land Rover became a model in its own right with the name of Land Rover One Two Seven. Nevertheless, it continued to be treated as a conversion of the One Ten, and still carried One Ten chassis coding. The standard engine in these vehicles was the 3.5-litre petrol V8.

Although the standard configuration for these vehicles consisted of a four-door Crew Cab, with a cut-down, high-capacity, pick-up body, Land Rover also offered the model in chassis-cab form for special bodywork, and in this guise it attracted MoD interest. As early as August 1984, two chassis were sent to Marshall of Cambridge for prototype Crash Ambulance bodywork to be built. Regardless, no further vehicles were purchased until early 1987, when a quantity of Marshall ambulances was ordered. These were followed, in late 1988, by a quantity of broadly similar ambulance bodies from Locomotors. There were 167 ambulances in all.

The largest order for One Two Seven chassis followed in 1989, when versions with special bodywork by Marshall were designated as replacements for the Rapier tractors used by the RAF Regiment. There were 257 of these vehicles in total. Only one other One Two Seven was taken into British military service; this was utilised as a mobile operations room for the RAF Police.

Marshall ambulances

In August 1984, the MoD placed a contract (FVE22A/140) with Marshall of Cambridge for two prototype Crash Ambulances for the RAF and RN. These were to have a large box body, and be capable of carrying two stretchers on the nearside and up to four seated, wounded, or medical personnel on the offside.

The box body was asymmetric, as it had a window on the offside with sliding vents at the top, but just plain panel work on the nearside. The roof was fitted with a rack for carrying personal equipment, scrim nets, and so on. The seating arrangement could also be reconfigured to accommodate a third stretcher.

After the two prototypes were purchased, almost three years passed before a production contract (FVE 22B/882) for 48 (45 RHD and 3 LHD) vehicles was placed with Marshall in February 1987. This brought the total of Marshall-bodied

Ambulance

08 KD 72 was one of two prototype vehicles, pictured here in Bosnia in 1997. It had been delivered in January 1986 by Marshall's and continued to serve until 2001. (RS)

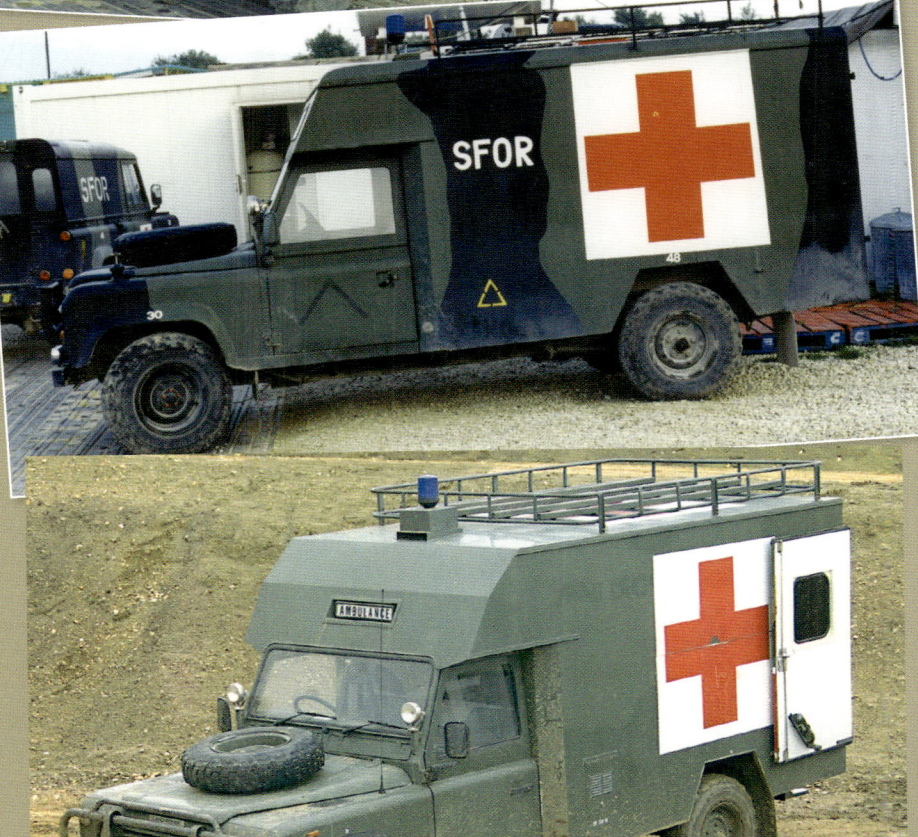

ambulances to 50. These Marshall ambulances had a number of differences from the later Locomotors type, and an obvious one was the large 'ambulance' sign, which was flush with the panelwork above the cab.

Locomotors ambulances

After that contract, the subsequent one (FVE 22B/939) was placed with Locomotors of Andover. Locomotors had won few military contracts at this stage, although it had built some van-bodied trucks for the services, and dental trailers for the navy. In practice, it appears that the actual construction of the bodies was sub-contracted to MMB (Macclesfield Motor Bodies), although all of them carried Locomotors identification plates.

The Locomotors body was similar to that of the Marshall ambulance, but had right-angled corners to the roof, rather than the chamfered style of the Marshall.. It also had a different arrangement to the Luton head over the driver's cab. The 'ambulance' sign over the cab was also much smaller and was recessed. There were also minor differences in the arrangement of the emergency blue lights. Locomotors built over 100 more ambulances, many of which were delivered on Defender 130 chassis (see Chapter 8).

Although both the Locomotors and Marshall ambulances on the One Two Seven chassis had been ordered as Crash Rescue types, many were pressed into active service in the former republic of Yugoslavia (FRY) in the early 1990s, where they served with army units, and in 1991, many were used on Operation Granby – the first Gulf war.

Left: 10 KJ 62 is from the contract with the Locomotors bodywork. Note the small recessed Ambulance sign in the revised angular bodywork head and the flat, rather than curved, roof. The box for the blue light on the roof has been revised and the twin blue lamps in the brush guard are circular, rather than rectangular. (GF)

Marshall Ambulance
The ambulance bodywork was asymmetric with a window on the offside and a plain metal panel on the nearside. The Marshall version featured a large, illuminated 'Ambulance' sign in the bodywork head – a feature that was much smaller in the Locomotors version. (CD)

Below left and right: This is an early production Marshall ambulance, still in almost as-delivered condition even though it was five years old when the photographs were taken at the International Tattoo. It then belonged to 4626 Aeromedical Evacuation Squadron, Royal Auxiliary Air Force. (GF)

10 KJ 62 was demonstrated at the Royal Navy and British Army Equipment Exhibition at Aldershot in September 1993. It is seen here on the Long Valley training area, picking up a simulated casualty. (GF)

Below: This view of 63 KG 84 illustrates how the body can carry three stretcher patients. The small, rearward-facing seat on the bulkhead, sometimes used by the medical attendant, is seen folded here. (CD)

Above: In July 1992, a number of vehicles were painted in overall white at Vehicle Depot Ashchurch for service with UK forces operating under the United Nations in Croatia as part of UNPROFOR. (VSM)

Top and above: The RAF Police had just one Mobile Operations Vehicle, 10 AY 22, based on the 127 chassis. The body manufacturer is unknown. This vehicle was equipped with awnings on both sides, which could provide additional external working space. It was occasionally seen at Airshows. (CD)

Mobile Operations Vehicle

The RAF purchased a single Mobile Operations Vehicle in 1988, which had similar bodywork to the Crash Rescue Ambulance. Although the bodywork was similar to Marshall's and Locomotors, it had a unique curved pantechnicon head. Internally, it was fitted with desks, and boards for displaying maps and details of incidents. The bodywork also included a folding awning on each side, providing additional, external working areas. The bodywork manufacturer is not known, but

some of the internal electronics are believed to have been provided by Saab Training Systems (UK) of Westbury.

It was used by Headquarters Provost & Security Services of the RAF as a mobile command centre, handling major events and incidents. It appeared at a number of air shows in the late 1990s and early 2000s.

Rapier Tractors

The RAF had a role providing air defence for US airfields in the UK, as well as protecting its own front-line airbases. To do this, it was equipped with the Rapier air defence missile, as were the army's air defence batteries of the Royal Artillery. The army had moved from the B1 version of Rapier, towed by the 1-ton Land Rover, to B2, which was towed by a Bedford 4-ton truck.

Although the RAF continued to be equipped with the B1 version, by the late 1980s, many of the 1-ton Land Rovers were beginning to show signs of age, and the decision was made to replace them with a new tractor.

A competition was held with the One Two Seven pitted against the Iveco 40-10WM – the One Two Seven won the production contract after trials ended in mid-1989. The first two were built in late October 1989, and were delivered to the Rapier Training Flight at West Raynham for trials. The remaining vehicles were built from late November 1989, and the final examples were completed in February 1990. All had been delivered by the end

In total, 257 tractors were purchased – a mix of 12-volt GS vehicles for towing the Rapier trailer, and 24-volt FFR vehicles for towing the tracking radar trailer. Both LHD and RHD types were purchased. All of them had the 3.5-litre V8 petrol engine, and all were fitted with a Warn 8274 electric winch within the front bumper to enable the vehicles to recover their trailers if they became bogged down during firing operations. The specialised soft-top bodywork to carry the missiles and other equipment was fitted to the bare chassis by Marshall's of Cambridge.

The operational life of these vehicles was not long, and, by the middle of the 1990s, many had been relegated to support duties within the RAF. A key reason for this, was that the early 1990s saw the USAF close down many of its facilities in Britain, where the Rapier units had been based, leaving the vehicles surplus to requirements. As petrol-engined vehicles, their redeployment was problematic within a military force that was now committed to a single-fuel (diesel) policy. The last examples were not withdrawn until around 2002, although, in the meantime, some had been redeployed to USAF bases in Europe and to other MoD units.

SUMMARY OF ONE TWO SEVEN DELIVERIES, 1983-1990

For brevity, the tables show only the serial numbers (and not the prefix code) of these vehicles, which were all built with VIN numbers.

Tri-Service

Serials	Contract	Chassis nos	Total	Remarks
08 KD 71 and 08 KD 72	FVE 22A/140	233503 and 233603	2	Crash Rescue Ambulance RHD; (Marshalls) Prototypes in Aug 1984
63 KG 47 to 63 KG 91	FVE 22B/882	295450 to 316166	45	Crash Rescue Ambulance RHD; (Marshall's) in February 1987
63 KG 92 to 63 KG 94	FVE 22B/882	N/K to 310862	3	Crash Rescue Ambulance RHD; (Marshall's) in February 1987
10 KJ 39 to 10 KJ 88	FVE 22B/939	Item 1 387241 to 402363	50	Crash Rescue Ambulance RHD; (Locomotors) in December 1988
10 KJ 89 to 10 KJ 99	FVE 22B/939	Item 2 407063 to 415036	11	Crash Rescue Ambulance LHD; (Locomotors) in December 1988
90 KJ 36	LP	215099	1	V8 HCPU RHD
		Total	112	

Note: The first Locomotors ambulances, delivered in KJ, were definitely Land Rover 127 types. The later order, placed in January 1990 and registered in KK, was fulfilled by a mixture of 127 and Defender 130 chassis. All those registered in KK are listed in Chapter 8 for convenience, although strictly some of them were 127s. The difference is largely academic.

RAF

Serials	Contract	Chassis nos	Total	Remarks
10 AY 22	FVE 22B/1004	371692	1	Mobile Operations Vehicle RHD; for RAF HQ P&SS in 1988
11 AY 78 to 12 AY 52	FVE 22A/424	N/K to N/K	75	GS Soft Top w/winch RHD; for RAF Regiment in June 1989
12 AY 53 to 12 AY 84	FVE 22A/424	N/K to 429829	32	GS Soft Top w/winch LHD; for RAF Regiment in June 1989
12 AY 85 to 13 AY 59	FVE 22A/424	418958 to 426742	75	FFR Soft Top w/winch RHD; for RAF Regiment in June 1989
13 AY 60 to 13 AY 91	FVE 22A/424	N/K to N/K	32	FFR Soft Top w/winch LHD; for RAF Regiment in June 1989
17 AY 52 to 17 AY 86	LV2A/165 Item 1	N/K to N/K	35	FFR Soft Top w/winch RHD; for RAF Regiment
17 AY 87 to 17 AY 94	LV2A/165 Item 2	931018 to N/K	8	GS Soft Top w/winch RHD; for RAF Regiment
		Total	258	

Left: By 2001, many surplus 127s had been transferred to other units. This LHD example served with Engineer Regiment (EOD), and the red wings are a standard feature of the EOD vehicle paint scheme. Doubtless the large load space in the rear was welcomed and utilised. (DP)

Right: This vehicle has been transferred from the RAF Regiment to the USAF in Europe (USAFE), based at RAF Mildenhall. Bearing the low visibility marking of 66 Squadron RAF Regiment on the door, it was based at RAF West Raynham, and supported RAF Mildenhall. It entered service in about 1990, and appears from the registration to have been transferred to USAFE in 1995. (GF)

ASSET CODES

The Asset Codes (in use from 1984 to around 1993) are:

1046-4100	Ambulance, Crash Rescue, 2/3 Stretcher, 4x4, Land Rover 127 (Prototype)
1046-4101	Ambulance, Crash Rescue, 2/3 Stretcher, 4x4, Land Rover 127
1046-4102	Ambulance, Crash Rescue, 2/3 Stretcher, 4x4, Land Rover 127 Locomotors Ltd
1046-9100	Ambulance, Crash Rescue, 2/3 Stretcher, 4x4, LHD, Land Rover 127
1046-9101	Ambulance, Crash Rescue, 2/3 Stretcher, 4x4, LHD, Land Rover 127 Locomotors Ltd
1703-3100	Ambulance, Crash Rescue, 2/3 Stretcher, 4x4, Land Rover 127 (Wadham Stringer)
1826-4100	Truck, Utility, Medium, Mobile Police Ops, 4x4, Land Rover 127
1826-9100	Truck, Utility, Medium, GS, Soft Top, w/winch, 12v, 4x4, Land Rover 127
1833-4100	Truck, Utility, Medium, GS, Soft Top, LHD, w/winch, 12v, 4x4, Land Rover 127
1833-9100	Truck, Utility, Medium, FFR, Soft Top, w/winch, 24v, 4x4, Land Rover 127
	Truck, Utility, Medium, FFR, Soft Top, LHD, w/winch, 24v, 4x4, Land Rover 127

The later Asset Codes (from around 1993) are:

RB1703-3100	Truck, Utility, Medium, Mobile Police Ops, 4x4, Land Rover 127 (Wadham Stringer)
RB1826-4100	Truck, Utility, Medium, GS, Soft Top, w/winch, 12v, 4x4, Land Rover 127
RB1826-9100	Truck, Utility, Medium, GS, Soft Top, LHD, w/winch, 12v, 4x4, Land Rover 127

Technical specifications, One Two Seven models

Engine
3528cc V8-cylinder petrol with two Zenith-Stromberg carburettors and 114bhp (to 1986) or 134bhp (1987 model-year and later)

Transmission
Permanent four-wheel drive with lockable centre differential
Four-speed main gearbox (1984-1985) or five-speed main gearbox (1986-1990)
Two-speed transfer gearbox, integral with main gearbox on four-speed models
Axle ratio: 3.54:1

Suspension, steering and brakes
Coil springs all round
Worm and roller steering
Disc brakes on the front wheels and drum brakes at the rear; dual hydraulic circuits; servo assistance; separate drum-type transmission parking brake

Electrical system
12-volt with alternator or (FFR models) 24-volt with 90-amp alternator; negative earth

Dimensions
Overall length:	198in (5029mm)
Wheelbase:	127in (3226mm)
Overall width:	70.5in (1791mm)
Unladen height:	80.1in (2034mm)
Track:	58.5in (1486mm)

Unladen weights
4167lb (1890kg) minimum

Performance
No performance figures available

Visit Veloce on the web:

www.velocebooks.com / www.veloce.co.uk
Details of all current books ● New book news ● Special offers

4

NINETY, 1986-1990

There was a delay of just over a year before Land Rover made available a short-wheelbase, coil-sprung model alongside the One Ten. The Ninety was announced in May 1984, but did not actually have the 90-inch wheelbase its name suggested. The wheelbase was, in fact, 92.9in (2360mm). From the beginning, it came with the 2.3-litre petrol engine, or the 2.5-litre diesel, with the 3.5-litre petrol V8, 2.5-litre petrol and 2.5-litre turbocharged diesel becoming later options. Not surprisingly, it shared as much common engineering as possible with the One Ten models. Civilian versions of the Ninety normally came with winding door windows but, like the One Ten, the model was made available for military users with the old style of removable door tops, incorporating sliding windows.

As sure as night follows day, the Army began to investigate the possibility of replacing its half-ton Lightweights with the new, coil-sprung Ninety. This seems to have been a lower priority than the three-quarter-ton replacement programme. The Lightweight had outlived its usefulness, anyway. Helicopter payloads had increased significantly since its introduction, and, by 1985, the

Puma HC1 and Chinook could lift a Land Rover without the need for removable panels. Similarly, the Hercules C1 no longer required the narrow track of the Lightweight. It was thus possible to move to a militarised version of the civilian Ninety, rather than the exclusively military Lightweight.

A contract was placed in September 1984 for eight validation vehicles – two GSs and two FFR Hard Tops in both LHD and RHD. These were delivered in March 1985, then subjected to trials by various organisations, including MVEE and Trials and Development Unit, RCT.

The only production contract (FVE 22A/340) duly followed in spring 1986, and eventually, after several amendments, amounted to around 3000 vehicles in various versions – Station Wagon, Aircraft Armament Support, GS Soft Top, CL Soft Top and FFR Hard Top. These began to enter service later in 1986, with front line units in the Army, RAF and Royal Navy. In service, the basic vehicle was often referred to as the 'TUL' – an acronym for Truck, Utility, Light and a term that would endure. All had the 2.5-litre, four-cylinder-naturally-aspirated diesel engine. Early examples gave the same

This was probably a validation example of the TUL FFR. Note the unpainted wheelarch 'eyebrows,' a feature of civilian models. (RLC Museum)

problems in service as the diesel One Tens, but there was never a Ninety equivalent of the One Ten 'interim' purchase of petrol V8 models. No orders seem to have been placed specifically for the Berlin Senät (XK series) or the RAF (AY Series). After the initial contract, subsequent deliveries of similar vehicles were badged as 'Defender 90s,' details of which are contained in Chapter 7.

Ninety variants
Aircraft Armament Support vehicle

The Aircraft Armament Support vehicles replaced the various diesel Lightweights and Series 3s that had served in that role with the RAF, although there was no longer a need for a non-standard diesel engine! All the vehicles were fitted with various forms of spark-suppression, and had a hard-top, with windows – externally, they looked extremely similar to the Station Wagon.

The 'Hardtop With Windows' version of the Ninety was visually very similar to the Station Wagon variant. The most obvious difference was that the Station Wagon had two-piece sliding windows in the rear body side while the hardtop had a single-piece fixed window. This is an Aircraft Armament Support version of the TUL, pictured in service at Coningsby in June 1993. The front bumper of 61 KF 61 is marked RUAS, standing for 'Ready Use Armament Section.' (GF)

57 KG 92 is a LHD example
of an Aircraft Armament
Support Ninety. It was seen
at RAF Cottesmore in
2001. (GF)

The competition was loosely based on the rigorous, annual Cambrian Patrol military exercise, and was turned into a programme for Central Television. The *Combat '89* competition was among four teams from infantry regiments that represented the four countries of Great Britain. A full list of those regiments has proved elusive, but it appears that the vehicles used in *Combat '89* were returned to Land Rover after six months. They had chassis numbers with three-digit serial numbers instead of the usual six-digit type, and were, therefore, clearly regarded as 'special' by Land Rover. It has not been possible to trace them in surviving Land Rover records.

There was a second competition in 1990, with four different teams: the Royal Regiment of Fusiliers, the Argyll and Sutherland Highlanders, the Royal Welch Fusiliers and the Irish Guards. There is no evidence that vehicles were allocated from Army stocks for the 1990 competition, or that further vehicles were borrowed from Land Rover, so the identities of the vehicles used remain unclear.

The Army's willingness to allow its rally teams use of soft-top Ninetys suggests that there was no pressing operational need for them. 56 KG 03 was a LHD example that was in use with one of the Scottish Transport Regiments RLC in June 1996. (GF)

CL Soft Top

The CL Soft Top version was purchased in small numbers, and was issued to administrative units of the Army, RAF and RN. Known users included Infantry Training Battalions and the Defence School of Transport. There was a plan to order CL Hard Top versions, as part of contract FVE 22A/340, but, before any were delivered, they were cancelled in favour of ordinary GS versions. Although an Asset Code was issued, this type of vehicle was never built.

'Combat' TV competition

The British military normally bought its Ninetys with the 2.5-litre, naturally-aspirated diesel engine, but, in 1989, acquired a group of five that were fitted with the turbocharged version of this engine. (The model was known on the civilian market as a Ninety Diesel Turbo.) These five were used by four army teams in a TV competition called *Combat*, and probably represented four team vehicles plus one spare.

FFR

The Fitted For Radio (FFR) version was issued to units that needed a vehicle capable of being fitted with radios (initially Clansman but later Bowman). Many command elements in Infantry Battalions, Armoured, Artillery and Engineer Regiments were issued with TUL FFRs. Where more than one radio was needed, a TUM FFR might be preferred. For example, in a Royal Artillery Field Regiment Battery in BAOR, the following were issued with a TUL FFR: the Signals Officer, the 2i/c, the Quartermaster, and the Quartermaster (Tech). As a further example, in a UK-based Royal Corps of Transport Regiment supporting a brigade, each Troop Headquarters was issued with a TUL FFR to carry a Clansman UK/VRC353 to enable it to communicate with Squadron HQ, and thus to brigade HQ.

Left: 53 KG 06 was a hardtop model that was pictured here when serving on the BATUS ranges in Canada. It later served with units in the UK including 47 Air Despatch Squadron RLC, HQ UK Force Artillery AMF(L) and 5 Regiment Royal Artillery before being sold in 2001 through MVS, Lichfield. Hardtops were favoured as they offered protection for valuable communications equipment. (Land Rover)

Below: Although looking like an RAF vehicle, 74 KF 60 was with the Army School of Mechanical Transport (ASMT) at Leconfield. From the damage to the bonnet, it looks like one of the learner drivers has been using it! (FMW)

Above: 63 KF 57 is a GS Soft Top model, pictured serving with the Royal School of Artillery in 1993. The School's fleet number of '125' is in white on the offside wing and is the only marking. (GF)

Left: Ninety Hard Top 52 KG 69 was pictured here in as-delivered condition inside Central Vehicle Depot Ashchurch. (VSM)

Right: Seen at Chelsea Hospital and driven by a member of the First Aid Nursing Yeomanry as part of a pageant to celebrate their centenary in 2007, 65 KF 96 was another TUL GS. It belonged to Headquarters Squadron of 71 Signal Regiment, RCS (V). (GF)

Above: 61 KF 88 was one of the first Ninetys to enter service and was receipted into Depot on 23 May 1986. It is a TUL GS Soft Top RHD of 1 Squadron RCT which supported 19 Brigade. (FMW)

Below: 64 KF 64, another TUL GS, was used by the British Forces Rally Team. Later it was preserved at the REME Museum reserve collection at Bordon. (GF)

Right: This Ninety in GS Soft Top form was in use at Battlesbury Bowl near Warminster during a Firepower Demonstration in 1992. (GF)

However, note that the Squadron HQ command vehicle was a TUM FFR, as it carried both a UK/VRC 353 to enable it to contact the Troop HQs and a UK/VRC321 to contact Brigade.

GS

The use of the General Service version of the Ninety was widespread, and it turned up with many different users in different roles. For example, in the Royal Artillery, it was issued to the Medical Officer in the A2 Echelon of an Artillery Battery, the Battery Sergeant Major in the RHQ of 50 Missile Regiment, and each Locating Battery is known to have had three. In the Infantry, it was issued to the MT Officer in Headquarters Company of an Armoured Infantry Battalion. However, it was also issued to many other units, where a command and liaison vehicle not specifically designed to carry radios was needed.

Station Wagon

The four Station Wagons in the contract all had RHD. The type was classified as a seven-seater – three in the front, and two facing inwards on each side at the rear – although it is doubtful if it ever carried that many personnel in service. Its potential users were limited in number – one went to Cyprus, another to the Inverness Training Centre, the third went to Defence Land Service Ammunition, and the user of the fourth is not known.

SAS 'Dinky'

During Operation Granby, the first Gulf war, units of 22 SAS quickly ran into a shortage of vehicles, as their One Ten long-range patrol vehicles were fully committed on operations. So, in early 1991, Longline quickly converted an unknown small quantity of TUL GS

vehicles for them. These vehicles were for proposed operations by B Squadron SAS, and were later also used to protect re-supply convoys towards the end of operations.

The modifications included: removing the windscreen, and adding a small, metal deflector plate to the bulkhead, the commander's seat was raised, as on the One Ten vehicles for the SAS, and a single GPMG was fitted ahead of that position, apparently using a footwell mount. At the rear, there was a pintle mount (possibly of the type used by the RAF regiment), which carried two more GPMGs, and there were panniers – made of wire mesh over a tubular framework – outside the rear body on each side. One spare wheel was carried on the bonnet, and one on a special mount above the tailgate at the rear. Some vehicles had rollover bars, although others appear not to have done.

The converted vehicles typically carried a crew of three.

These special conversions acquired the punning nickname of 'Dinky:' the word was created by replacing a 'D' (for diesel) to the 'P' of 'Pinky,' the nickname used for the One Ten Desert Patrol Vehicles, and of course, the word 'dinky' can mean 'small' as well. Pictures of these vehicles are extremely rare, although at least one (62 KF 44) did return to the UK intact. Like its fellows, this Dinky was later stripped of its modifications, and sold on in the usual way. Worth noting is that the vehicle which has been displayed at the IWM in Duxford as a Dinky, was not, in fact, a real one, but a former Land Rover demonstrator vehicle. It may also be of interest that the infamous 'Bravo Two Zero' patrol declined to take a Dinky, despite urging by both the 22 SAS commanding officer and the Regimental Sergeant Major!

Photographs of the SAS 'Dinky' are extremely rare. This illustration of 62 KF 44 is composed of two pictures taken in summer 1991 after it had returned from convoy escort duty in Iraq. The vehicle was delivered to the Regiment in December 1986. Its special equipment was later removed, and the vehicle was struck off in 2002. (JT)

The Asset Codes (in use until around 1993) are as follows. Note that the records for 1617-3100 and 1617-8100 show the name Defender, which strictly refers to later models (see Chapter 7).

1150-3100	Car, Utility, 4x4, 7 seater, Land Rover 90 (Diesel)
1617-3100	Truck, Utility, Light, Aircraft Armament Support, Hard Top w/windows, 12v, 4x4, Land Rover 90 Defender (Diesel)
1617-8100	Truck, Utility, Light, Aircraft Armament Support, Hard Top w/windows, 12v, 4x4, LHD, Land Rover 90 Defender (Diesel)
1620-3101	Truck, Utility, Light, GS, Cargo, Soft Top, 12v, 4x4, Land Rover 90 (Diesel)
1620-8100	Truck, Utility, Light, GS, Cargo, Soft Top, 12v, 4x4, LHD, Land Rover 90 (Diesel)
1621-3101	Truck, Utility, Light, CL, Plain Hard Top, 12v, 4x4, Land Rover 90 (Diesel)
1625-3100	Truck, Utility, Light, FFR, Plain Hard Top, 12/24v, 4x4, Land Rover 90 (Diesel)
1625-8100	Truck, Utility, Light, FFR, Plain Hard Top, 12/24v, 4x4, LHD, Land Rover 90 (Diesel)
1627-3100	Truck, Utility, Light, CL, Soft Top, 12v, 4x4, Land Rover 90 (Diesel)
1627-8100	Truck, Utility, Light, CL, Soft Top, 12v, 4x4, LHD, Land Rover 90 (Diesel)

The later Asset Codes (from around 1993) are:

NB1620-3101	Truck, Utility, Light, GS, Cargo, Soft Top, 12v, 4x4, Land Rover 90 (Diesel)
NB1620-8100	Truck, Utility, Light, GS, Cargo, Soft Top, 12v, 4x4, LHD, Land Rover 90 (Diesel)
NB1625-3100	Truck, Utility, Light, FFR, Plain Hard Top, 12/24v, 4x4, Land Rover 90 (Diesel)
NB1625-8100	Truck, Utility, Light, FFR, Plain Hard Top, 12/24v, 4x4, LHD, Land Rover 90 (Diesel)
NB1628-8100	Truck, Utility, Light, FFR, Soft Top, 12/24v, 4x4, LHD, Land Rover 90 (Diesel)
NB1627-3100	Truck, Utility, Light, CL, Soft Top, 4x4, 12V, Land Rover 90
NB1627-8100	Truck, Utility, Light, CL, Soft Top, 12v, 4x4, LHD, Land Rover 90 (Diesel)
RB1627-3100	Truck, Utility, Light, CL, Soft Top, 4x4, 12V, Land Rover 90
RB1620-3101	Truck, Utility, Light, GS, Cargo, Soft Top, 12v, 4x4, Land Rover 90 (Diesel)
RB1620-810	Truck, Utility, Light, GS, Cargo, Soft Top, 12v, 4x4, LHD, Land Rover 90 (Diesel)
RB1625-3100	Truck, Utility, Light, FFR, Plain Hard Top, 12/24v, 4x4, Land Rover 90 (Diesel)
RB1625-8100	Truck, Utility, Light, FFR, Plain Hard Top, 12/24v, 4x4, LHD, Land Rover 90 (Diesel)

SUMMARY OF NINETY DELIVERIES, 1983-1990
Tri-Service

Serials	Contract	Chassis nos	Total	Remarks
25 KD 06 to 25 KD 13	FVE 22A/78	227399 to 228294	8	Validation vehicles GS and FFR, LHD and RHD; September 1984
60 KF 85 ZZZ 60 KF 86	FVE 22A/340	274334 ZZZ 274340	2	Station Wagon RHD
60 KF 87 to 61 KF 22	FVE 22A/340	269764 to 276809	36	Aircraft Armament Support RHD
61 KF 23 to 61 KF 53	FVE 22A/340	269765 to 275068	31	Aircraft Armament Support LHD
61 KF 54 to 61 KF 74	FVE 22A/340	N/K to N/K	21	Aircraft Armament Support RHD
61 KF 75 to 69 KF 59	FVE 22A/340	259718 to 270505	785	GS Soft Top RHD
69 KF 60 to 74 KF 18	FVE 22A/340	N/K to N/K	459	GS Soft Top LHD

74 KF 19 to 74 KF 21	FVE 22A/340	270508 to 272257	3	GS Soft Top RHD
74 KF 22 to 75 KF 04	FVE 22A/340	270514 to 272172	83	GS Soft Top RHD [planned CL Hard Top RHD]
75 KF 05 to 75 KF 13	FVE 22A/340	N/K to 269558	9	CL Soft Top RHD
75 KF 14 to 76 KF 13	FVE 22A/340	258709 to 272229	100	FFR LHD
76 KF 14 to 78 KF 78	FVE 22A/340	260495 to 267675	265	FFR RHD
91 KF 16	LP	N/K	1	Station Wagon LHD; for SAAS
51 KG 00 to 52 KG 99	FVE 22A/340	288074 to 312090	200	FFR LHD
53 KG 00 to 54 KG 92	FVE 22A/340	288056 to 311741	193	FFR RHD
54 KG 93 to 56 KG 36	FVE 22A/340	287950 to 311791	144	GS LHD
56 KG 37 to 57 KG 74	FVE 22A/340	287942 to 313179	138	GS RHD
57 KG 75 to 57 KG 76	FVE 22A/340	298716 to N/K	2	Station Wagon RHD
57 KG 77	FVE 22A/340	290065	1	CL Soft Top LHD
57 KG 78 to 57 KG 85	FVE 22A/340	N/K to N/K	8	CL Soft Top RHD
57 KG 86 to 57 KG 96	FVE 22A/340	295355 to 304724	11	CL Soft Top LHD
57 KG 97 to 58 KG 14	FVE 22A/340	295344 to	18	Aircraft Armament Support RHD
63 KG 29 to 63 KG 33	FVE 22A/340	N/K to 310815	5	Aircraft Armament Support LHD
59 KH 96 to 60 KH 00	LP	179 to 183	5	GS Soft Top RHD; for TV Programme 'Combat' in March 1989, then returned to Land Rover

Note: There were no deliveries directly to the RAF or for the Berlin Senät.

The RAF was also a user of the TUL GS, although like this one they were often adorned with hi-vis fluorescent stripes for airfield movements. 69 KF 40 was on strength at RAF Abingdon in September 1987. (GF)

Technical specifications, Ninety models

Engines
2495cc four-cylinder diesel with indirect injection and 67bhp
2495cc four-cylinder turbocharged diesel with indirect injection
and 85bhp ('Combat' motorsport vehicles only)

Transmission
Permanent four-wheel drive with lockable centre differential
Five-speed manual main gearbox
Two-speed transfer gearbox
Axle ratio: 3.54:1

Suspension, steering and brakes
Coil springs all round
Worm and roller steering
Disc brakes on the front wheels and drum brakes at the rear;
dual hydraulic circuits; servo assistance; separate drum-type
transmission parking brake

Electrical system
12-volt with alternator or (FFR models) 24-volt with 90-amp
alternator; negative earth

Dimensions
Overall length:	146.5in (3720mm)
Wheelbase:	92.9in (2360mm)
Overall width:	70.5in (1791mm)
Unladen height:	7.3in (1963mm) for truck cab
	77.4in (1966mm) for soft-top
	77.6in (1971mm) for hardtop and Station Wagon
Track:	58.5in (1486mm)

Unladen weight
3622lb (1643kg) minimum

Performance
0-60mph:	25secs approximately
Maximum:	70mph (112km/h)
Fuel consumption:	23mpg approximately

(Figures for standard non-turbocharged engine)

Towards the middle of the 1980s, the MoD issued a requirement for a new two-ton general purpose load carrier that it hoped would enter service towards the end of that decade. One of its intended uses was to replace the Land Rover 101 Forward Control models that were then in service.

The requirement went out during 1984 through EASAMS (Elliott Automation Space and Advanced Military Systems), acting as sub-contractor for the MoD, and manufacturers were invited to offer two types of vehicle: a GS cargo truck and a 24-volt box-body communications truck within the two-ton class, known as TUH (Truck, Utility, Heavy). It was clear from this that the MoD was thinking long-term, and wanted its new TUH to have a great deal of commonality with its other vehicles in the half- to two-ton load classes. As Land Rovers were already the standard vehicles in the lighter load classes, the idea that a two-tonner from Land Rover would win the contract was almost written into the request for proposals.

Land Rover decided that the most effective way of meeting the TUH requirement was to develop a new vehicle on the basis of the current production One Ten model, allowing a high proportion of the mechanical items to be identical to, or adapted from, existing production items. Back in the early 1960s, the company had created a 30cwt load-carrier from the then-current 109-inch model, by re-engineering it with forward control (see Chapter 7 of *British Military Land Rovers, vol 1*). This basic idea was now brought up to date, as the new two-ton truck was designed around the existing One Ten chassis. Although both the cab and the body would have to be specially designed, Land Rover later claimed that 85% of the

new vehicle's chassis and drivetrain components were taken from existing Land Rover models.

A first feasibility prototype was built in 1984, on a modified production One Ten chassis. Like the later 'full' prototypes, this had a carburettor V8 engine; it probably also had the heavy-duty Salisbury axles used on Shorland armoured-car derivatives of the One Ten. It was fitted with an extended HCPU-type back body, and an all-new cab design, which used GRP panels bonded to a steel tube space-frame. Experience with this prototype underpinned the formal programme proposal that was completed in mid-September, 1984.

Land Rover management approved the development programme, which was known as 'Project Llama,' in the full knowledge that there were risks. Firstly, Land Rover would have to underwrite all the development costs itself on this project, and MVEE, as it still was, would not provide the design input, which had contributed so much to the development of the Lightweight and 101 models for the military. Secondly, although the contract would be for 2000 or more vehicles, those costs were only likely to be justified if the vehicle could be sold to overseas military forces and civilian customers. There was no guarantee of either, and a market study showed that existing competitors in this class of vehicle were all sold in worryingly low volumes. The viability of the Llama project, therefore, depended on obtaining the MoD contract.

Land Rover then submitted its technical proposals to the MoD for approval, and received a request to deliver four vehicles for

Below: The only sales brochure for the Llama showed the vehicle towing a 105mm Light Gun. This was an important role carried out by the 1-Tonne for which a replacement was needed. (JT Collection)

LAND ROVER FORWARD CONTROL

Above: The Llama chassis had a distinctive triangulated feature at the front, which served as the pivot for the tilting cab. (JT)

the trials, scheduled to begin in August 1985. The development period was now very short, and building of the vehicles actually began around June 1985. In the longer term, Land Rover had hoped to launch commercial versions of the vehicle in June 1986. The military versions, meanwhile, would start to enter service in April 1987.

The initial prototype had made clear that the modified One Ten chassis was not up to the job, so a special, straight-frame, truck-type chassis had to be designed. This came to a point at the front, providing a pivot and mounting for the cab, which was designed to tilt forwards (as in some heavy trucks) to give access to the engine. Instead of the One Ten's rear-mounted fuel tank, there was a side-mounted one, taken from the Leyland truck division, and several other Leyland light-truck components were also incorporated into the design, saving both time and costs.

Meanwhile, the HCPU-style rear body had been rejected in favour of a bought-in, aluminium, platform-style body. This was more readily adaptable to the GS cargo truck and the 24-volt box-body communications truck configurations that the MoD

wanted, and was also flexible enough to suit anticipated civilian applications.

Land Rover completed a total of seven vehicles as a first stage, retaining the first three for its own development work, and delivering four to the MoD for trials, all with the GS cargo configuration (although at least one had a different design of dropside rear body). These trials were conducted over the winter of 1985-1986, and the Llama was competing with two other vehicles: the Reynolds-Boughton RB44 (a 4x4 adaptation of the Dodge 50-series truck), and the Stonefield, built by a small Scottish company, and dependent on Land Rover running components. On the face of it, neither looked like a promising contender for the contract.

Two of the four Llama prototypes began trials at RARDE (the newly re-named MVEE) in Chertsey during February 1986, and immediately hit a problem. They would not meet the tilt and stability criteria. So one was rushed back to Solihull for a re-work while the other was put through performance trials.

The re-worked Llama came back to Chertsey two months later, by which time it would pass the tilt and stability tests but was not actually complete; the wider front axle that Land Rover wanted was

The contract for the RB44 was formally placed in June 1988; this was for 846 vehicles and worth around £25 million. It was a decision that the MoD was later to regret, when braking problems grounded the RB44s in the early 1990s. Ironically, many of the Land Rover 101s the Llama had been intended to replace were refurbished to keep the army mobile.

THE LLAMA TRIALS VEHICLES, 1985-1986

None of these vehicles ever wore a military serial number. All four carried civilian registration plates throughout the trials. The chassis prefix numbers had a distinctive letter code (K), but the serial numbers were simply prototype numbers; LFC stood for Llama (or possibly Land Rover) Forward Control.

This Llama, with box body, is now preserved at the British Motor Museum at Gaydon. In this form it might have been used as an Ambulance or a Radio vehicle. (GF)

The full set of Llama prototypes were registered as A238 KHP, C412 SNP to C418 SNP, D543 YAB, D544 YAB and D873 GDU. The enthusiast-built vehicle became G11 AMA.

Trials no	Registration no	Chassis nos	Remarks
T5	C416 SNP	SALLKHAV7AA-LFC005	Low-mounted dropside body and 24-volt electrical system; alternator mounted behind cab and shaft-driven.
T6	C417 SNP	SALLKHAV7AA-LFC006	Low-mounted dropside body.
T7	C415 SNP	SALLKHAV7AA-LFC004	High-mounted dropside body.
T8	C418 SNP	SALLKHAV7AA-LFC007	Low-mounted dropside body.
(None)	D543 YAB	SALLKHAV7AA-LFC008	Built with turbocharged 2.5-litre engine for second-stage trials.

Technical Specifications, 'Llama' 110 Forward Control

Petrol engine
3528cc V8-cylinder with two Zenith-Stromberg carburettors and 134bhp

Diesel engine
2495cc turbocharged four-cylinder with indirect injection and 85bhp

Transmission
Permanent four-wheel drive with lockable centre differential
Five-speed manual main gearbox
Two-speed transfer gearbox
Axle ratio: 4.7:1

Suspension, steering and brakes
Coil springs all round, with anti-roll bars front and rear
Recirculating-ball steering with power assistance
Disc brakes on the front wheels and drum brakes at the rear; servo assistance; separate drum-type transmission parking brake

Electrical system
12-volt with alternator, or 24-volt with 90-amp alternator

Dimensions
Overall length:	197in (5000mm)
Wheelbase:	110in (2794mm)
Overall width:	73in (1850mm)
Unladen height:	90in (2290mm)
Track:	59in (1511mm)
Ground clearance:	9.4in (240mm) on 9.00 x16 tyres

Unladen weights
4409lb (2000kg) in civilian trim

Performance
(V8 petrol engine):
0-60mph:	9.45secs
Maximum:	95mph (105km/h)
Fuel consumption:	15mpg approx

6

Defender 110, 1990 onwards

By mid-1990, Land Rover had a package of changes ready to introduce on its utility models. The most important of these was a new turbocharged, 2.5-litre direct-injection diesel engine, known as 200Tdi, which was to become the standard powerplant. Power-assisted steering was also to become standard, and modifications to the front seat mountings allowed the seats to be fitted closer together in order to provide more room between seats and doors. For commercial reasons, the new models would be known as Land Rover Defender types, and the long-wheelbase models became Defender 110 models. One reason for the choice of the Defender name was that it reflected the model's widespread military use, but in a politically correct description!

However, the new 200Tdi engine (also known by its development name of Gemini), had been designed as a civilian-market engine, and its design did not allow for fitting the large 90-amp alternator used on 24-volt FFR vehicles. There were two consequences of this; one was that the MoD continued to purchase its Land Rovers with the older 2.5-litre naturally-aspirated diesel engine; the other was that Land Rover embarked on a second-stage development of the new engine (internally codenamed Gemini 2), with a modified front end design that would accommodate the military alternator. Meanwhile, the 200Tdi engine was also being further refined for civilian vehicles, and, before long, the 'military' and 'refinement' programmes were amalgamated as the

A new grille badge distinguished the Defender models from earlier coil-sprung Land Rovers – but it was not impossible to transfer a Defender badge to an earlier vehicle. Civilian models like this one also had a green Land Rover oval badge on the grille bars, and black plastic headlamp surround panels. On British military vehicles, the Defender badge was often carried on the nose of the bonnet rather than above the grille. (LR)

'Gemini 3' programme, the resulting engine entering production in March 1994 with the name 300Tdi.

Although Land Rovers delivered to the MoD in the early 1990s carried the new name above the grille (the nameplate simply read 'Defender'), they did not have the same specification as the civilian models of the time. They also retained the earlier military asset codes unchanged. As new types received asset codes, sometimes the word 'Defender' appeared, but there seems to have been no absolute consistency about this! As far as it is possible to tell, the only Defenders purchased by the MoD with the 200Tdi engine were a batch of ten long-range desert patrol vehicles for the SAS – although it is likely that some of those purchased for SAAS use also had this engine.

British military Defenders of the early 1990s, nevertheless, did have the repositioned front seats of the civilian

models, and from 1994 they also had the new R380 five-speed gearbox, in place of the earlier LT77 type. This was a completely redesigned gearbox, with a different 'gate' (placing reverse gear behind fifth, instead of on a spur next to first) and a smoother gear-change action.

From 1994, the standard engine in civilian Defenders was the 300Tdi, which was mounted further forward in the chassis and had a relocated turbocharger. This invariably came with the R380 gearbox, and the combination remained in use until 1998. However, very few examples with this specification were delivered to the MoD (probably around 70 in all), and just three types have been identified. These were Station Wagons for the RAF; 'Anti-Spark' vehicles (initially for the RAF, but later with Tri-Service serials); and vehicles fitted with air conditioning. The 300Tdi engine, nevertheless, became standard on the special military Wolf models

Above: The 200Tdi engine in the Defender models had a distinctive ribbed top cover. This picture shows it in an early Discovery, which had a differently mounted turbocharger. (LR)

Above: A CAV 100 as originally used as 'Snatch' in Northern Ireland. 31 KK 92 is now preserved at the RLC Museum. (GF)

Left: This is a typical MoD identification plate, seen on 58 KK 62. Note that the manufacturer is shown as the Rover Group, of which Land Rover Ltd was then a part. (GF)

that began to enter service in 1995 and are covered in Chapters 10, 11 and 12.

Civilian models, meanwhile, went through several more changes. From 1998, they had a 122bhp, five-cylinder, 'Td5' turbocharged diesel engine, and a number of these entered British military service. This engine remained available until mid-2006, which is the cut-off date for this book. Later civilian Defenders had a 122bhp, 2.4-litre, four-cylinder 'Puma' or TDCi engine made by Ford (who by then owned Land Rover) which, from mid-2011, was replaced by a similarly powerful 2.2-litre derivative. Both versions of the Puma engine were accompanied by a Ford six-speed gearbox. There were a few deliveries with the Puma engine in late 2006.

Defender 110 variants

As usual, there were both 12-volt GS and 24-volt FFR variants of the Defender 110. In addition, there were multiple special variants, some created by user units. The major in-service refurbishment programme, TITHONUS, is dealt with later.

CL types

There were also purchases of civilian-specification vehicles, particularly for use by the Royal Air Force and Royal Navy. There were many Station Wagons (some for the SAAS) and Hard Tops, but some batches for the RAF were purchased with an Anti-Spark specification, to permit operations close to aircraft carrying bombs and within bomb dumps. Many CL Hard Tops seem to have served with RAF Police detachments, and others with the RAF Mountain Rescue Service (see below).

Purchases of civilian-specification Land Rovers continued after the introduction of Wolf XD. Because the use of some

Above: The Snatch as used in Northern Ireland was deployed unchanged to Bosnia where it provided troops with small arms protection during that conflict. This one was photographed in Bosnia in 1997. (RS)

Above: The armoured body of the Snatch was built to very close tolerances – so close that Land Rover had to prepare a special version of the Defender 110 chassis to suit it. (Courtaulds)

Left: A line of Snatch 1 vehicles ready to deploy during training during exercise Desert Dragon in 2006. The Perspex box on the bonnet normally fits over the rear hatch but can only protect from dust and debris. (GF)

more recent vehicles may be sensitive, the following tables listing these vehicles end in 2006. There were large numbers of purchases of Station Wagons for Cyprus, British Gurkhas Nepal (BRIGNEPAL) and the Falklands. There were also purchases of CL Hard Tops for the Falklands, the RAF JETS Radar Simulator unit based at RAF Spadeadam and the 'Dagger' Satellite Communications vehicle operated by 30 Signal Regiment, Royal Corps of Signals.

Composite Armoured Vehicle (CAV) or 'Snatch'

One of the more elaborate conversions of the One Ten was the Composite Armoured Vehicle (CAV) produced by Courtaulds as a replacement for the 109-inch Land Rovers used in Northern Ireland with Vehicle Protection Kits (VPKs).

The original requirement was for a more modern, demountable armour kit, to suit existing Land Rovers. At this stage, plastic armour technology was emerging, and Land Rover identified Courtaulds as able to meet the MoD requirement – but with a self-contained box body rather than a demountable kit of parts. The MoD was prepared to accept this change in specification, but it did cause problems for Land Rover.

The Courtaulds armoured body was made to very precise tolerances – far more precise than those Land Rover used for its chassis. The upshot of this was that there were major difficulties fitting bodies to chassis. So the Land Rover military engineering team drew up a new chassis with the necessary 3600kg GVW, using the existing design, but with the dimensional tolerances removed. The design was then supplied to GKN, who built the chassis specially for the Courtaulds vehicles. As these special chassis were expensive to build, the close-tolerance version was not adopted for all Defenders but remained unique to the Snatch.

The CAV offered significant protection to the crew against small arms fire through Courtaulds' patented armour system. However, the additional weight of the armoured body necessitated the use of the V8 petrol engine instead of the naturally-aspirated diesel engine favoured by the MoD for other Land Rover deliveries. In service, the vehicle became known as 'Snatch,' because of its role in collecting terrorist suspects from the streets of Northern Ireland. When Snatch was later deployed to Iraq and Afghanistan, its vulnerability to mines and improvised explosive devices (IEDs), led to campaigns in the press to have it replaced.

The first modifications saw the vehicle 'desertised' to enable more effective operation in these hotter climates. There was then an upgrade to Snatch 2 which involved fitting the 300Tdi engine in place of the V8, and in this form there were three variants: a 12-volt LHD, a 24-volt RHD and a 24-volt RHD for Northern Ireland, where some stocks were maintained even after the peace agreement.

Finally, 100 of the CAVs were rebuilt by Ricardo under contract SUVC/0156 to a new standard (known as 'Snatch 3,' or 'Vixen'). This involved fitting extra underbody protection including a belly-plate beneath the driver and commander, as well as a comprehensive set of enhancements to the engine, suspension, transmission and chassis. The increase in the GVW to 4.7 tons necessitated a more powerful engine; the swept volume increased from 2.5 to 2.8 litres, delivering around 20% more power. These engines were modified by Ricardo and were not bought in from South America, where Maxxion was also producing a 2.8-litre derivative of the 300Tdi engine.

The manual transmission was replaced by an automatic, offering not only greater ease of operation for the driver in difficult conditions but also promising better reliability. The chassis received a complete overhaul, with extra stiffening throughout. The front axle was modified, and the rear axle replaced completely with a unit supplied by Dynatrac. A heavily-revised suspension was fitted.

Snatch 2

Right: 33 KK 00 represents the CAV in Snatch 2 form. The heavy-duty wheels used on this version were distinguished by perforations around the rim. (GF)

Big Bird

Left: 'Big Bird' (30 KK 91) is a Composite Armoured Vehicle after it had been reconfigured to Snatch 2 form and fitted with Counter-IED equipment on the front windows and wings. It is seen at Basrah International Airport with 2 Squadron RAF Regiment. (RS)

Vixen

Right: The final version of CAV for Afghanistan was Snatch 3, known as Vixen. It can be differentiated from Snatch 2 by the alloy wheels although mechanically Vixen differed in several ways, among them being an engine enlarged to 2.8 litres. (AB)

This Station Wagon was purchased for use by NATO's Joint Electronic Warfare Core Staff (JEWCS). It is marked MIJA for Mobile Interceptor/Jammer. It carries a RACAL ULQ 19 jammer, which can operate while moving and can also act in an intercept capacity, scanning up to sixteen channels and indicating their strength. (DP)

73 KJ 08 was a RHD FFR Soft Top and was pictured at Basrah International Airport during Operation Herrick in 2008. (RS)

This rear view of a MIJA Station Wagon belonging to NATO JEWCS shows the roof-mounted aerials. (AB)

CG 14 AA is a well-used RHD FFR Soft Top, seen here marked up for Warminster Training Centre. (WTC) (RS)

with new springs and Bilstein dampers. In this form, the Snatch is regarded as High Specification (HS), and equivalent to the Wolf.

Some of the Snatch vehicles (a total of 153), were also rebuilt by Ricardo as Weapons Mount Installation Kit (WMIK) vehicles, but built to 'Wolf' specification, and are known as R-WMIK (Rebuilt WMIK). More details on WMIK are in Chapter 11.

Other vehicles underwent much more dramatic conversions, including 30 that became Project PANAMA remotely-controlled counter-IED vehicles, and 10 that were fitted with Station Wagon bodies by Ricardo designated as Media Ops Support Vehicles. Details of the media ops variants follow.

Glover Webb APV

A batch of 109 Armoured Patrol Vehicles was made in 1996 for use in Northern Ireland. Although the earlier Glover Webb APVs purchased as One Tens (see Chapter 2) were up-armoured later in life by fitting slabs of armour on the outside of the crew doors and body sides, much thicker slabs of armour were used on the Defenders in this purchase.

Grade A armoured staff car

In June 1996, two armoured County Station Wagons were ordered from Penman Engineering Ltd. These were for senior officers of four-star rank and above (ie Generals) and are presumed to have been purchased for senior officers serving in Bosnia.

Helicopter ground support

A special version of the leaf-sprung 109-inch Land Rover had been developed to provide ground handling support for

Top Right: Amongst the most dramatic conversions of CAV is Project PANAMA, which created a remotely operated vehicle with ground penetrating radar as part of a complex Counter-IED team of vehicles deployed for route clearance in Afghanistan. This is 28 KK 04. (GF)

Centre: This is PANAMA being towed by the Buffalo Mine Protected Clearance Vehicle. Note how the front detection beam folds up over the bonnet. (DP)

Bottom: Built as a CAV, 32 KK 41 has been converted to a Station Wagon by Hobson Industries. It is in use as a Media Ops vehicle and is fitted with a snorkel for deep wading. (GF)

helicopters, and this was now replicated on the long-wheelbase, coil-sprung chassis. The vehicle was capable of providing 24 volts at 90 amps for ground starting of helicopters, and was fitted with a Hard Top. Above the Hard Top was a working platform with a fold-down safety rail and a ladder to the left of the rear door. There was also an external socket in the Hard Top to the rear of the driver's door; this was for the 'heli-start' connection. The platform enabled technicians to work on the engines and tail rotors of helicopters in the field without needing specialist platforms. These vehicles equipped helicopter units of the RAF, principally 33 Squadron at Odiham and 230 Squadron at Gütersloh.

Media Ops

The Media Operations Group (MOG) is a specialist Army Reserve unit recruited from across the UK. Its members regularly form part of the deployed British Army on operations in all theatres, delivering specialist media training on exercises. Two types of vehicle were created for this group by Hobson Industries in 2006; one was a Media Ops Support Vehicle, based on a Station Wagon, and the other was a long wheelbase (130) box van as a base operation vehicle. The base operation vehicle is described in Chapter 12. The Station Wagons were created in most cases from surplus Snatch vehicles, although at least one was created based on a One Ten GS Soft Top. All had a heavy-duty chassis (already standard on the Snatch), to which were added a 2.2-litre Puma engine and the six-speed manual gearbox used with it on civilian production models. The known examples are: 80 KE 39, 80 KE 87, 82 KE 06, 27 KK 38, 27 KK 55, 28 KK 90, 28 KK 95, 30 KK 54, 30 KK 61, 32 KK 41, 32 KK 87, 33 KK 23, 33 KK 29, 38 KL 42 and CF 66 AA.

Top left: A Glover Webb Armoured Patrol Vehicle in its final form as used in Northern Ireland. 90 KL 47 is an example from the Defence School of Transport used for driver training and the 'Confidential Telephone Freephone – 0800 666 999' – has been painted over. (CD)

Centre: 59 KK 97 is a LHD Helicopter Ground Support vehicle and was pictured at RAF Cottesmore in 2001. (GF)

Bottom: 80 KE 87 is one of five Media Ops Station Wagons based on a One Ten GS rather than a Snatch. (DP)

RAF Mountain Rescue

The RAF Mountain Rescue Service (MRS) has used Land Rovers since the mid-1950s, when they were introduced as replacements for the service's wartime Jeeps. During the late 1990s, the MRS had teams at Kinloss, Stafford, Valley, St Athan, Leeming and Lossiemouth. These teams had a complement of Land Rovers, each of which performed a particular function – for example ambulance, command vehicle, or team support vehicle. The V8 Station Wagon proved popular with the teams, presumably because of its higher top speed, and a number served with the MRS. In 1999 these were replaced with a batch of civilian-specification white Station Wagons with standard modifications and the 300Tdi engine.

R-WMIK

As explained, a number of Snatch vehicles were later rebuilt to R-WMIK standard. (For more details of this specification, please see

Right: RAF Mountain Rescue Teams clearly liked the V8 Station Wagon and a further batch was purchased after the introduction of the Defender name. Here is 73 KJ 63, clearly wearing its 'Defender 110' decal badge above the rear grab handle. (GF)

Main picture: Two later examples of the Mountain Rescue Station Wagon are seen here in white livery. RX 31 AA is a Td5-engined vehicle; the rear view shows JP 01 AA. (GD)

Chapter 11.) In total, 153 CAVs were converted to WMIKs. Some went through a series of evolutions, beginning with the fitting of the roll-cage and enhancements to enable a higher payload to be carried; these became E-WMIK types. The next stage was refurbishment as R-WMIK, and the final evolution was R-WMIK+, with a further increase in payload, a larger engine, and automatic transmission.

SAS Desert Patrol Vehicle

A batch of ten Desert Patrol Vehicles was ordered in May 1992, based on the Defender chassis. These differed from their One Ten predecessors (see Chapter 2) in having a 200Tdi engine. The precise reason for this particular purchase is not known but since no losses occurred during Operation Granby – the first Gulf War – it may have been to strengthen overall numbers.

Winterised

It had been standard practice to convert normal vehicles with 'Winterisation Kits', but for the first time vehicles were now purchased in 'Winterised' form. Such vehicles are identifiable by Velcro strips around the windows, turnbuckles over the windscreen, and an additional heater between the front seats. Winterised vehicles were issued to units intended for service in Arctic areas, particularly northern Norway. They included units serving with ACE Mobile Force (Land) or 3 Commando Brigade.

ACE Mobile Force (Land) was a NATO force created in the 1960s to defend against a Warsaw Pact advance on the northern or southern flanks of Europe. The northern flank was northern Norway whilst the southern flank was Turkey.

From the 1950s until the end of the Cold War, 3 Commando Brigade had an increasing role in support of possible Arctic warfare in Norway. While 45 Commando at Arbroath maintained the core skills in mountain and Arctic warfare (MAW), other units deployed to northern Norway on a regular basis for training. Winterised versions of both GS and FFR types were available, and both were fitted with Hard Tops.

Many of the 3 Commando Brigade vehicles were subsequently fitted with a waterproofing kit to enable them to drive in deep water – for example, coming ashore from a landing craft. The most obvious feature of the kit was the snorkel fitted to the windscreen frame.

Above left and right: This is a Winterised GS Hard Top. Note the Velcro strips around the windows of 62 KJ 18 to enable window blinds to be fitted, the 'access hatch' or sun roof over the crew positions, and the cover over the fuel filler. The vehicle is marked 'OC 1 Tp' and was the OC's vehicle of 1 Troop of the REME Workshop of the Commando Logistic Regiment. (GF)

Right: The snorkel on this Winterised GS Hard Top suggests that a full waterproofing kit has also been fitted, as happened to many Defender 110s issued to 3 Commando Brigade units. This one was in use with the Medical Squadron of the Commando Logistic Regiment at the Royal Navy and British Army Equipment Exhibition in August 1997. (GF)

Main picture: CC 65 AA is a TITHONUS rebuild, with the later (Wolf) pattern Hard Top and an external roll-cage to protect the cab, as well as checker-plate additions on the sills, bonnet and wings. Unusually, it does not have the heavy-duty wheels. The picture was taken at RAF Coningsby in July 2011. (JT)

A Winterised FFR Hard Top of 29 Commando Regiment, Royal Artillery, which supports 3 Commando Brigade. The vehicle is marked "X" on the bumper, indicating a Battery Commander, and the roof rack is a unit modification. (GF)

CG 44 AA is a revitalised RHD FFR Soft Top, seen after it had undergone the Life Extension Programme (Project TITHONUS) including the fitting of a roll-cage over the crew positions. The vehicle was in use at Bovington. (BM)

Project Tithonus

Announced in 2007 and completed in 2010, Project Tithonus saw around 2700 Land Rover Defender vehicles upgraded by DSG. The work was intended to extend the in-service life of the fleet by up to ten years. The scope of work included refurbishment of bulkheads and chassis, renewal of all brake components, pipes, wheel bearings, hub seals and shock absorbers, and painting inside and out.

To improve occupant comfort and safety, a rollover protection system was also fitted, and all seat belts, driver and passenger seats were renewed. A new-style Hard Top, or canopy (as seen on the Wolf vehicles), was also to be fitted.

In Greek mythology, the goddess Eos, who loved Tithonus, wished for him to be given immortality. When Eos asked Zeus to grant her request, she forgot to ask for eternal youth, so legend has it that Tithonus was indeed immortal but existed as a withered and weak shadow of his former self, begging for his own demise!

(*) The same chassis serial number is recorded on MERLIN for both CU 88 AA and CV 44 AA. It seems likely that the vehicle was rebodied and re-serialled at the same time.

36 AY 38 is an RAF CL Hard Top Anti-Spark vehicle. It seems that various RAF units were equipped with such vehicles where they needed to visit hazardous areas. This example was seen in service with the RAF Police at the International Air Tattoo at Fairford in 1996, and has the civilian pattern headlamp surrounds, albeit painted over. (GF)

36 AY 37 was pictured in 'traditional' white livery with the RAF Police. (NH)

JM 83 AA is a later RAF Police vehicle, seen here in civilian colours, apart from the red stripe. (RC)

ASSET CODES

Note: Military record-keepers seem to have maintained a rather lax attitude to the differences between a Land Rover One Ten and a Land Rover Defender 110. The descriptions associated with the relevant Asset Codes are, therefore, somewhat haphazard in their use of the correct model names, but are shown here as they are recorded in MERLIN and JAMES computer records.

The Asset Codes in use up to around 1993 were:

1155-3102	Car, Utility, Medium, 12 seater, 4x4, 2.5 Litre Turbo Diesel, Land Rover 110 Station Wagon
1155-4104	Car, Utility, Medium, 4x4, 12 seater, Land Rover 110 (V8) Petrol
1155-4105	Car, Utility, Medium, 4x4, 11/12 seater, 2.5 Petrol, Land Rover 110 County
1161-3100	Car, Utility, SAAS, Medium, 4x4, 12 seater, Land Rover 110
1161-4104	Car, Utility, SAAS, Medium, 4x4, Land Rover 110 Defender
1161-9106	Car, Utility, SAAS, Medium, 4x4, LHD, Land Rover 110 Defender
1705-3100	Truck, Utility, Medium, GS, Plain Hard Top, 12/24v, 4x4, Land Rover 110
1705-8100	Truck, Utility, Medium, GS, Plain Hard Top, 12/24v, 4x4, LHD, Land Rover 110
1706-3100	Truck, Utility, Medium, Helicopter Ground Support, Plain Hard Top 12/24v, 4x4, Land Rover 110 Defender (Diesel)
1708-3100	Truck, Utility, Medium, (Winterised), GS, Plain Hard Top, 12v, 4x4, LHD, Land Rover 110 (Diesel)
1710-3103	Truck, Utility, Medium, GS, Cargo, Soft Top, 12v, 4x4, Land Rover 110 (Diesel)
1710-3104	Truck, Utility, Medium, GS, 4x4, Land Rover 110 2.5 Litre Mk 6B
1714-3101	Truck, Utility, Medium, CL, Cargo, 4x4, Hard Top, 12v, Land Rover 110
1716-3100	Truck, Utility, Medium, CL, Hard Top, (Winterised), 4x4,12v, Land Rover 110 (Diesel)
1717-3100	Truck, Utility, Medium, GS, Plain Hard Top, 12v, 4x4, Land Rover 110
1717-8100	Truck, Utility, Medium, GS, Plain Hard Top, 12v 4x4, LHD, Land Rover 110
1720-3100	Truck, Utility, Medium, FFR, Plain Hard Top, 12/24V, 4x4, Land Rover 110 (Diesel)
1720-3101	Truck, Utility, Medium, FFR, Plain Hard Top, Land Rover 110 2.5 Litre Mk 6B
1720-8100	Truck, Utility, Medium, FFR, Plain Hard Top, 12/24V, 4x4, LHD, Land Rover 110 Defender (Diesel)
1721-3100	Truck, Utility, Medium, (Winterised), FFR Plain Hard Top, 12/24v 4x4, Land Rover 110 (Diesel)
1722-4102	Truck, Utility, Heavy Duty, Armoured Patrol, 4x4, Land Rover 110 (US) Version, Internal Security, Land Rover Chassis
1722-4103	Truck, Utility, Heavy Duty, Armoured Patrol, 4x4, Land Rover 110 (US) Version, Internal Security, Courtaulds Chassis
1724-3102	Truck, Utility, CL, Anti-Spark, Medium, Aircraft Armament Support, 12v, Hard Top w/windows, Land Rover 110 Diesel Defender
1725-3101	Truck, Utility, Medium, SAS, (Pink Panther), 4x4, 3600Kg GUW, Gemini, Turbo Diesel, Land Rover 110 HC DV
1731-3100	Truck, Utility, Medium, FFR, Soft Top, 12/24v, 4x4, Land Rover 110 (Diesel)
1731-8100	Truck, Utility, Medium, FFR, Soft Top, 12/24v, 4x4, Land Rover 110 Diesel
1734-3100	Truck, Utility, Medium, GS, Mould, 4x4, 12v, Hard Top, Land Rover 110 (Diesel)
1738-3100	Truck, Utility, HT 3600 Kg, Land Rover 110 V8, Courtaulds Fibres Ltd
1738-3101	Truck, Utility, HT 3600 Kg, Land Rover 110 V8, Courtaulds Fibres Ltd

The later Asset Codes (from around 1993) are:

FB1090-3100	Car, Utility, CL, 4x4, BCU, 2.5-litre Diesel, Land Rover Defender 110
FB1091-3100	Car, Utility, CL, 4x4, Police Patrol, 2.5-litre Diesel, Land Rover Defender 110
FB1093-3100	Car, Utility, CL, 4x4, Medium, Hard Top, 2.5-litre Diesel, Land Rover Defender 110
FB1093-3101	Car, Utility, CL, 4x4, Medium, Station Wagon, 2.5-litre Diesel, Land Rover Defender 110
NB1126-9108	Car, Saloon, Grade A, Special Body, Penman, Land Rover Defender 110 Tdi County Station Wagon
NB1155-3102	Car, Utility, Medium, 12 seater, 4x4, 2.5-litre Turbo Diesel, Land Rover 110 Station Wagon
NB1710-3104	Truck, Utility, Medium, GS, 4x4, Land Rover 110 2.5-litre Mk 6B
NB1720-3101	Truck, Utility, Medium, FFR Hard Top, 4x4, Land Rover 110 Defender 2.5-litre Mk 6B
NB1720-3103	Truck, Utility, Medium, FFR, Plain Hard Top, 12/24V, 4x4, 2.5-litre Mk 6B Diesel, R380 Gearbox, Land Rover 110
NB1720-8102	Truck, Utility, Medium, FFR, Plain HT, 12/24V, 4x4, 2.5-litre Mk 6B Diesel, R380 Gearbox, LHD, Land Rover 110
NB1721-3100	Truck, Utility, Medium, (Winterised), FFR Plain Hard Top, 12/24v 4x4, Land Rover 110 (Dsl)
NB1731-3104	Truck, Utility, Medium, FFR, Soft Top, 12/24V, 4x4, 2.5-litre Mk 6B Diesel, R380 Gearbox, Land Rover 110
NB1731-8101	Truck, Utility, Medium, FFR, Soft Top, 12/24V, 4x4, 2.5-litre Mk 6B Diesel, R380 Gearbox, LHD, Land Rover 110
NB5004-3100	Truck, Utility, Medium, HS, Hard Top, w/VPK, 24v (with ACU), Refurbished 2008, GVW 4100 Kg, GTW 7000 Kg, Front Axle 1580 Kg, Rear Axle 2550 Kg
QB1714-3107	Truck, Utility, Medium, CL, Hard Top, 12-Volt, 4x4, Land Rover 110 JETS
RB1155-3102	Car, Utility, Medium, 12 seater, 4x4, 2.5-litre Turbo Diesel, Land Rover 110 Station Wagon
RB1155-3106	Car, Utility, ¾ Tonne, 4x4, 2.5L Turbo Dsl, Land Rover Defender 110 Station Wagon
RB1155-3107	Car, Utility, Medium, CL, 4x4, Land Rover 110 Station Wagon 12-seater
RB1155-4104	Car, Utility, Medium, 4x4, 12-seater, Land Rover 110 (V8) Petrol
RB1155-3115	Car, Utility, Medium, CL, 4x4, RHD, 9 seats, Land Rover 110 Station Wagon, 2.5-litre TD5 Diesel
RB1155-3117	Car, Utility, Medium, CL, 4x4, Land Rover 110 Station Wagon, 2.5-litre TD5, 11-seater, Cubby Box, LN Tow Hook
RB1702-3100	Truck, Utility, Medium, (HT), 4x4, RHD, Diesel, Land Rover TD5 110, Mechanical Transport Small Support Vehicle (MTSSV)
RB1714-3102	Truck, Utility, Medium, CL, 4x4, Hard Top, 2.5 Dsl, Land Rover 110
RB1714-3105	Truck, Utility, Medium, 4x4, Land Rover Defender 110, Double Cab, Hard Top w/Side Windows, 2.5-litre TD5 Diesel, 9 Seats, Cubby Box, LN Tow Hook
RB1724-3103	Truck, Utility, Medium, CL, 4x4, Hard Top, Anti-Spark, Land Rover 110 2.5-Ltr Tdi
RB1920-3100	Truck, Utility, Medium, Heavy Duty, CL, 4x4, Land Rover Station Wagon Bird Control Unit (BCU)
SB1155-3101	Car, Utility, Medium, 4x4, 12-seater, Land Rover 110
XB1701-8100	Truck, Utility, Medium, Sat Com, 4x4, HT, LHD, Diesel, Land Rover Defender 110 TD5 Dagger

WB1100-4105	Car, Utility, Large, 4x4, Land Rover Defender County Station Wagon TDi 300
WB1100-8102	Car, Utility, 4x4, LHD, 2.5-litre TDI, 8 seats, Land Rover Defender 110
WB1100-9103	Car, Utility, 4x4, LHD, Hard Top, 5 seats, 2.5-litre Diesel, Land Rover Defender 300Tdi Station Wagon
WB1100-9104	Car, Utility, 4x4, LHD, Hard Top, 2 seats with Cargo Area, 2.5-litre Diesel, Land Rover Defender 300Tdi Station Wagon
WB1147-8125	Car, Utility, Large, Indigenous, (LP), 4x2 or 4x4, Up to 6-Litre, Land Rover
WB1155-3102	Car, Utility, Medium, 4x4, 12-str, 2.5-Ltr Turbo, Land Rover Defender 110 Station Wagon
WB1155-3108	Car, Utility, Medium, CL, 4x4, Land Rover Defender 110, Station Wagon w/50mm Ball CL 7-pin ELE Int/change w/NATO T/H 12PE
WB1155-3111	Car, Utility, Medium, 4x4, LWB, 12-seater, Air Conditioned, Land Rover Defender 110 County Station Wagon, 2.5-Ltr Tdi
WB1155-3113	Car, Utility, Medium, 4x4, 9 seat, Land Rover Defender 110 Station Wagon, 2.5-litre Turbo Diesel Injection
WB1155-3114	Car, Utility, Medium, 4x4, 2.5-litre TDI, Land Rover Defender 110
WB1155-3115	Car, Utility, Medium, 4x4, RHD, 9 seat, Land Rover Defender 110 Station Wagon, 2.5-litre TD5 Diesel
WB1155-8102	Car, Utility, Medium, CL, 4x4, LHD, 9 seats, Land Rover 110 Station Wagon, 2.5-litre TD5 Diesel
WB1155-8103	Car, Utility, Medium, 4x4, LHD, 9 seats, 2.5 TD5 Dsl, Motorola Fit, Police Light Bar, Land Rover Defender 110 Station Wagon
WB1155-8104	Car, Utility, Medium, 4x4, LHD, 9 seats, 2.5 TD5 Diesel, Tow Hook, Roof Rack, Land Rover Defender 110 Station Wagon
WB1155-8105	Car, Utility, Medium, 4x4, LHD, 9 seats, 2.5 TD5 Diesel, Roof Rack for Smart Fit, Land Rover Defender 110 Station Wagon
WB1155-8106	Car, Utility, Medium, 4x4, LHD, 8 seats, 2.5-litre TD5 Diesel, Land Rover Defender 110
WB1155-8108	Car, Utility, Medium, 4x4, LHD, 10 seats plus Driver, 2.5-litre Diesel, Land Rover Defender 300Tdi Station Wagon
WB1155-8109	Car, Utility, Medium, 4x4, LHD, 7 seat, 2.75-litre Diesel,Land Rover Defender 110
WV1155-8110	Car, Utility, Medium, (HT), 4x4, LHD, 9 Seats, 2.5-Litre Diesel, Land Rover Defender 300Tdi Station Wagon
WB1155-4109	Car, Utility, Medium, 4x4, (MoD Police) 2.5 Ltr Petrol, Land Rover 110 Station Wagon
WB1157-3100	Car, Utility, Medium, 4x4, w/Winch, 2.5-litre Diesel, 9-seater, Land Rover Defender 110 Station Wagon
WB1711-8100	Truck, Utility, Medium, CL, w/Cab, 12V, 4x4, LHD, Land Rover 110

Below and inset: One of just two such vehicles procured, this is DE 80 AA, specially equipped for EOD duties in Northern Ireland. The basic vehicle is a Defender 110 High-Capacity Pick-Up model with standard truck cab. (CE)

SUMMARY OF DELIVERIES
Tri Service

Serials	Contract	Chassis nos	Total	Remarks
61 KJ 78	LV2A/004 Item 27	466656	1	GS Hard Top 12/24v RHD; 25 May 1990
61 KJ 79	LV2A/004 Item 28	469821	1	GS Hard Top LHD; 25 May 1990
61 KJ 80 to 61 KJ 97	LV2A/004 Item 29	467944 to 470294	18	Helicopter Ground Support RHD; 25 May 1990
61 KJ 98 to 64 KJ 18	LV2A/004 Item 30	467421 to 483456	221	GS Hard Top Winterised RHD; 25 May 1990
64 KJ 19 to 64 KJ 83	LV2A/004 Item 31	465036 to 470513	65	GS Soft Top RHD; 25 May 1990
64 KJ 84	LV2A/004 Item 32	474028	1	CL Hard Top RHD; 25 May 1990
64 KJ 85 to 64 KJ 92	LV2A/004 Item 33	901254 to 901386	8	CL Hard Top Winterised RHD; 25 May 1990
64 KJ 93	LV2A/004 Item 34	471577	1	GS Hard Top RHD; 25 May 1990
64 KJ 94	LV2A/004 Item 35	470597	1	GS Hard Top LHD; 25 May 1990
64 KJ 95 to 66 KJ 74	LV2A/004 Item 36	477907 to 900728	180	FFR Hard Top RHD; 25 May 1990
66 KJ 75 to 71 KJ 19	LV2A/004 Item 37	466704 to 483403	445	FFR Hard Top LHD; 25 May 1990
71 KJ 20 to 72 KJ 89	LV2A/004 Item 38	472796 to 901249	170	FFR Hard Top Winterised RHD; 25 May 1990
72 KJ 90 to 72 KJ 99	LV2A/004 Item 39	470075 to 472062	10	Aircraft Armament Support RHD; 25 May 1990
73 KJ 00 to 73 KJ 44	LV2A/004 Item 40	480992 to 900754	45	FFR Soft Top RHD; 25 May 1990
73 KJ 45 to 73 KJ 53	LV2A/004 Item 41	480969 to 900562	9	FFR Soft Top LHD; 25 May 1990
73 KJ 62 to 73 KJ 67	LV2A/004 Item 16	465931 to 474456	6	Station Wagon (V8) RHD; 25 May 1990; for RAF
79 KJ 05	LP	363069	1	Station Wagon RHD; 30 May 1990; for SAAS
90 KJ 36	LP	215099	1	HCPU RHD
90 KJ 63 to 90 KJ 70	LV2A/004	467512 to 467681	8	GS Soft Top RHD; 25 July 1990
00 KK 55 and 00 KK 56	LV2A/004 Item 31	470594 and 470586	2	GS Soft Top RHD; 6 September 1990
00 KK 57	LV2A/004 Item 36	485194	1	FFR Hard Top RHD; 6 September 1990
02 KK 49	LP	901855	1	Station Wagon RHD; 14 August 1990; for SAAS
09 KK 41	LP	288034	1	This was a 1987-model One Ten; the plates were used for only seven days, possibly to enable a vehicle captured during Operation Granby to be brought to the UK.
12 KK 34	LP	436294	1	Hard Top; used as Mobile Cinema on Op Granby; 28 November 1990
19 KK 60 to 19 KK 64	LV2A/004 Item 48	904228 to 904532	5	GS Hard Top Winterised RHD; 28 November 1990
19 KK 65 to 19 KK 95	LV2A/004 Item 49	903341 to 903773	31	FFR Hard Top LHD; 28 November 1990
19 KK 96 to 20 KK 09	LV2A/004 Item 50	903614 to 903773	14	FFR Hard Top RHD; 28 November 1990
20 KK 10 to 20 KK 15	LV2A/004 Item 51	903195 to 903529	6	Aircraft Armament Support RHD; 28 November 1990
20 KK 16	LV2A/004 Item 52	904496	1	Helicopter Ground Support RHD; 28 November 1990
21 KK 63 to 21 KK 65	LP	319105 to 286099	3	County Station Wagon RHD (2.5 petrol); 13 March 1991; for BRIGNepal
25 KK 32	LP	305457	1	Safari Station Wagon RHD (diesel); for NATO
25 KK 33	LP	273417	1	Safari Station Wagon RHD (petrol); for NATO
25 KK 34	LP	271298	1	Station Wagon RHD (petrol); for NATO
25 KK 35	LP	466135	1	Station Wagon RHD (diesel); for NATO
25 KK 36	LP	273467	1	Station Wagon RHD (petrol); for NATO
25 KK 45 to 25 KK 47	LV2A/044 Item 1	449135 to 473513	3	Composite Armoured Vehicle (CAV) RHD; 8 April 1991; for trials
25 KK 48 to 35 KK 41	LV2A/044 Item 3	910879 to 931027	994	Composite Armoured Vehicle (CAV) RHD; 8 April 1991
39 KK 03	FVE 22A/373 LR/BA 188/121	906477	1	Station Wagon RHD; 3 July 1991; for SAAS

41 KK 51	LP	25988	1	2 August 1991; for trials; like 09 KK 41, this may have been a vehicle captured during Operation Granby; it was certainly a pre-1987 One Ten and not a Defender
45 KK 44	LV2A/115 Item 1	907881	1	Station Wagon LHD; 1 October 1991; for SAAS
45 KK 45	LV2A/115 Item 2	909740	1	Station Wagon RHD; 1 October 1991; for SAAS
46 KK 07 to 46 KK 12	LV2A/123 LR/ BA35/005	910701 to 911371	6	Station Wagon RHD; 11 November 1991; for RAF
55 KK 53	LV2A/044	N/K	1	Composite Armoured Vehicle (CAV) RHD; 9 December 1991; for Trials at RARDE
59 KK 00 to 59 KK 89	LV2A/004 Item 58	915610 to 917819	90	FFR Hard Top RHD; 3 October 1989; 3 October 1989
59 KK 90 to 59 KK 96	LV2A/004 Item 59	916461 to 917883	7	Helicopter Ground Support RHD; 3 October 1989
59 KK 97 to 59 KK 99	LV2A/004 Item 60	917499 to 917801	3	Helicopter Ground Support RHD; 3 October 1989
77 KK 37	LP	443877	1	HCPU; 10 May 1992; for Trials
78 KK 53 to 78 KK 62	LV2A/117	921205 to 921277	10	Desert Patrol Vehicle (diesel) RHD
82 KK 43 to 82 KK 52	LV2A/123 LR/ BR59/020	922658 to 922714		Station Wagon RHD; for RAF
89 KK 36 to 89 KK 43	LV2A/123 LR/ BN56/019	922640 to 922799	8	Station Wagon RHD; for Royal Navy
99 KK 61 to 99 KK 65	LV2A/004 Rapier 61	926847 to 926878	5	FFR Hard Top RHD; for USAF Rapier Squadrons
99 KK 66 to 99 KK 87	LV2A/004 Rapier 62	924655 to 926907	22	FFR Soft Top RHD; for USAF Rapier Squadrons
27 KL 15 to 27 KL 26	LV2A/123 LR/ BN60/037	934288 to 934432	12	Station Wagon RHD; for Royal Navy
27 KL 27 to 27 KL 39	LV2A/123 LR/ BR71/038	933711 to 933803	13	Station Wagon RHD; for Royal Air Force
29 KL 05 to 29 KL 65	LV2A/004 Item 65	933464 to 936544	61	FFR Soft Top RHD
29 KL 66 to 29 KL 85	LV2A/004 Item 65	936870 to 938021	20	FFR Soft Top LHD
36 KL 22 to 38 KL 48	LV2A/181 Item 3	935377 to 939870	227	GS Soft Top RHD
58 KL 49 to 59 KL 55	LV2A/101 Item 4	937737 to 939930	87	FFR Hard Top RHD
45 KL 92 to 46 KL 01	LV2A/123 LD/ BR71/051	938954 to 938813	10	Station Wagon RHD; for RAF
49 KL 79 to 49 KL 86	LV2A/123 LR/ BR71/069	941331 to N/K	8	Station Wagon RHD; for COBRA Radar Trials
49 KL 88	LP	282710	1	Station Wagon RHD; for MoD Police; this was an early (circa 1984) One Ten and not a Defender; it was presumably second-hand
90 KL 21 to 90 KL 32	LV2A/216	938246 to 938144	12	Glover Webb APV RHD (Courtaulds Chassis)
90 KL 33 to 91 KL 29	LV2A/215	958265 to 958194	97	Glover Webb APV RHD
91 KL 59 and 91 KL 60	LP	968998 to 977512	2	County Station Wagon; Grade A Armoured Staff Car
04 KM 96 to 04 KM 97	LP	122527 to 122534	2	County Station Wagon Air-Con RHD
05 KM 07 to 05 KM 08	LP	991813 to 979321	2	Station Wagon RHD; for BATLSK
07 KM 42 to 07 KM 43	LP	823395 to 823394	2	Station Wagon RHD; for BATLSK
07 KM 47 to 07 KM 49	LP	826066 to 826063	3	Station Wagon RHD; for BATLSK
07 KM 63	LP	182297	1	Station Wagon RHD; for BATLSK
07 KM 65 to 07 KM 67	LP	181808 to 181795	3	Station Wagon RHD; for BATLSK
07 KM 77	LP	N/K	1	Model not known; for BATKEN
07 KM 78 to 07 KM 82	LP	607762 to 608351	5	Td5, model not known; for Project Dagger
48 KM 27 to 48 KM 28	LP	N/K to N/K	2	Station Wagon RHD; as MIJA; for NATO JEWCS

49 KM 71 to 49 KM 74	LP	749743 to 747570	4	Station Wagon RHD
50 KM 39 to 50 KM 40	LP	732825 to 732837	2	Model not known (VIN record appears corrupt); for Afghanistan
62 KM 66 to 62 KM 83	LP	781193 to 792075	18	Station Wagon RHD; for BATLSK
BZ 91 AA to CB 80 AA	LV2A/211	955294 to 959427	190	FFR Hard Top LHD
CB 81 AA to CE 66 AA	LV2A/211	959419 to 957219	286	FFR Hard Top RHD
CE 67 AA to CE 96 AA	LV2A/211	N/K to 961604	30	FFR Soft Top LHD; CE 68 AA had chassis serial 961183
CE 97 AA to CG 46 AA	LV2A/211	958186 to N/K	150	FFR Soft Top RHD
CG 47 AA to CG 51 AA	BA573/087	953589 to 954482	5	Station Wagon RHD
CU 88 AA	LP	443877 (*)	1	HCPU; for trials with ITDU
CV 44 AA	LP	443877 (*)	1	GS RHD; for trials with ITDU
DE 79 AA and DE 80 AA	LP	903055 and 910378	2	HCPU; for EOD work
DZ 15 AA	LP	960592	1	Station Wagon RHD; for Cyprus
DZ 17 AA	LP	960089	1	Station Wagon RHD; for Cyprus
DZ 23 AA and DZ 24 AA	LP	960546 and 960040	1	Station Wagon RHD; for Cyprus
GU 28 AA	Loan	N/K	1	FFR RHD; for 45 Cdo RM
GU 29 AA	Loan	976285	1	GS RHD; for 45 Cdo RM
GW 59 AA to GW 72 AA	LV2A/265	983855 to 984412	14	Station Wagon RHD
JH 07 AA	LV2A/265	106613	1	Station Wagon RHD
JM 00 AA and JM 01 AA	LV2A/265	105174 and 105434	2	Station Wagon RHD; for RAF
JM 02 AA to JM 16 AA	LV2A/265	106403 to 106702	15	CL Cargo Hard Top RHD; for RAF
JM 17 AA and JM 20 AA	LV2A/265	105207 and 105186	4	Station Wagon RHD; for RAF
JM 21 AA to JM 28 AA	LV2A/265	N/K to N/K	8	CL Cargo Hard Top RHD; for RAF
JM 29 AA to JM 46 AA	LV2A/265	N/K to 105601	18	CL Cargo Hard Top Anti-Spark RHD; for RAF
JM 47 AA to JN 06 AA	LV2A/265	N/K to 106737	60	CL Cargo Hard Top RHD; for RAF
JN 07 AA to JN 12 AA	LV2A/265	N/K to N/K	6	CL Cargo Hard Top Cab RHD; for RAF
JN 17 AA	LV2A /265	989826	1	County Station Wagon RHD
JN 97 AA to JP 11 AA	LV2A/265	105674 to N/K	15	Station Wagon RHD; 17 July 1996
JP 45 AA	LP	989984	1	County CL Cargo Hard Top RHD; for RAF
JP 51 AA	LP	990342	1	County CL Cargo Hard Top RHD; for RAF
JR 07 AA to JR 21 AA	LV2A/265	N/K to 105157	15	Station Wagon RHD; for RAF
JS 42 AA and JS 43 AA	LP	987080 and 987780	2	Station Wagon RHD
JT 64 AA	LV2A/265	107590	1	Station Wagon RHD 29 May 1996
JW 32 AA and JW 33 AA	LV2A/265	108161 and 103402	2	County Station Wagon 300Tdi RHD
JZ 45 AA to JZ 53 AA	LV2A/265	N/K to N/K	9	Station Wagon RHD; for RAF; 10 October 1996
LE 57 AA and LE 58 AA	LV2A/265	111240 and 111354	2	Station Wagon RHD; for RAF as Bird Control Unit
LF 13 AA and LF 14 AA	BA154/024	107657 and 107749	2	County Station Wagon 300Tdi RHD;
LJ 08 AA andf LJ 09 AA	LP	991059 and 991069	2	Station Wagon RHD; 21 February 1997
NA 06 AA to NA 15 AA	LV2A/265	N/K to 131736	10	CL Cargo Hard Top RHD
NB 38 AA and NB 39 AA	LV2A/265	131934 and 131585	2	CL Hard Top Anti-Spark RHD; for RAF 16 June 1997
NB 40 AA to NB 46 AA	LV2A/265	131752 to 131501	7	Station Wagon RHD; for RAF; 16 June 1997
NB 47 AA to NB 53 AA	LV2A/265	N/K to N/K	7	CL Hard Top RHD; for RAF 16 June 1997
NB 54 AA	LV2A/265	131560	1	Station Wagon RHD; for RAF; 16 June 1997

NE 17 AA	LV2A/265	132734	1	CL Soft Top RHD; for RAF
NE 18 AA to NE 29 AA	LV2A/265	N/K to 132111	12	CL Hard Top RHD; for RAF
NF 57 AA to NF 61 AA	LV2A/265	132226 to 133623	5	CL Hard Top RHD; for RAF; 23 July 1997
NF 91 AA and NF 92 AA	LV2A/265	132508 and 132431	2	Station Wagon RHD; for RAF 23 July 1997
NG 16 AA and NG 17 AA	LV2A/265	131106 and 132286	2	Station Wagon RHD; for RAF 29 July 1997
NG 51 AA and NG 52 AA	LP	N/K and N/K	2	County Station Wagon Aircon RHD; 1 August 1997
NG 53 AA and NG 54 AA	LP	N/K and N/K	2	County Station Wagon 300Tdi RHD; 1 August 1997
NG 59 AA	LV2A/265	N/K	1	Station Wagon RHD
NL 92 AA and NL 93 AA	LP	122491 and 123445	2	Station Wagon RHD; 25 September 1997
NM 74 AA and NM 75 AA	LV2A/265	138735 and 138654	2	CL Cargo Hard Top RHD; for RAF
NN 22 AA to NN 24 AA	LP	117530 to 127600	3	County Station Wagon Aircon RHD; 21 October 1997
NS 25 AA to NS 28 AA	LV2A/265	141015 to 141171	3	CL Cargo Hard Top RHD; for RAF
NZ 15 AA	LP	138699	1	Station Wagon RHD
PT 10 AA to PT 21 AA	LV2A/265	N/K to N/K	12	Station Wagon RHD; for RAF
PT 22 AA to PT 48 AA	LV2A/265	155123 to 156048	27	CL Cargo Anti-Spark RHD; for RAF; 29 April 1998
PT 49 AA to PT 62 AA	LV2A/265	155888 to 156108	14	CL Cargo Hard Top RHD; for RAF
PT 63 AA to PT 92 AA	LV2A/265	155241 to 156676	30	CL Cargo Soft Top RHD; for RAF
PX 97 AA to PX 99 AA	LV2A/265	157114 to 157407	3	Station Wagon RHD; for RAF; 29 May 1998
PY 14 AA to PY 26 AA	LV2A/265	156394 to 156724	14	CL Cargo Hard Top RHD; for RAF; 29 May 1998
PZ 05 AA	LV2A/265	145895	1	Station Wagon RHD
RL 16 AA	LV2A/265	168106	1	CL Cargo Hard Top RHD; for RAF; 1 October 1998
RS 01 AA and RS 02 AA	LR004-98/99	167161 and 167075	2	CL Cargo Hard Top Cab RHD; 18 November 1998
RW 72 AA	LR008-98/99	167574	1	CL Cargo Hard Top Cab RHD;
RX 15 AA to RX 20 AA	MN1	N/K to N/K	6	Station Wagon MRT RHD; for RAF
RX 21 AA to RX 32 AA	MN2	N/K to 170911	12	Station Wagon MRT RHD; for RAF
RX 60 AA to RX 65 AA	LP	163702 to 163837	6	Station Wagon RHD; for Cyprus
RY 88 AA	9	170813	1	Station Wagon RHD
RY 89 AA and RY 90 AA	LR015-98/99	N/K and 166479	2	Station Wagon RHD; for RAF; 16 March 1999
SM 51 AA and SM 52 AA	LR033-99/00	N/K and N/K	2	CL Hard Top Anti-Spark RHD; for RAF
SM 53 AA to SM 55 AA	LR033-99/00	188445 to N/K	3	Station Wagon RHD; for RAF
SN 63 AA to SN 83 AA	LR022-99/00	181924 to 182156	21	CL Cargo Hard Top RHD; for RAF
TD 99 AA to TE 05 AA	LP	177873 to 154998	7	County Station Wagon LHD; for Kosovo; 12 January 2000
TE 10 AA to TE 14 AA	LP	176122 to 186815	5	County Station Wagon LHD; for Kosovo; 12 January 2000
TN 05 AA and TN 06 AA	LP	189574 and 189652	2	Station Wagon RHD; for Cyprus
TN 09 AA and TN 10 AA	LP	172335 and 173375	2	Station Wagon RHD; for Cyprus
TT 64 AA to TT 69 AA	LP	192183 to 191913	6	Station Wagon RHD; for Bosnia; 26 May 2000
TU 20 AA	LP	162417	1	Station Wagon LHD; for Kosovo
TU 22 AA	LP	124957	1	Station Wagon LHD; for Kosovo
TV 69 AA to TV 83 AA	LP	192238 to N/K	15	Station Wagon RHD; for BRIGNEPAL
UA 78 AA and UA 79 AA	LR045	602849 and 603267	2	Station Wagon RHD
UP 98 AA to UR 02 AA	N/K	N/K to N/K	5	Station Wagon Td5 RHD; for RAF
VC 15 AA to VC 34 AA	N/K	627109 to 627533	20	CL Cargo Hard Top w/windows Td5 RHD; for RAF

VF 88 AA to VF 92 AA	N/K	627146 to 627872	5	Station Wagon Td5 RHD
VM 22 AA to VM 27 AA	LP	629321 to 629167	6	Station Wagon 300Tdi LHD; for Kosovo; 10 January 2002
VM 28 AA and VM 29 AA	LP	621487 to 618708	2	CL Cargo Hard Top LHD; for Kosovo; 10 January 2002
VM 85 AA to VM 94 AA	N/K	632211 to 633497	10	Station Wagon Td5 RHD; for RAF; January 2002
VN 19 AA to VN 34 AA	LR007	631467 to 631202	16	Station Wagon Td5 RHD; for RAF; January 2002
VP 69 AA to VP 72 AA	LR008	N/K to N/K	4	CL Cargo Hard Top RHD; for RAF; February 2002
VP 83 AA to VP 88 AA	LP	630873 to 630895	6	Station Wagon Police fit LHD; for Op Resolute
VP 89 AA and VP 90 AA	LP	631338 and 631364	2	Station Wagon LHD; for Op Resolute
VP 91 AA	LP	631364	1	Station Wagon LHD; for Op Resolute
VR 38 AA and VR 65 AA	LP	632984 to 632020	28	Station Wagon LHD; for Op Resolute
VR 94 AA to VS 04 AA	N/K	632099 to 632965	11	Station Wagon LHD; for Op Resolute
VS 40 AA	N/K	627174	1	Station Wagon 300Tdi RHD; for BRIGNEPAL
VT 62 AA	LP	616816	1	Station Wagon Td5 RHD; for Kosovo
VV 98 AA	LP	631572	1	Station Wagon 300Tdi LHD; for Kosovo; 28 May 2002
VW 60 AA	N/K	640326	1	Station Wagon RHD
WA 33 AA	LP	632227	1	Station Wagon LHD; for Kosovo
WV 68 AA to WV 74 AA	LP	639025 to 637981	7	Station Wagon 300Tdi LHD; for Op Resolute; 19 September 2002
WX 98 AA to WY 08 AA	N/K	984905 to 984036	11	Station Wagon Td5 LHD; for Op Resolute; 19 September 2002
WY 52 AA	LP	986036	1	Station Wagon LHD; for Op Resolute; 3 October 2002
WY 53 AA	LP	986049	1	Station Wagon Td5 LHD; for Op Resolute; 3 October 2002
WY 54 AA	LP	986031	1	CL Cargo with Cab LHD; for Op Resolute; 3 October 2002
WY 55 AA	LP	985122	1	Station Wagon 300Tdi LHD; for Op Resolute; 3 October 2002
WY 56 AA	LP	986254	1	Station Wagon Td5 LHD; for Op Resolute; 3 October 2002
WY 58 AA	LP	986373	1	Station Wagon Td5 LHD; for Op Resolute; 3 October 2002
ZZ 50 AA to ZZ 56 AA	LP	645210 to 645319	7	Station Wagon RHD; for Cyprus; December 2002
AK 19 AB to AK 23 AB	LP	648349 to 647993	5	Station Wagon Police RHD; for RAF Police Falklands Islands; 15 April 2003
AK 65 AB	LP	N/K	1	CL Hard Top RHD; for Dagger Satcomms; 7 March 2003
AR 72 AB and AR 73 AB	LP	631459 and 631423	2	CL Cargo Hard Top RHD; for RAF JETS radar simulator; 21 May 2003
AW 97 AB to AX 00 AB	LP	623770 to 647406	4	CL Hard Top RHD; for Dagger Satcomms; 7 March 2003
AY 88 AB to AY 93 AB	LP	667298 to 667824	6	Station Wagon RHD; for Cyprus; December 2003
BD 27 AB	LP	667308	1	Station Wagon RHD; for Cyprus; December 2003
BF 72 AB to BF 81 AB	LP	669731 to 670591	10	Station Wagon Td5 RHD; for RAF Falkland Islands; February 2004
BF 91 AB to BF 99 AB	LP	669795 to 670549	9	Station Wagon Td5 RHD; for RAF Falkland Islands; February 2004
BJ 33 AB to BJ 37 AB	LP	670279 to 670770	5	CL Cargo Hard Top RHD; for Falkland Islands; March 2004
BJ 38 AB to BJ 43 AB	LP	669968 to 670947	6	Station Wagon RHD; for Falkland Islands; March 2004
BR 93 AB and BR 94 AB	LP	675262 and 676043	2	Station Wagon RHD; for Falkland Islands; July 2004
CY 93 AB to CZ 05 AB	LP	685315 to 685556	13	Station Wagon RHD; for Falkland Islands;
DD 15 AB and DD 16 AB	LP	687201 and 687070	2	Station Wagon RHD; for Falkland Islands;
DE 82 AB and DE 83 AB	LP	684043 and 684185	2	Station Wagon RHD; for BRIGNEPAL
DU 79 AB to DU 89 AB	LP	681799 to 697595	11	Station Wagon RHD; for Cyprus

DV 08 AB to DV 12 AB	LP	696718 to 696299	5	Station Wagon w/Winch RHD; for BATLSK; 11 April 2005
DW 02 AB to DW 05 AB	LP	697544 to 696040	4	Station Wagon RHD; for BRIGNEPAL
ED 60 AB and ED 61 AB	LP	708767 and N/K	2	Station Wagon RHD; for Cyprus; November 2005
EF 84 AB and EF 85 AB	LP	710097 and 709652	2	Station Wagon RHD; for Falkland Islands;
EF 97 AB	LP	709322	1	Station Wagon RHD; for Falkland Islands;

RAF

Serials	Contract	Chassis Nos	Total	Remarks
29 AY 06 to 29 AY 10	LV2A/123	956230 to N/K	5	Station Wagon RHD
30 AY 00 to 30 AY 09	LV2A/211	N/K to 957944	10	FFR Hard Top RHD
34 AY 04 to 34 AY 28	LV2A/227	956315 to N/K	25	CL Hard Top RHD
34 AY 42 to 34 AY 45	LV2A/123	959062 to 959837	4	Station Wagon RHD
34 AY 46 to 34 AY 49	LV2A/221	965225 to N/K	4	Helicopter starting
34 AY 50 to 34 AY 52	LV2A/221	966764 to N/K	3	GS Hard Top Winterised 12/24v RHD
34 AY 63 to 34 AY 82	LV2A/227	960762 to N/K	20	CL Hard Top RHD
35 AY 46 to 35 AY 49	LV2A/221	N/K to 967389	4	GS Hard Top Winterised 12/24v RHD
36 AY 37 to 36 AY 40	LV2A/265	983118 to 983080	4	CL Hard Top Anti-Spark RHD
36 AY 41 to 36 AY 71	LV2A/265	N/K to 983512	31	Station Wagon RHD
36 AY 92 to 37 AY 37	LV2A/265	982976 to 983619	46	CL Hard Top RHD

RN

Serials	Contract	Chassis Nos	Total	Remarks
00 RN 18	N/K	N/K	1	Station Wagon RHD
02 RN 66 to 02 RN 76	N/K	N/K to N/K	11	Cargo CL Hard Top RHD; March 1996
03 RN 36	N/K	931082	1	Station Wagon RHD; March 1994
04 RN 84	N/K	N/K	1	Station Wagon RHD; 1996
08 RN 64	N/K	N/K	1	Carmichael RIV
18 RN 94	N/K	N/K	1	Cargo CL Hard Top RHD
21 RN 80	N/K	N/K	1	Cargo CL Hard Top Cab RHD
22 RN 98	N/K	N/K	1	Cargo CL Hard Top Cab RHD
24 RN 89	N/K	N/K	1	Cargo CL RHD
26 RN 77	N/K	N/K	1	Cargo CL Hard Top RHD
28 RN 96	N/K	N/K	1	Station Wagon RHD
33 RN 35 to 33 RN 39	N/K	N/K to N/K	5	Station Wagon RHD; November 1994
51 RN 15 to 51 RN 19	N/K	N/K to N/K	5	Station Wagon RHD V8
54 RN 53 to 54 RN 54	N/K	N/K to N/K	2	FFR Hard Top RHD
71 RN 64	N/K	N/K	1	Cargo CL RHD
88 RN 37 to 88 RN 88	N/K	N/K to N/K	52	Station Wagon RHD V8
99 RN 28 to 99 RN 33	N/K	N/K to N/K	6	Cargo CL Hard Top RHD

This Station Wagon of the Royal Navy's Southern Diving Unit 2 at Portsmouth has various items of extra equipment fitted including a roof rack to carry an inflatable boat, a Warn winch and a light bar. (CE)

99 RN 28 is a Royal Navy Station Wagon in a civilian colour scheme, photographed at a petrol station and towing a boat trailer. (CE)

Berlin Senät

Serials	Contract	Chassis nos	Total	Remarks
10 XK 92 to 10 XK 98	-	356337 to 356348	7	CL Hard Top LHD
11 XK 16 and 11 XK 17	-	356779 and 365051	2	GS Soft Top LHD
13 XK 04 to 13 XK 13	-	386137 to 387110	10	CL Hard Top LHD
13 XK 37 to 13 XK 44	-	404137 to 413908	8	FFR Hard Top LHD
13 XK 45 to 13 XK 51	-	399064 to 405289	7	GS Soft Top LHD
15 XK 04 to 15 XK 16	-	438821 to 447979	13	GS Soft Top LHD
15 XK 17 to 15 XK 27	-	443340 to 459144	11	FFR Hard Top LHD
16 XK 04	-	901899	1	GS Soft Top LHD
16 XK 06	-	903216	1	GS Soft Top LHD

When Berlin Garrison closed, some Land Rovers were transferred and re-serialled. The new Tri-service serials included 43 KL 20 to 43 KL 27, 56 KL 31 and 56 KL 32, 60 KL 52 to 60 KL 55, BS 11 AA to BS 50 AA, and CH 71 AA to CJ 04 AA

Technical specifications, Defender 110 models

Petrol engine
3528cc V8-cylinder with two Zenith-Stromberg carburettors and 134bhp

Diesel engines
2495cc four-cylinder with indirect injection and 67bhp
2495cc turbocharged four-cylinder with direct injection and 107bhp (200Tdi)
2495cc turbocharged four-cylinder with direct injection and 111bhp (300Tdi)
2495cc turbocharged five-cylinder with direct injection by electronic unit injectors, 122bhp (Td5)
2401cc turbocharged four-cylinder with common-rail injection and 122bhp (Puma)

Transmission
Permanent four-wheel drive with lockable centre differential
Five-speed manual main gearbox (to 2006); six-speed manual gearbox (with Puma engine)
Two-speed transfer gearbox
Axle ratio: 3.54:1

Suspension, steering and brakes
Coil springs all round
Worm and roller steering
Disc brakes on the front wheels and drum brakes at the rear (1991-1993 models); disc brakes on all four wheels (1993 on); servo assistance; separate drum-type transmission parking brake

Electrical system
12-volt with alternator or 24-volt with 90-amp alternator; some vehicles with 12/24v specification

Dimensions
Overall length:	175in (4445mm) for truck cab and Soft Top
	180.3in (4580mm) for Station Wagon
	184in (4674mm) for HCPU
Wheelbase:	110in (2794mm)
Overall width:	70.5in (1791mm)
Unladen height:	80.1in (2034mm)
Track:	58.5in (1486mm)

Unladen weights
3858lb (1750kg) minimum with Puma engine
3981lb (1806kg) minimum with V8 petrol engine
4030lb (1828kg) minimum with naturally-aspirated diesel engine
4127lb (1872kg) minimum with Tdi diesel engine
4156lb (1885kg) minimum with Td5 engine

Performance
(110 with 300Tdi engine):
0-60mph:	Not quoted
Maximum:	Not quoted
Fuel consumption:	29mpg

(110 with Td5 engine):
0-60mph:	Not quoted
Maximum:	Not quoted
Fuel consumption:	27mpg

7

DEFENDER 90, 1990 onwards

Just as the One Ten became a Defender 110 during 1990, so did the Ninety become a Defender 90. Although the new 200Tdi turbocharged diesel engine was standard for civilian models, the UK armed forces continued to buy their Land Rovers with the old naturally-aspirated diesel engine, right through until 1994. The next short-wheelbase models to enter British military service were Defender XD or Wolf types (see Chapter 11), which had the 300Tdi turbocharged diesel derived from the earlier 200Tdi. Despite these differences from the civilian specification, short-wheelbase Land Rovers delivered after mid-1990 wore Defender badges.

It is hardly surprising, then, that the existing Asset Codes for short-wheelbase, coil-sprung Land Rovers remained unchanged. As new vehicle types received Asset Codes, the Defender name sometimes appeared, but also sometimes did not. For the MoD, a production change that was very significant for Land Rover actually made almost no difference at all.

Note that the Berlin Senät purchased only three Defender 90s in total. This was because the demise of the Berlin Garrison was anticipated under 'Options for Change' – the restructuring of the British armed forces after the end of the Cold War in 1990. After the Berlin Garrison closed in 1994, some of its vehicles were transferred to the normal registration system for use elsewhere with British Forces.

This standard GS version was pictured in use by 10 Gurkha Transport Regiment, Royal Logistic Corps – note the Kukri and the fluorescent 'X' on the windscreen. The picture was taken at the Aldershot Show in April 1995. (GF)

This later GS model is perfectly standard except for the unusual 'Defender 90' badging. It is one of the last Tri-Service batch before the introduction of the Wolf. It was seen at Defence Vehicle Dynamics in 2002. (GF)

Another late GS model is put through its paces on the Long Valley Test Track. Note that this example has been fitted with a wading snorkel.(GF)

Defender 90 variants

The Defender 90 was purchased in much smaller numbers than its long-wheelbase equivalent. The armed forces took both 12-volt GS and 24-volt FFR variants, together with a few CL-specification deliveries. In addition, there were several specially built variants, and unit modifications led to other variants, although these were not necessarily given a new Asset Code.

The MoD continued to purchase the civilian-specification Defender 90 after the introduction of the Wolf, or 90 HS as it was known to the military. The first orders were placed for the 90 HS in 1996 (see Chapter 10), and orders for the Defender 90 continued until at least 2000, mainly for the RAF. These were CL Hard and Soft Top models, and civilian-specification Station Wagons for various roles. Note that no Defender 90s were put through the Life Extension Programme called TITHONUS. This may have been because of their relatively limited range of military uses. For example, when the military introduced a requirement for forward-facing seats for all passengers, there was a limited role for 90s as radio vehicles, because there was insufficient room for the radio operators to travel behind the radio racks.

All vehicles (except for CL models) had a military-pattern front bumper with central towing aperture and radio tuner mounts on the front wings. The RAF had Armament Support versions, which were essentially diesel-engined Hard Top models with windows.

Aircraft Armament Support vehicle

Aircraft Armament Support versions of the Defender 90 followed similarly named variants of the earlier Land Rover Ninety into service. Once again, these vehicles had spark-suppression equipment and were bodied as Hard Tops with windows.

CL

A small number of CL versions was purchased in 1990, some of which had Hard Tops. All were for the use of the RAF. CL purchases continued after the introduction of the Wolf, and most of these were also for RAF use, although some went to the Military Provost Guard Service (MPGS) for patrol duties at various garrisons.

FFR

The FFR version was purchased in both Hard Top and Soft Top forms. The Hard Top was the more common and equipped the majority of units. However, the Soft Top version was purchased for the units of 5 Airborne Brigade and 24 Airmobile Brigade. Some of these were subsequently converted to the 'air-droppable' version

PT 98 AA is typical of CL Defenders purchased after the introduction of the Wolf. Note the reflective number plate and lack of radio tuner mounts on the front wings. (GF)

This Winterised Aircraft Armament Support was issued to RAF Coltishall in 1992, and was photographed at the International Air Tattoo in 1996. No.41(F) Squadron Jaguars from Coltishall deployed regularly to Bardufoss airbase, over 150 miles north of the Arctic circle in the far north of Norway, as part of the Squadron's NATO role. (GF)

This is an FFR Hard Top of 7 Regiment, Royal Horse Artillery. 58 KK 91 was photographed during preparations for an exercise at Air Mounting Centre, South Cerney in April 1993. (GF)

Also modified for the airborne role, FFR Soft Top 61 KJ 43 wears UN markings after operations abroad. It was photographed during preparations for the exercise at Air Mounting Centre, South Cerney in April 1993, at the same time as other vehicles in this chapter. (FMW)

A CL Defender in use at Royal Military College of Science (RMCS) Shrivenham for garrison security. Such vehicles were used by the Military Provost Guard Service (MPGS). (CE)

Two Defender 90 FFR Soft Tops on a Medium Stressed Platform. Note how the front wheel of the rear one fits on the cutaway rear body of the one in front. (CE)

which had demountable upper rear body sides so that two such vehicles could be stacked on a Medium Stressed Platform (MSP). These vehicles were air-dropped to provide reconnaissance troops (Pathfinders and Observation Post parties) with vehicles that could be dropped two at a time by parachute.

GS

All of the GS vehicles were purchased in Soft Top form, and had 12-volt electrics. They were used for light liaison and communication duties.

58 KK 20 was another FFR Hard Top attached to 7 Regiment RHA, and was pictured at the same event as 58 KK 91 on the previous page. (GF)

This is a Soft Top version of the Defender 90 FFR. 61 KJ 44 has been modified for the airborne role – note the removable sections at the top of the rear bodywork. This permits two such vehicles to be loaded on a standard Medium Stressed Platform (MSP) for parachute dropping, as shown on the opposite page. (GF)

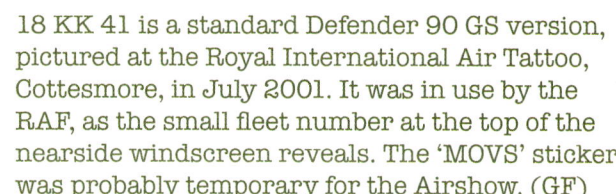

18 KK 41 is a standard Defender 90 GS version, pictured at the Royal International Air Tattoo, Cottesmore, in July 2001. It was in use by the RAF, as the small fleet number at the top of the nearside windscreen reveals. The 'MOVS' sticker was probably temporary for the Airshow. (GF)

The blue lights and badge on the door indicate that 56 KK 34, a standard GS Soft Top, is in use by a Fire Officer of the Defence Fire Service. It was photographed at Artillery Day, Larkhill, in May 1995. (GF)

This standard GS model, 35 KL 33, was photographed while being driven by a member of the First Aid Nursing Yeomanry (FANY) at their centenary in June 2007. It was on the strength of 47 Squadron of 71 Signal Regiment, Royal Corps of Signals (V). (GF)

As if to prove that the White Fleet was not always white, the RAF painted this 2008-model Defender 90 in the yellow it always used for visibility on airfields. The vehicle has the 2.4-litre 'Puma' engine, made by Ford – a tall engine which necessitated the inclusion of the visible bulge in the vehicle's bonnet. (GF)

Winterised

As with the Defender 110, Defender 90s were purchased in 'Winterised' form for the first time, rather than converting standard vehicles with Winterisation Kits. The details of their specification were essentially the same as those for Defender 110s, and the Winterised Defender 90s were for use with ACE Mobile Force (Land) (AMF(L)) and 3 Commando Brigade (see Chapter 6 for more details on these formations). Winterised versions of both GS and FFR types were available, and both were fitted with Hard Tops.

Many of the 3 Commando Brigade vehicles were subsequently fitted with a waterproofing kit to enable them to wade in deep water, for example, when wading ashore from a landing craft. As on the equivalent Defender 110, the most obvious feature of the kit was the snorkel fitted to the windscreen frame.

Pictured in May 1992 during an exercise at Larkhill, this Winterised FFR Hard Top was in use with 29 Commando Regiment, Royal Artillery. The 'M' just visible above the headlamp identifies 61 KJ 00 as the Signals Officer's vehicle attached to one of the gun groups. (GF)

The body on this Defender 90 is what Land Rover calls a 'Window Hardtop,' and 56 KJ 79 is an Aircraft Armament Support vehicle. The turnbuckles along the top of the windscreen and the Velcro strips for the window covers identify it as a Winterised version. (GF)

This Winterised GS was in use by 42 Squadron RCT at Middle Wallop in May 1992. The Velcro strips for the window covers can just be seen above the back door and side windows. 42 Squadron had an Arctic role with the ACE (Allied Command Europe) Mobile Force. (GF)

ASSET CODES

The Asset Codes (in use until around 1993) are:

1150-3100	Car, Utility, 4x4, 7 seater, Land Rover 90 (Diesel)
1155-3103	Car, Utility, Medium, 7 seater, 4x4, 2.5 Litre Diesel, air conditioned, Land Rover 90 Station Wagon
1613-3100	Truck, Utility, Light, (Winterised), Aircraft Armament Support, 12v, 4x4, Land Rover 90 (Diesel)
1617-3100	Truck, Utility, Light, Aircraft Armament Support, Hard Top w/windows, 12v, 4x4, Land Rover 90 Defender (Diesel)
1617-8100	Truck, Utility, Light, Aircraft Armament Support, Hard Top w/windows, 12v, 4x4, LHD, Land Rover 90 Defender (Diesel)
1619-3100	Truck, Utility, Light, GS, (Winterised), 4x4, 12v, Land Rover 90 (Diesel)
1620-3101	Truck, Utility, Light, GS, Cargo, Soft Top, 12v, 4x4, Land Rover 90 (Diesel)
1621-3102	Truck, Utility, Light, CL, Plain Hard Top, 12v, 4x4, 2.5 Litre Mk 6B Diesel, Land Rover 90 Defender
1620-8100	Truck, Utility, Light, GS, Cargo, Soft Top, 12v, 4x4, LHD, Land Rover 90 (Diesel)
1625-3100	Truck, Utility, Light, FFR, Plain Hard Top, 12/24v, 4x4, Land Rover 90 (Diesel)
1625-8100	Truck, Utility, Light, FFR, Plain Hard Top, 12/24v, 4x4, LHD, Land Rover 90 (Diesel)
1626-3100	Truck, Utility, Light, FFR, (Winterised), 12/24v, 4x4, Land Rover 90 (Diesel)
1628-3100	Truck, Utility, Light, FFR, Soft Top, 12/24v, Land Rover 90 (Diesel)

The later Asset Codes (from around 1993) are:

NB1619-3100	Truck, Utility, Light, GS, (Winterised), 4x4, 12v, Land Rover 90 (Diesel)
NB1620-3101	Truck, Utility, Light, GS, Cargo, Soft Top, 12v, 4x4, Land Rover 90 (Diesel)
NB1620-8100	Truck, Utility, Light, GS, Cargo, Soft Top, 12v, 4x4, LHD, Land Rover 90 (Diesel)
NB1625-3100	Truck, Utility, Light, FFR, Plain Hard Top, 12/24v, 4x4, Land Rover 90 (Diesel)
NB1625-8100	Truck, Utility, Light, FFR, Plain Hard Top, 12/24v, 4x4, LHD, Land Rover 90 (Diesel)
NB1626-3100	Truck, Utility, Light, FFR, (Winterised), 12/24v, 4x4, Land Rover 90 (Diesel)
NB1628-3100	Truck, Utility, Light, FFR, Soft Top, 12/24v, Land Rover 90 (Diesel)
RB1147-3106	Car, Utility, Large, Indigenous, 4x4, LP, Land Rover 90 County SWB 3-Door Hard Top, Side Seats, 2.5-Ltr Dsl
RB1613-3100	Truck, Utility, Light, (Winterised), Aircraft Armament Support, 12v, 4x4, Land Rover 90 (Diesel)
RB1617-3100	Truck, Utility, Light, Aircraft Armament Support, Hard Top w/windows, 12v, 4x4, Land Rover 90 Defender (Diesel)
RB1617-8100	Truck, Utility, Light, Aircraft Armament Support, Hard Top w/windows, 12v, 4x4, LHD, Land Rover 90 Defender (Diesel)
RB1620-3101	Truck, Utility, Light, GS, Cargo, Soft Top, 12v, 4x4, Land Rover 90 (Diesel)
RB1620-8100	Truck, Utility, Light, GS, Cargo, Soft Top, 12v, 4x4, LHD, Land Rover 90 (Diesel)
RB1621-3103	Truck, Utility, Light, CL, 4x4, Land Rover 90, Hard Top, 2.5-litre Tdi
RB1621-3104	Truck, Utility, Light, 4x4, Land Rover Defender 90, Hard Top, 6 seats, cubby box, LN Tow Hook
RB1625-3100	Truck, Utility, Light, FFR, Plain Hard Top, 12/24v, 4x4, Land Rover 90 (Diesel)
RB1625-8100	Truck, Utility, Light, FFR, Plain Hard Top, 12/24v, 4x4, LHD, Land Rover 90 (Diesel)
WB1150-3100	Car, Utility, 4x4, 7 seater, Land Rover 90 Diesel
WB1621-3101	Truck, Utility, Light, CL, Plain Hard Top, 12v, 4x4, Land Rover 90 (Diesel)

SUMMARY OF DELIVERIES, 1990 onwards

As noted elsewhere, military records are sometimes rather lax about the distinction between Land Rover Ninety and Land Rover Defender 90. All vehicles in the tables below have nevertheless been confirmed as genuine Defenders (with HA or later VIN dating codes).

Tri-Service

Serials	Contract	Chassis nos	Total	Remarks
56 KJ 78 and 56 KJ 79	LV2A/004 Item 17	900832 and 901221	2	Aircraft Armament Support Winterised RHD; May 1990
56 KJ 80 to 57 KJ 00	LV2A/004 Item 18	484972 to 790463	21	Aircraft Armament Support RHD; May 1990
57 KJ 01 to 57 KJ 14	LV2A/004 Item 19	900019 to 701050	14	Aircraft Armament Support LHD; May 1990
57 KJ 15 to 57 KJ 77	LV2A/004 Item 20	482695 to 901230	63	GS Hard Top Winterised RHD; May 1990
57 KJ 78 to 59 KJ 17	LV2A/004 Item 21	473969 to 900604	140	GS Soft Top RHD; May 1990
59 KJ 18 to 59 KJ 69	LV2A/004 Item 22	479910 to 700505	52	GS Soft Top LHD; May 1990
59 KJ 70 to 60 KJ 08	LV2A/004 Item 23	700524 to 701061	39	FFR Hard Top RHD; May 1990
60 KJ 09 to 60 KJ 95	LV2A/004 Item 24	484129 to 700913	87	FFR Hard Top LHD; May 1990
60 KJ 96 to 61 KJ 39	LV2A/004 Item 25	485364 to 901092	44	FFR Hard Top Winterised RHD; May 1990
61 KJ 40 to 61 KJ 77	LV2A/004 Item 26	484776 to 701043	38	FFR Soft Top RHD; May 1990
90 KJ 35	FVE 22A/373 LR/ BA47/098	700089	1	Station Wagon RHD; August 1990
90 KJ 51 to 90 KJ 53	FVE 22A/373 LR/ BA45/0106	700255 to 700202	3	Station Wagon RHD; August 1990
00 KK 53	LV2A/004 Item 21	485003	1	GS Soft Top RHD; September 1990
00 KK 54	LV2A/004 Item 23	485136	1	FFR Hard Top RHD; September 1990
17 KK 68	LV2A/004 Item 44	904695	1	Aircraft Armament Support Winterised RHD; November 1990
17 KK 69 to 17 KK 82	LV2A/004 Item 45	904065 to 904491	14	Aircraft Armament Support RHD; November 1990
17 KK 83 to 18 KK 96	LV2A/004 Item 46	903393 to 904145	114	GS Soft Top RHD; November 1990
18 KK 97 to 19 KK 59	LV2A/004 Item 47	903692 to 904525	63	GS Soft Top LHD; November 1990
56 KK 00 to 57 KK 43	LV2A/004 Item 55	911595 to 914678	144	GS Soft Top RHD; January 1992
57 KK 44 to 57 KK 99	LV2A/004 Item 56	912483 to 915241	56	GS Soft Top LHD; January 1992
58 KK 00 to 58 KK 99	LV2A/004 Item 56	914188 to 917174	100	FFR Hard Top RHD; January 1992
33 KL 69	LP	927671	1	Station Wagon RHD; for Brunei June 1993
34 KL 02	LP	927628	1	Station Wagon RHD; for Brunei July 1993
34 KL 85 to 35 KL 19	LV2A/181 Item 1	937800 to 939376	35	FFR Hard Top RHD; August 1993
35 KL 20 to 36 KL 21	LV2A/181 Item 2	935477 to 938663	102	GS Soft Top RHD; August 1993
49 KL 87	LV2A/123 LR/BN78/070	940960	1	CL Soft Top, with 300Tdi engine; for Royal Navy November 1993; to 10 RN 13
06 KM 64	LP	N/K	1	County (see note below) 2.5TD Air Con LHD; for Op Loadstar February 1998
HT 63 AA to HT 65 AA	LP	288361 to 287459	3	CL Hard Top RHD; February 1996
JN 13 AA to JN 16 AA	LV2A/265	N/K to 106249	4	CL Hard Top RHD; for RAF July 1996
JP 12 AA to JP 31 AA	LV2A/265	106476 to N/K	20	CL Soft Top RHD; in July 1996
JP 46 AA to JP 53 AA	LP	990647 to 990605	8	County Station Wagon RHD for RAF Mount Pleasant in July 1996
MZ 95 AA to NA 05 AA	LV2A/265	131984 to N/K	11	CL Hard Top RHD; for RAF in May 1997
NE 16 AA	LV2A/265	131298	1	CL Hard Top RHD; for RAF in July 1997
PT 93 AA to PU 32 AA	LV2A/265	154817 to 154988	40	CL Hard Top RHD; for RAF in April 1998
PY 00 AA to PY 13 AA	LV2A/265	157902 to 158709	14	CL Hard Top RHD; for RAF May 1998
RS 60 AA	LV2A/265	169965	1	CL Hard Top RHD; November 1998

S 62 AA and RS 63 AA	LV2A/265	169968 and 170125	2	CL Hard Top RHD; November 1998
RY 53 AA	LR009-98/99	170346	1	CL Hard Top RHD; March 1999
SN 84 AA to SP 03 AA	LR021-99/00	182260 to 182878	20	CL Hard Top RHD; October 1999
TE 06 AA to TE 09 AA	LP	102107 to 138052	4	Station Wagon RHD; Kosovo January 2000
TE 15 AA to TE 16 AA	LP	137826 to 138041	2	Station Wagon RHD; Kosovo January 2000
UC 76 AA to UC 82 AA	LR046	N/K to N/K	7	CL Hard Top RHD; for RAF; 2000
		Total	1277	

Note: The County model was the most luxurious civilian specification available and would not normally have become a military purchase. It appears in these tables only as a Local Purchase.

RAF

Serials	Contract	Chassis Nos	Total	Remarks
20 AY 01 to 20 AY 02 LV2A/133	BR110/71	940853 to 940788	2	CL Soft Top; for RAF AT in April 1994
34 AY 53 to 34 AY 62	LV2A/221	N/K to N/K	10	GS Hard Top Winterised; in November 1994
36 AY 72 to 36 AY 91	LV2A/265	983018 to 983567	20	CL Soft Top
		Total	32	

Berlin Senät

Serials	Contract	Chassis Nos	Total	Remarks
16 XK 03	–	701585	1	GS Soft Top LHD; April 1991
16 XK 05	–	902864	1	GS Soft Top LHD; April 1991
16 XK 07	–	903273	1	FFR Hard Top; July 1991
		Total	3	

Technical specifications, Defender 90 models

Engines

2495cc four-cylinder with indirect injection and 67bhp
2495cc turbocharged four-cylinder with direct injection and 107bhp (200Tdi)
2495cc turbocharged four-cylinder with direct injection and 111bhp (300Tdi)

Transmission

Permanent four-wheel drive with lockable centre differential
Five-speed manual main gearbox
Two-speed transfer gearbox
Axle ratio: 3.54:1

Suspension, steering and brakes

Coil springs all round
Worm and roller steering
Disc brakes on the front wheels and drum brakes at the rear (1991-1993 models); disc brakes on all four wheels (1993 on); servo assistance; separate drum-type transmission parking brake.

Electrical system

12-volt with alternator, or 24-volt with 90-amp alternator; some vehicles with 12/24v system.

Dimensions

Overall length:	146.5in (3720mm)
Wheelbase:	92.9in (2360mm)
Overall width:	70.5in (1791mm)
Unladen height:	77.3in (1963mm) for truck cab
	77.4in (1966mm) for soft-top
	77.6in (1971mm) for hardtop and Station Wagon
Track:	58.5in (1486mm)

Unladen weights

3651lb (1656kg) minimum with naturally-aspirated diesel engine
3734lb (1694kg) minimum with Tdi diesel engine

Performance

No exact figures are available, but performance was generally similar to that of a similarly engined Defender 110 (see Chapter 6).

DEFENDER 130 1990 onwards

The Land Rover 127 became a Defender 130 for the 1991 model year. Despite the name, there was no increase in the wheelbase, which remained at the original 127 inches. All that had happened was that the name had changed, to give a neat coherence to the naming of the three sizes of Defender chassis then on offer. However, the Defender 130 did come with the same fundamental specification changes as other Defenders.

The MoD purchased a number of Defender 130 models in the early 1990s for a variety of uses. The focus of its purchases then changed to the 130 HS, or Wolf derivative, when this became available (see Chapter 12), but small purchases of civilian-specification Defender 130 models continued to be made.

All Defender 130 purchases, once the Locomotors Ambulance contract was complete, had Tdi engines instead of the naturally-aspirated diesel engines in most other MoD purchases. The Locomotors ambulances themselves had V8 petrol engines, like their predecessors.

Crash Rescue Ambulance

As Chapter 3 explains, the contract for later RAF Crash Rescue Ambulances was placed with Locomotors of Andover. The contract was still open when Land Rover switched from building One Two Seven to Defender 130 chassis and, as a result, it is far from clear which of the Locomotors ambulances delivered in KK were built on Land Rover 127 chassis, and which were built on Defender 130 chassis.

The difficulty arises because what should in theory be 127 chassis (in the 400000 serial range) are mixed in some batches with what should in theory be Defender 130 chassis (in the 900000 serial range). This difficulty could well be compounded by clerical errors in the MERLIN records.

For clarity, we have listed all Locomotors ambulances in KK as Defenders, while accepting that some of the KK chassis may actually have been 127s. The difference is in any case largely academic.

These ambulances were among the last military orders for Locomotors, who called in the receivers in December 1992, closing shortly afterwards.

Although the Crash Ambulance was intended for use on RAF stations, it appears that many of the late deliveries were drawn from depot and issued to army units deploying to the Former Republic of Yugoslavia (FRY).

Crew Cab pick-ups

Several Crew Cab pick-ups have been purchased over the years. These have been used in Cyprus, at RAF Mount Pleasant on the Falkland Islands and by the Brigade of Gurkhas (BRIGNEPAL) in Dharan, Nepal.

In addition, a small number was purchased for Operation Resolute in the Former Republic of Yugoslavia (FRY). Resolute was the British military operation from 1995 until 2004 to enforce

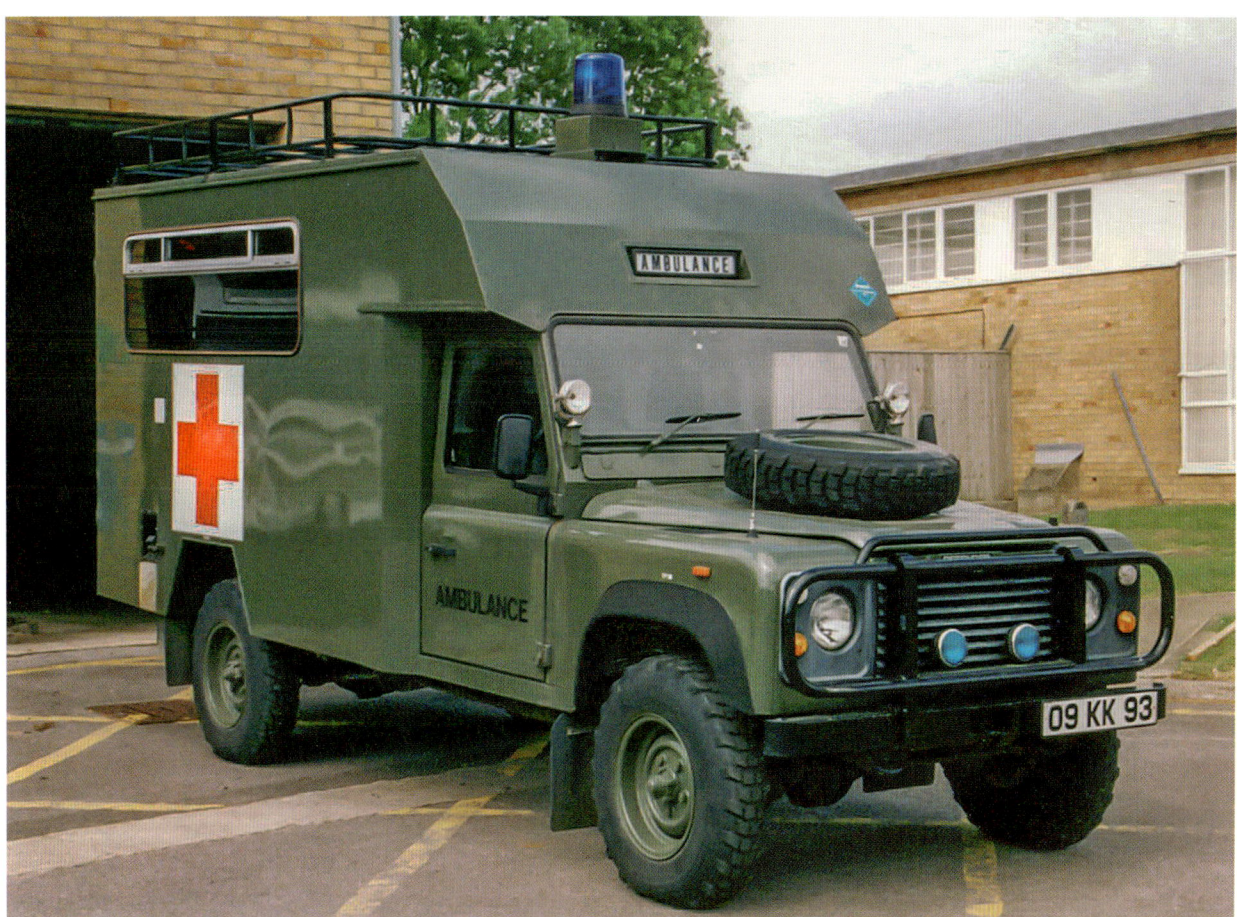

09 KK 93 is typical of the Crash Ambulances and this one is photographed on an RAF Station. It is known to have served at RAF Lyneham. Note the large roof-rack, and the additional wording 'Ambulance' on the driver's door. (CD)

This Locomotors ambulance served at RAF Brampton. Note that on the nearside the bodywork had provision for two vertically stacked stretchers and so had no window. (CD)

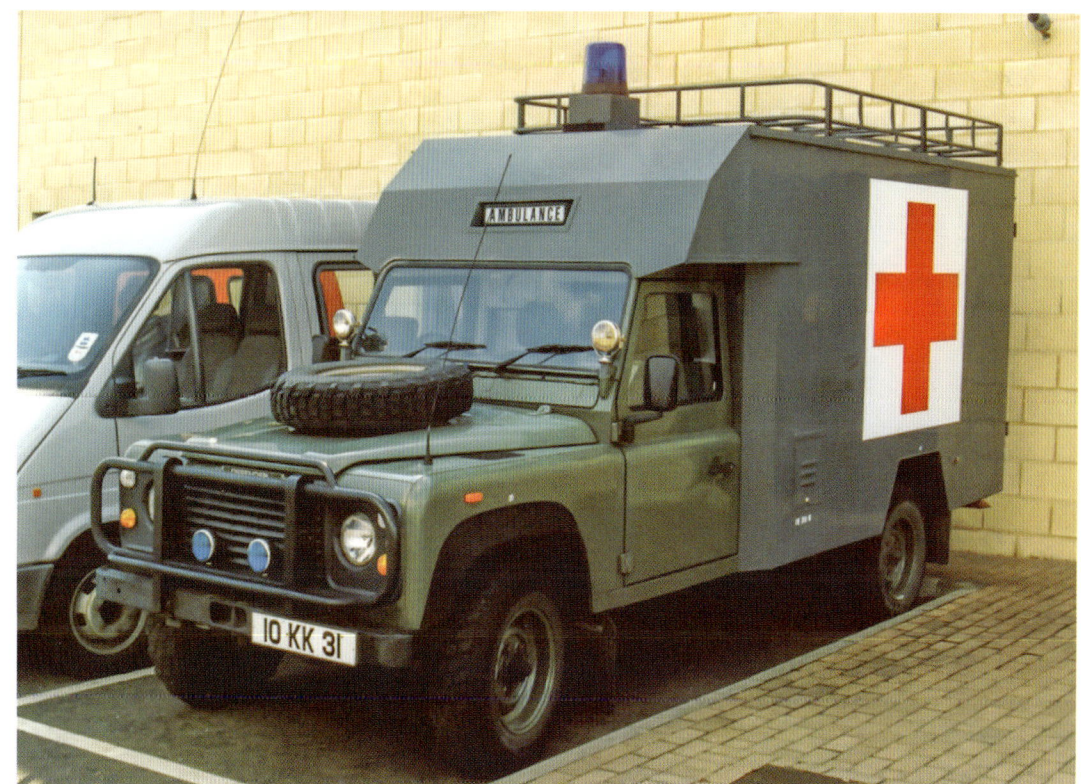

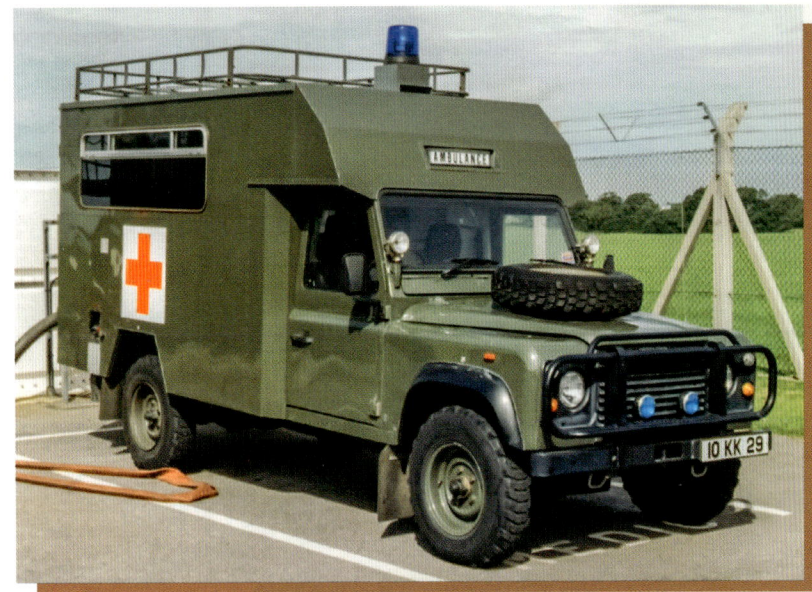

Crash Ambulances were dedicated to the role of reaching injured aircrew in air accidents on or near RAF airbases. The front bull bars enabled them to break through timber crash gates, and the spotlights on the windscreen pillars enabled the accident scene to be illuminated. (CD)

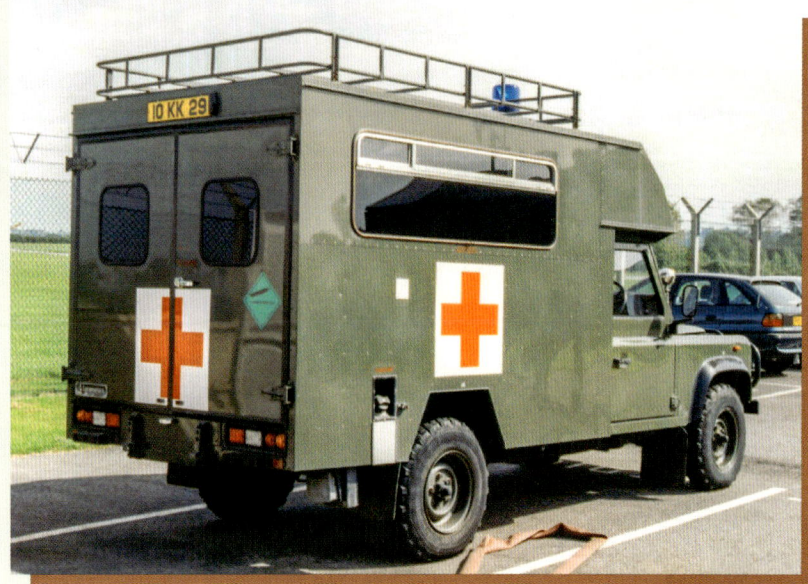

The large high window on the ambulance body is an unusual feature, and military ambulances had traditionally had very small windows up to this time. The roof rack was rarely used by the RAF crews although the Army used it to stow camouflage nets and personal kit. (CD)

the Dayton Agreement, by which the agreed political divisions of Bosnia and Herzegovina were to be ensured. Its vehicles were initially part of the Implementation Force (IFOR), and this became the Stabilisation Force (SFOR) in 1996. The Defender 130s that served there wore identification of both types. From 2004, the role of SFOR was absorbed by the European Althea Force (EUFOR).

NATO JEWCS

Two Defender 130 vehicles, with Quadtec box bodies by Land Rover Special Vehicles, were delivered in September 2006. Both were equipped as Mini Radar Vans (MRV) to provide radar jamming and radar simulations. The MRV can be used to train radar and electronic warfare operators in basic skills, and also in advanced, multi-threat scenarios. The highly mobile nature of the MRV allows it to reach training audiences that cannot be reached by traditional containerised systems.

It is not clear how these vehicles were deployed between delivery and their attachment to the newly-formed NATO Joint Electronic Warfare Core Staff (JEWCS), which was officially activated on 1 October 2013 and is based at Royal Naval Air Station Yeovilton. However, it is likely that they were used by NATO staff in a similar role to the one for which JEWCS has used them.

JEWCS is a capability centre for Electronic Warfare (EW),

providing Supreme Allied Command Europe (SACEUR) with EW expertise and training, in support both of the planning and execution of NATO operations and exercises. In addition, NATO JEWCS provides the same level of exercise support to the nine member nations – France, Germany, Greece, Italy, Netherlands, Norway, Poland, United Kingdom and the United States of America – that all signed the original Memorandum of Understanding (MoU).

NATO JEWCS supports all NATO Headquarters and Commands in the development of NATO EW Policy, doctrine, concepts and experimentations. NATO JEWCS is, and was, the unit which ensures that NATO forces have the significantly enhanced capability to operate in today's hostile EW environment.

JEWCS is also equipped with the Mobile Interceptor/Jammer (MIJA), based on the Defender 110 Station Wagon (see Chapter 6). MIJAs provide Electronic Support Measures (ESM), ie: jamming and deception, on the move. The ULQ 19 is a RACAL-based jammer, which can operate whilst mobile. It can also act in an intercept capacity, scanning up to sixteen channels and indicating their strength. Installing an agile receiver can enhance the interception capability.

Recovery vehicle

At least one civilian-specification Defender 130 was purchased locally, and bodied as a recovery vehicle for Cyprus.

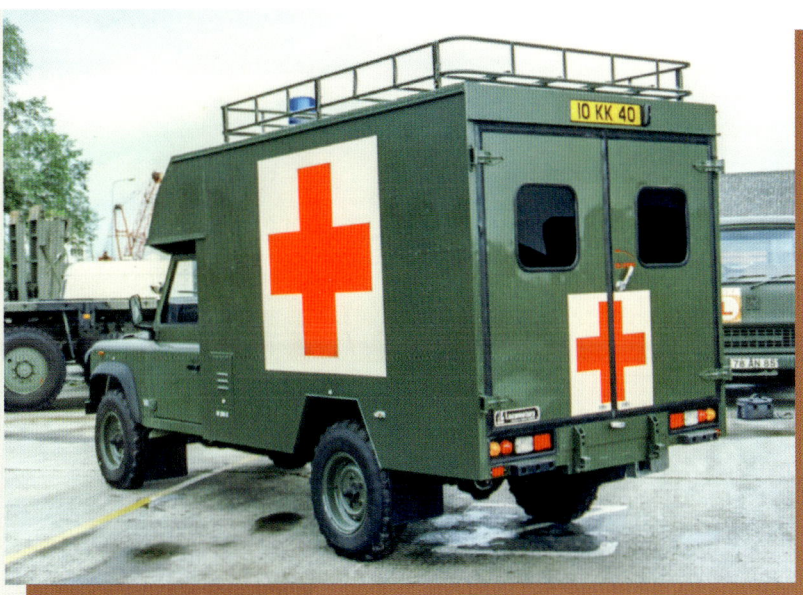

This brand new ambulance stands in Ashchurch prior to delivery. It went on to serve on Operation RESOLUTE with the Combat Services Support Battalion. The Locomotors build plate is very clearly visible above the left-hand cluster of tail lights. (VS)

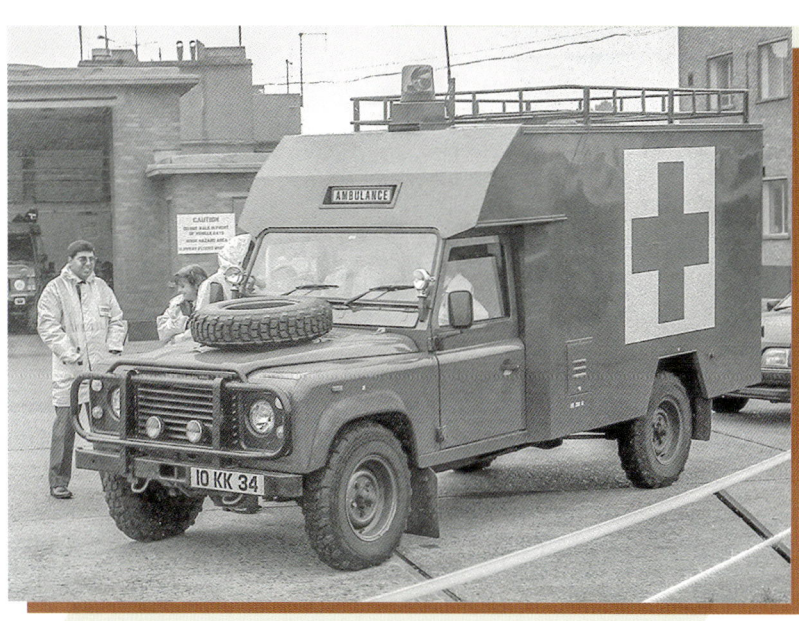

This ambulance was delivered to depot in April 1991, then went to RAF Coningsby where it was photographed at an Air Day in June 1993. It was sold at auction in November 2000. (GF)

ASSET CODES

Note that military records for the Locomotors-bodied ambulances make no distinction between Land Rover One Two Seven models and Defender 130s.

The Asset Codes (in use from 1990 to around 1993) are:

1046-4102	Ambulance, Crash Rescue, 2/3 Stretcher, 4x4, Land Rover 127 Locomotors Ltd
1046-9101	Ambulance, Crash Rescue, 2/3 Stretcher, 4x4, LHD, Land Rover 127 Locomotors Ltd

The later Asset Codes (from around 1993) are:

FB1094-3100	Car, Utility, CL, 4x4, Large, Crew Cab Pickup, 2.5-litre Diesel, Land Rover Defender 130
NB1046-4102	Ambulance, Crash Rescue, 2/3 Stretcher, 4x4, Land Rover 127 Locomotors Ltd
NB1046-9101	Ambulance, Crash Rescue, 2/3 Stretcher, 4x4, LHD, Land Rover 127 Locomotors Ltd
NB1302-3101	Recovery Vehicle, Wheeled, Light, 4x4, Land Rover 130 2.5-litre Tdi
QB1147-3122	Car, Utility, Large, Indigenous, (LP), 4x4, Land Rover 130 Td5, Crew Cab
RB1046-4102	Ambulance, Crash Rescue, 2/3 Stretcher, 4x4, Land Rover 127 Locomotors Ltd
RB1046-9101	Ambulance, Crash Rescue, 2/3 Stretcher, 4x4, LHD, Land Rover 127 Locomotors Ltd
WB1115-8111	Car, Utility, Medium, 4x4, LHD, 3.5-tonne GVW, 2.5-litre Diesel, Double Cab/HCPU, Land Rover Defender 130
WB1147-3122	Car, Utility, Large, Indigenous, (LP), 4x4, Land Rover 130 Td5, Crew Cab

Stanford pick-ups

Stanford Training Area was equipped with at least three High-Capacity Pick-up (HCPU) bodied versions of the Defender 130.

These were used for a variety of duties by the Wardens on the training area.

SUMMARY OF DELIVERIES
Tri-Service

Serials	Contract	Chassis nos	Total	Remarks
09 KK 88 to 10 KK 09	FVE 22B/939 Item 7	476619 to 900470	22	Crash Rescue Ambulance RHD; (Locomotors); ordered Jan 1990
10 KK 10 to 10 KK 15	FVE 22B/939 Item 8	485315 to 485489	6	Crash Rescue Ambulance LHD; (Locomotors); ordered Jan 1990
10 KK 16 to 10 KK 34	FVE 22B/939 Item10	900743 to 900820	19	Crash Rescue Ambulance RHD; (Locomotors); ordered Jan1990
10 KK 35 to 10 KK 37	FVE 22B/939 Item11	900888 to 900943	3	Crash Rescue Ambulance LHD; (Locomotors); ordered Jan1990
10 KK 38 to 10 KK 43	FVE 22B/939 Item14	901476 to 901853	6	Crash Rescue Ambulance RHD; (Locomotors); ordered Jan 1990
61 KK 43 to 61 KK 49	FVE 22B/939	909495 to 910748	7	Crash Rescue Ambulance LHD (Locomotors); September 1991
18 KL 53 and 18 KL 54	LP	916191 and 916371	2	High Capacity Pick-up with cab RHD; for Stanford Training Area; February 1993
21 KL 16 and 21 KL 17	LP	916338 and 916409	2	High Capacity Pick-up with cab RHD; for Stanford Training Area
48 KM 35 to 48 KM 36	LP	N/K to N/K	2	Box Van MRV; for NATO JEWCS; September 2006
CU 89 AA	LP	927059	1	Crew-Cab Pick-up RHD; for ITDU Trials; October 1994
JU 74 AA and JU 75 AA	LP	990874 and 991057	2	Recovery RHD; for Cyprus; August 1996
WY 51 AA	LP	987092	1	Crew-Cab Pick-up LHD; for Op Resolute; October 2002
WY 57 AA	LP	987290	1	Crew-Cab Pick-up LHD; for Op Resolute; October 2002
AK 94 AB to AL 03 AB	LP	651728 to 652957	10	Crew-Cab Pick-up RHD; for RAF Mount Pleasant; March 2003
BF 82 AB to BF 90 AB	LP	669617 to 670797	9	Crew-Cab Pick-up RHD; for RAF Mount Pleasant; February 2004
BJ 44 AB	LP	671197	1	Crew-Cab Pick-up RHD; for Mount Pleasant; 8 March 2004
DD 17 AB to DD 28 AB	LP	687956 to 689308	12	Crew-Cab Pick-up RHD; for RAF Mount Pleasant; Dec 2005
DE 81 AB	LP	683975	1	Crew-Cab Pick-up RHD; for BRIGNEPAL; Dec 2004
DN 21 AB	LP	687855	1	Crew-Cab Pick-up RHD; for Mount Pleasant; Dec 2004
		Total	154	

RN

Serials	Contract	Chassis nos	Total	Remarks
03 RN 73	N/K	N/K	1	Pick-up Dsl; July 1992
		Total	1	

Above and right:: Seen at a Yeovilton Air Day, 48 KM 35 is a Mini Radar Van (MRV) of NATO's Joint Electronic Warfare Core Staff (JEWCS). The body is a version of the Quadtec type produced by Land Rover Special Vehicles for civilian applications, and the protruding grille panel indicates that an air conditioning system is fitted to the vehicle. (AB)

MRV

Above and right: The aerial and dish array of the MRV is certainly distinctive. Note, too, that this is a LHD vehicle. (AB)

Above: Packed with electronic equipment, this is the interior of 48 KM 35. (AB)

Technical specifications, Defender 130 models

Petrol engine
3528cc V8-cylinder with two Zenith-Stromberg carburettors and 134bhp

Diesel engines
2495cc turbocharged four-cylinder with direct injection and 107bhp (200Tdi)

2495cc turbocharged four-cylinder with direct injection and 111bhp (300Tdi)

2495cc turbocharged five-cylinder with direct injection by electronic unit injectors. 122bhp (Td5)

Transmission
Permanent four-wheel drive with lockable centre differential

Five-speed manual main gearbox (to 2006); six-speed manual gearbox (with Puma engine)

Two-speed transfer gearbox

Axle ratio: 3.54:1

Suspension, steering and brakes
Coil springs all round

Worm and roller steering

Disc brakes on the front wheels and drum brakes at the rear (1991-1993 models); disc brakes on all four wheels (1993 on); servo assistance; separate drum-type transmission parking brake

Electrical system
12-volt with alternator

Dimensions
Overall length:	198in (5029mm)
Wheelbase:	127in (3226mm)
Overall width:	70.5in (1791mm)
Unladen height:	80.1in (2034mm)
Track:	58.5in (1486mm)

Unladen weights
4167lb (1890kg) minimum with V8 petrol engine

Performance: No performance figures available

9

DISCOVERY

The Land Rover Discovery was launched in 1989 with a choice of the then-new 200Tdi turbocharged diesel engine or the 3.5-litre V8 petrol engine. It was based on the Range Rover chassis, and initially offered a lower-priced, family-oriented alternative to the more luxurious Range Rover, along with a seven-seat option. The original Discovery used some Range Rover inner panels as well as parts from other Rover Group vehicles (including Freight Rover, Maestro and Montego cars). For the first year, only three-door models were available (two side doors plus one tail door), but from autumn 1990, a five-door model rapidly became the popular choice (four side doors plus one tail door). After autumn 1993, a 3.9-litre, V8 petrol engine replaced the original 3.5-litre.

The MoD did not initially have a role for the Discovery, but the first examples were acquired as Local Purchases for Operation Granby – the name given to military operations during the 1991 Gulf War. The type's value as transport for senior commanders was recognised, and several were subsequently purchased as less costly alternatives to the Range Rover. In general, however, the Discovery was purchased for special roles, in many of which it became a replacement for the Range Rover, as that model's cost and luxury features increased.

During 1991, Land Rover also began work on what it called Project Challenger, which was intended to deliver a new military Land Rover based on an extended Discovery chassis. As Chapter 10 explains, this was unsuccessful and, in the end, the MoD bought the specially-developed Wolf, or Defender XD, instead.

The original Discovery was replaced by a Series II model in 1998, which was very similar in appearance but considerably more sophisticated. This again consisted of five doors, retained coil springs (although top models had air springs on the rear axle), and remained in production until 2004. Most examples were powered by a new, five-cylinder turbocharged diesel engine called the Td5, although a 4.0-litre petrol V8 was also available. These vehicles were mostly used in roles similar to those allocated to the earlier (Series I) types.

After 2004, air suspension became standard on new Discovery models. Although a few examples of the Discovery 3 were built with coil springs for less sophisticated civilian markets, none of these is known to have entered British military service.

Below: Five 1994-model Discoverys of the Queen's Flight, pictured here with four of the dedicated Scania/Carmichael Helicopter Operations Foam Tenders. (CD)

Above: The Queen's Flight took delivery of several examples of the Discovery. This one dates from 1994 and is a five-door 'facelift' model. The basic specification is civilian, complete with alloy wheels, although the additional lights on the grille and roof, and the paintwork, were all added by the RAF. The vehicle is wearing civilian registration plates. (CD)

Below: This is another 1994 Queen's Flight Discovery, in this case, hitched to a Thompson refuelling trailer. (CD)

Land Rover proudly issued this picture when the first Discoverys were delivered to the Queen's Flight in 1991. The pictured vehicle really is one of those that were used; they had standard civilian-pattern side decals and, when wearing their civilian registration plates, the only obvious special feature was the roof-mounted light bar. (Land Rover)

Despite attempts to promote the Discovery through military equipment exhibitions, Land Rover was unable to interest the MoD in buying any at first. This is an early three-door diesel model, with little special about it except the light bar on the roof. (PH)

Queen's Flight

The Queen's Flight acquired five Discovery models for helicopter support duties in October 1991. These were three-door diesel models in full civilian colours, complete with standard side decals. They were given RAF serials 16 AY 34 to 38, but also had civilian registrations, probably all with the H-prefix numbers then current. Among them was H384 DJC.

There was at least one later purchase of Discovery models for the Queen's Flight. This again consisted of five vehicles: all five-door models, which carried the civilian registration identities L603 OFW, L154 JRW, L176 SDU, L912 VCC, and L521 ARU. They were painted in the special dark blue associated with the Queen's Flight, and carried Hazmat markings. The evidence suggests that they were registered in the summer of 1994, but no military evidence of the purchase has so far come to light. It therefore seems likely that they may have been part of a pioneering 'white fleet' contract.

These vehicles carried both firefighting and medical equipment, a paramedic being part of the regular crew. The emergency light bar at the rear of the roof incorporated the green lights associated with paramedic vehicles, and there were blue emergency lights in the grille. They towed refuelling trailers (Trailer, Tanker, Refuelling, Helicopter Support, 4-wheeled, 300-gallon, 1700 Kg, NEI Thompson Ltd) of which four were purchased, taking the serials immediately following those allocated to the first batch of Discovery models and becoming 16 AY 39 to 16 AY 42.

RAF Police

The RAF Provost & Security Service purchased a number of Discoverys over the years, although full details are unfortunately not available. As an example, the two four-door models ordered in July 1997 had blue lights in the grille, a light bar mounted over the cargo area, and a Hy-Light Floodlight system just behind the rear seats. The Floodlight System consisted of a telescopic mast and four floodlights mounted at the top. These two vehicles were painted white overall with day-glo panels, and left service in 2005.

RMP

A purchase of 12 five-door diesel Discovery models was made in March 1996. These equipped the Special Investigation Branch of the Royal Military Police, as well as providing a commander's car for the bomb disposal teams of 11 Explosive Ordnance Disposal Regiment, Royal Logistic Corps. The vehicles were unremarkable in appearance, apparently having an entirely civilian specification, and were not fitted with external blue lights.

Left (DP) and opposite (ID): The two 1997 deliveries for the RAF Police are seen here, each one a diesel-engined, five-door model.

SAAS

The Service Attaché and Adviser Service (SAAS) provides vehicles for Military Attachés in Embassies all over the world, and it found that the Discovery offered a useful compromise between an off-road vehicle and a prestigious British vehicle.

SAAS took on quite large numbers of these vehicles, which bore military registrations, until the service ceased using military registrations around 1996. The SAAS used both diesel- and petrol-engined versions, with both RHD and LHD, with and without air conditioning systems.

Senior Commanders' vehicles

In 1990, as the British army was preparing for Operation Granby, the first military Discovery models were purchased locally in Saudi

Arabia for senior military commanders. Among these were four, LHD five-door examples, fitted with roof-racks and bull bars. Not all Local Purchases during the Gulf War were given military registrations, but these four became 12 KK 52 to 12 KK 55. They were painted sand overall and had the rear windows painted out, while black chevrons (the recognition mark used by UK, US and allied forces) were painted on the front doors.

After the Gulf War, the Discovery became popular with Senior Commanders and further examples were purchased locally in Bosnia, Kosovo and Iraq for their use during the conflicts in these regions. The ones in Kosovo initially wore serials in a local system UK 00 ZZ to UK 999 ZZ, although at least two were transferred later to the normal 'Census' system. Many of those used in Iraq were associated with the Multi-National Division (South East) (MND(SE)) and wore serials in the locally allocated 00 MD 01 to 99 MD 99 series.

RM 13 AA was a Local Purchase for BMLO Ethiopia, and later went to the Brunei Garrison. The steel wheels and absence of roof bars show that this vehicle has a relatively low specification, even though it would have been used by a Senior Commander. (CS)

Not all Senior Commanders' vehicles were painted in military colours. This 1996 example retained its civilian colour scheme. (GF)

Pictured in service with SFOR, the NATO Stabilisation Force in Kosovo, this 'facelift' Discovery – probably with 300Tdi engine – carries one of the locally applied serials. It has been given an all-over military green colour scheme. (RS)

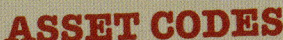

ASSET CODES

The usual inconsistencies are apparent within the descriptions applied to these Asset Codes, where the Discovery is sometimes a 'large' car and sometimes 'medium' or even a 'light' one.

The Asset Codes (in use up to around 1993) are:

1097-3100	Car, Utility, Large, 4x4, 5dr, 2.5 Litre Turbo Diesel, Land Rover Discovery
1097-8100	Car, Utility, Large, 4x4, 5dr, 2.5 Litre Turbo Diesel, LHD, Land Rover Discovery
1100-3100	Car, Utility, Non-Standard, 4x4, 2.5 Litre Diesel, Land Rover Discovery
1100-9100	Car, Utility, 4x4, LHD, Land Rover Discovery 2.5 Tdi
1147-9126	Car, Utility, 4x4, LHD, Land Rover Discovery 2.5 Tdi Base
1160-3100	Car, Utility, Large, Indigenous, LP, 4x4, LHD, Land Rover Discovery
1160-3101	Car, Utility, SAAS, Medium, 4x4, Airconditioned, 2.5-Litre Turbo Diesel, Land Rover Discovery
1160-3104	Car, Utility, SAAS, Medium, 4x4, Airconditioned, 2.5-Litre Turbo Diesel, Land Rover Discovery Tdi (Estate)
1160-4100	Car, Utility, SAAS, Medium, 4x4, Air Conditioned, 2.5-Litre Turbo Diesel, Land Rover Discovery
1160-8101	Car, Utility, SAAS, Medium, 4x4, Air Conditioned, 3.5 Litre V8 Petrol, Land Rover Discovery
1160-8102	Car, Utility, SAAS, Medium, 4x4, LHD, Air Conditioned, 2.5 Litre Turbo Diesel, Land Rover Discovery
1160-8103	Car, Utility, SAAS, Medium, 4x4, LHD, 2.5 Litre Turbo Diesel, Land Rover Discovery
1160-8107	Car, Utility, SAAS, Medium, 4x4, LHD, 2.5 Litre Turbo Diesel, Land Rover Discovery
1160-8108	Car, Utility, SAAS, Medium, 4x4, LHD, 2.5-Litre Diesel, Land Rover Discovery
1160-9100	Car, Utility, SAAS, 4x4, LHD, 2.5 Litre Diesel, Land Rover Discovery
1160-9101	Car, Utility, SAAS, Medium, 4x4, 3.5 Litre V8 Petrol, Land Rover Discovery
1160-9102	Car, Utility, SAAS, Medium, 4x4, LHD, Air Conditioned, 3.5-Litre V8 Petrol, Land Rover Discovery
	Car, Utility, SAAS, Medium, 4x4, LHD, Air Conditioned, 3.9-Litre Petrol (Low Octane), Land Rover Discovery (Note: MERLIN records this as '2.5-litre petrol')
1160-9104	Car, Utility, SAAS, Medium, 4x4, LHD, 3.9-Litre Petrol, Land Rover Discovery 3.9 EFi
1160-9105	Car, Utility, SAAS, Medium, 4x4, LHD, 3.9-Litre Petrol, Land Rover Discovery
1160-9106	Car, Utility, SAAS, Medium, 4x4, LHD, 3.9-Litre Petrol, Land Rover Discovery
1160-9107	Car, Utility, SAAS, Medium, 4x4, LHD, Air Conditioned, Land Rover Discovery Estate, V8 Automatic 3.9-Litre Petrol
1161-4105	Car, Utility, SAAS, Medium, 4x4, 3.5 Litre V8 Petrol, Air Conditioned, Land Rover Discovery
1161-8102	Car, Utility, SAAS, Medium, 4x4, LHD, 2.5 litre Diesel, Land Rover Discovery
1161-9108	Car, Utility, SAAS, Medium, 4x4, LHD, 3.6, Land Rover Discovery
1164-4102	Car, Utility, SAAS, 4x4, 3.5-litre V8 Petrol, Land Rover Discovery
1164-9106	Car, Utility, SAAS, 4x4, 3.9-litre Petrol, LHD, Land Rover Discovery (Note: the MERLIN record shows this as a '3.8' engine)
1172-8100	Car, Utility, SAAS, LHD, 4x4, 2.5-Litre Diesel, Land Rover Discovery
1707-3100	Truck, Utility, Helicopter Support, 4x4, 2.5 Litre Diesel, Land Rover Discovery

The later Asset Codes (from around 1993) are:

NB1160-3100	Car, Utility, SAAS, Medium, 4x4, Air Conditioned, 2.5-Litre Turbo Diesel, Land Rover Discovery
NB1160-3101	Car, Utility, SAAS, Medium, 4x4, Air Conditioned, 2.5-Litre Turbo Diesel, Land Rover Discovery
NB1160-3102	Car, Utility, SAAS, Medium, 4x4, 2.5-Litre Diesel, 7-seat Configuration, Land Rover Discovery
NB1160-3103	Car, Utility, SAAS, Medium, 4x4, 2.5 Litre Diesel, Land Rover Discovery
NB1160-3104	Car, Utility, SAAS, Medium, 4x4, Air Conditioned, 2.5-Litre Turbo Diesel, Land Rover Discovery Tdi (Estate)
NB1160-8104	Car, Utility, SAAS, Medium, 4x4, LHD, 2.5-Litre Diesel, 7-seat Configuration, Land Rover Discovery
NB1160-8105	Car, Utility, SAAS, Medium, 4x4, LHD, 2.5-Litre Diesel, Land Rover Discovery
NB1160-8106	Car, Utility, SAAS, Medium, 4x4, LHD, 2.5-Litre Diesel, Land Rover Discovery
NB1160-8107	Car, Utility, SAAS, Medium, 4x4, LHD, 2.5-Litre Diesel, Land Rover Discovery
NB1160-8108	Car, Utility, SAAS, Medium, 4x4, LHD, Air Conditioned, 3.5-Litre V8 Petrol, Land Rover Discovery
NB1160-9101	Car, Utility, SAAS, Medium, 4x4, LHD, 3.9-Litre Petrol, Air Conditioned, Land Rover Discovery
NB1160-9103	Car, Utility, SAAS, Medium, 4x4, LHD, 3.9-Litre Petrol, Land Rover Discovery 3.9EFi
NB1160-9104	Car, Utility, SAAS, Medium, 4x4, LHD, 3.9-Litre Petrol, Land Rover Discovery
NB1160-9105	Car, Utility, SAAS, Medium, 4x4, LHD, 3.9-Litre Petrol, Land Rover Discovery
NB1160-9106	Car, Utility, SAAS, Medium, 4x4, LHD, 3.9-Litre Petrol, Land Rover Discovery

NB1172-8100	Car, Utility, SAAS, LHD, 4x4, 2.5-Litre Diesel, Land Rover Discovery
RB1097-3100	Car, Utility, Land Rover Discovery
RB1097-8100	Car, Utility, Light, 2.5-Litre Turbo Diesel, 4x4, 5 Door, LHD, Land Rover Discovery
RB1147-3105	Automobile, Utility, Large, Indigenous (LP), 4x4, Land Rover Discovery Estate 2.5-Litre Tdi
RB1147-9156	Car, Utility, Large, Indigenous, 4x4, LHD, 3.9 Litre Petrol, Land Rover Discovery
RB1168-3100	Car, Utility, Police Special, 4x4, Land Rover Discovery Turbo Diesel, c/w Hy-Light Floodlight System
SB1155-3118	Car, Utility, Medium, 4x4, TD5, 2.5-Ltr Dsl, Land Rover Discovery XS (Note: This is recorded on MERLIN as a TDS rather than TD5, and X5, rather than XS. This is clearly a Series II model. Bizarrely, the same Asset Code is used for a Discovery 3!)
WB1100-3100	Car, Utility, Non-Standard, 4x4, 2.5-litre Diesel, Land Rover Discovery
WB1100-3108	Car, Utility, CL, 4x4, Land Rover Discovery V8 EFi
WB1100-3111	Car, Utility, C/L, 4x4, Land Rover Discovery Estate 2.5 Tdi
WB1100-3112	Car, Utility, CL, 4x4, Land Rover Discovery 200 2.5 Tdi
WB1100-8101	Car, Utility, CL, 4x4, LHD, Land Rover Discovery 2.5-Litre Tdi 5-door Estate, Automatic, Air Conditioning Fitted
WB1100-9100	Car, Utility, 4x4, LHD, Land Rover Discovery 2.5 Tdi
WB1147-3114	Car, Utility, Large, LP, Indigenous, 4x4, Land Rover Discovery 2.5 Litre Tdi
WB1147-9126	Car, Utility, Large, Indigenous, LP, 4x4, LHD, Land Rover Discovery 2.5 Tdi Base
WB1160-9107	Car, Utility, Large, Indigenous, LP, 4x4, Air Conditioning, Land Rover Discovery Estate, V8 Automatic 3.9-Ltr Petrol
	Car, Utility, SAAS, Med, 4x4, LHD, Air Conditioning, Land Rover Discovery

Note: Asset Codes NB1160-3100 and NB1160-3101 appear to be for identical vehicles and the reason for the two different codes is unclear.

SUMMARY OF DELIVERIES
Army

Serials	Contract	Chassis nos	Total	Remarks
12 KK 52 to 12 KK 55	LP	46375 to 459178	4	3.5P V8 LHD; for Operation Granby Nov 1990
21 KK 89	LP	462079	1	3.5P V8 RHD; for SAAS March 1991
38 KK 38	LP	009936	1	3.5P V8 LHD; for SAAS June 1991
46 KK 04 and 46 KK 05	LV2A/123 LR/BA184/003	021741 and 021950	2	3.5P V8 RHD; for SAAS November 1991
46 KK 06	LV2A/123 LR/BA271/004	020535	1	2.5D RHD; in November 1991
55 KK 17	LP	008601	1	3.5P V8 RHD; for SAAS November 1991
60 KK 00	LP	018884	1	Model not known; for trials in January 1992
63 KK 83	LP	016692	1	2.5D LHD; for SAAS January 1992
74 KK 23	LV2A/123 LR/BA286/009	027853	1	2.5D Air-Con LHD; for SAAS February 1992
76 KK 99	LP	016808	1	2.5D Air-Con LHD; for SAAS March 1992
79 KK 00	LP	015430	1	2.5D Air-Con LHD; for Defence Attaché, Accra May 1992
81 KK 61	LP	019366	1	3.9P V8 LHD; for SAAS July 1992
82 KK 13	LV2A/123 LR/BR46/016	088386	1	3.5P V8 Air-Con RHD; for SAAS
82 KK 53	LV2A/123 LR/BR337/021	038237	1	3.5P V8 Air-Con RHD; for SAAS
91 KK 00	LP	009956	1	3.5P V8 LHD; for SAAS October 1992
00 KL 53	LV2A/123 LR/BA363/026	047007	1	3.5 V8 Air-Con LHD; for SAAS February 1993
00 KL 59	LV2A/123 LR/BA397/029	047038	1	2.5D LHD; for SAAS March 1993
12 KL 57	LP	032105	1	3.5P V8 Air-Con RHD; for SAAS December 1992
18 KL 55	LP	046785	1	2.5D RHD; for Stanford Training Area in February 1993
26 KL 58 and 26 KL 59	LV2A/123 LR/BR70/036	063988 and 064655	2	2.5D RHD; use not known
43 KL 28 to 43 KL 36	LV2A/123 LR/BA410/043	076142 to 076221	9	2.5D RHD; for N Ireland
46 KL 02	LV2A/123 LR/BR70/053	077122	1	2.5D RHD; for RAF January 1994
60 KL 46	LV2A/123 LR/BA421/055	081952	1	2.5D Air-Con LHD; for SAAS

60 KL 47	LV2A/123 LR/BA427/056	081811	1	2.5D Air-Con LHD; for SAAS
60 KL 48	LV2A/123 LR/BA431/057	081983	1	2.5D Air-Con RHD; for SAAS
60 KL 49	LV2A/123 LR/BA420/058	080950	1	2.5D LHD; for SAAS
60 KL 50	LV2A/123 LR/BA436/059	080946	1	2.5D Air-Con RHD; for SAAS
60 KL 51	LV2A/123 LR/BA445/060	081883	1	2.5D Air-Con LHD; for SAAS
71 KL 36	LV2A/123 Warrant N/K	116632	1	2.5D RHD; for SIB in October 1994
83 KL 78	Ex-BZ 74 AA	116612	1	2.5D RHD
		Total	43	

Army – Others

UK xx ZZ	Assumed LP	N/K	1	for SFOR
01 MD 92	Assumed LP	N/K	1	for Op TELIC
02 MD 45	Assumed LP	N/K	1	for Op TELIC
		Total	3	

RAF

Serials	Contract	Chassis nos	Total	Remarks
16 AY 34 to 16 AY 38	A68A/4404	N/K to N/K	5	2.5D Helicopter Support RHD; for Queen's Flight March 1991
29 AY 04 and 29 AY 05	LV2A/123	N/K and N/K	2	2.5D LHD;
30 AY 20	LV2A/123	N/K	1	2.5D RHD; September 1994
38 AY 81 and 38 AY 82	LV2A/236	N/K and N/K	2	2.5D RHD;
		Total	10	

Royal Navy None known.

Tri-Service
a) Series I models

Serials	Contract	Chassis nos	Total	Remarks
04 KM 14	LP	N/K	1	2.5D RHD; 2-week loan to Eqt Support, Andover
07 KM 45	LP	765293	1	2.5D RHD; for Kosovo June 1999
09 KM 36	LP	764832	1	for Defence Attaché, Skopje
09 KM 37	LP	729992	1	for Asst Defence Attaché, Tirana
AB 78 AA	LP	045835	1	3.5P V8 Air-Con LHD; for SAAS November 1993
AW 09 AA to AW 12 AA	BA517/072	088677 to 088913	4	2.5D RHD; for British Gurkhas in Nepal (BRIGNEPAL)
BL 31 AA	LV2A/203	087095	1	2.5D Air-Con RHD; for SAAS
BZ 54 AA	Loan	N/K	1	2.5D RHD; loan to 5 RRF (V) for 2 weeks on 2 August 1994
BZ 72 AA to BZ 74 AA	BA569/01	N/K	3	2.5D RHD; use unknown
CJ 34 AA	LP	089237	1	2.5D RHD; for SAAS
CR 72 AA	BA620/095	N/K	1	2.5D RHD; for SAAS
CR 73 AA	BA623/096	129111	1	2.5D LHD; for SAAS
CR 74 AA	BA618/094	N/K	1	3.9P V8 Air-Con LHD; for SAAS
CR 75 AA	LP	095336	1	2.5D LHD; for SAAS
CY 90 AA	LP	077958	1	2.5D LHD; for SAAS February 1994
CY 92 AA	LP	068741	1	2.5D LHD; for SAAS in February 1994

DD 60 AA	LV2A/225	123078	1	2.5D Air-Con; for SAAS
DE 11 AA and DE 12 AA	BA657/002	N/K and N/K	2	2.5D RHD; for Army
DG 91 AA	LP	092968	1	3.9P V8 LHD; for SAAS
DG 94 AA	LP	071093	1	3.9P V8 LHD; for SAAS
DP 43 AA	LP	091999	1	3.9P V8 LHD; for SAAS
DP 44 AA	LP	133644	1	2.5D LHD; for SAAS
DP 47 AA	LP	070119	1	2.5D LHD; for SAAS
DZ 42 AA and DZ 43 AA	LP	N/K and N/K	2	2.5D LHD; for BATUS April 1995
EB 07 AA	LP	133271	1	2.5D LHD; for SAAS in March 1995
ES 63 AA to ES 70 AA	BA030/008	505766 to 506381	8	2.5D RHD; for N Ireland in January 1996
ET 86 AA to ET 87 AA	BA004/009	175594 and 509797	2	2.5D RHD; for N Ireland in April 1996
EW 43 AA and EW 44 AA	BA046/013	509778 and 509970	2	2.5D RHD; for N Ireland in April 1996
EW 61 AA to EW 63 AA	BA046/013	509789 to 509866	3	2.5D RHD; for N Ireland in April 1996
EX 82 AA and EX 83 AA	LR/BR041/14	511042 and 510929	2	2.5D RHD; for RAF in March 1996
FL 87 AA	BA042/4/015	517397	1	2.5D Air-Con RHD; use not known; April 1996
GC 40 AA to GC 51 AA	BA004/016	517190 to 517202	12	2.5D RHD; for Army in February 1996
HS 99 AA	BA042/4/019	189863	1	3.9P V8 Auto RHD; for SAAS; April 1996
JH 91 AA and JH 92 AA	LP	117958 and 119991	2	2.5D LHD; use unknown; June 1996; probably originally had serials in UK xx ZZ series; re-serialled as TM 13 AA and TM 14 AA in 2000
JK 54 AA	LP	055608	1	2.5D RHD; RAF use unknown; July 1996
JR 22 AA	LR/BR083020	N/K	1	2.5D RHD; for RAF Mt Pleasant in August 1996
JV 59 AA	BA139/021	543643	1	2.5D RHD; for Land Command in December 1996
JX 26 AA	LP	990041	1	2.5D RHD; RAF, use unknown; September 1996
ND 48 AA and ND 49 AA	LV2/DBG/64	751140 and 751078	2	2.5D Police Special RHD; for RAF P&SS
NG 60 AA	LP	100183	1	2.5D RHD; for Joint Police Unit, Cyprus Aug 1997
NJ 55 AA	LR/BA185/026	504877	1	2.5D Air-Con Auto LHD; use unknown, in September 1997
NU 06 AA	LR/BR110/01	N/K	1	2.5D RHD; for Falklands
NW 02 AA to NW 04 AA	LR/BA177/03	775424 to 775688	3	2.5D RHD; for Northern Ireland in March 1998
PY 96 AA to PZ 00 AA	LR/BA217/05	777337 to 781883	5	2.5D RHD; for Northern Ireland in June 1998
RK 62 AA	LR/BA217/09	151281	1	2.5D RHD; for Northern Ireland in September 1998
RM 13 AA	LP	778335	1	2.5D RHD; for BMLO Ethiopia and later Brunei Garrison
SU 12 AA	LR028-99/00	238020	1	V8 RHD; for 46 Squadron RLC in October 1999
SU 22 AA	LP	N/K	1	3.9P LHD; for RAF November 1999
TF 41 AA to TF 43 AA	LP	565389 to 565096	3	2.5D RHD; use unknown; Jan 2000 but 1998 build
TM 13 AA and TM 14 AA	Re-serialled (see Remarks)	117958 and 119991	2	2.5D RHD; re-serialled from JH 91 AA and JH 92 AA in 2000; for Pontrilas Training Area
		Total	89	

b) Series II models

11 KM 07 to 11 KM 12	LP	712490 to 707163	6	Td5 (11 KM 07 to 11 KM 10) or 4.0 V8 (11 KM 11 and 11 KM 12); for Op FINGAL
TT 70 AA and TT 71 AA	LP	267362 and 270456	2	2.5D LHD; use unknown, in May 2000
TT 93 AA and TT 94 AA	LP	274449 and 268824	2	2.5D LHD; use unknown
UC 83 AA and UC 84 AA	LR050	N/K and N/K	2	2.5D RHD; For Falklands in February 2001
UF 06 AA	LP	294188	1	2.5D LHD; use not known; October 2000

UP 96 AA	LP	706471	1	Td5 XS RHD; for Cyprus in January 2001
UU 77 AA	LP	714153	1	2.5D RHD; use unknown
VW 55 AA	JM029	N/K	1	2.5D LHD; RAF, use unknown
XA 14 AA	LP	783550	1	2.5D RHD; for Brunei Garrison
AN 84 AB	LP	N/K	1	2.5D RHD; use unknown; April 2003
AS 27 AB	LR1CSS0304	828124	1	2.5D RHD; for Northern Ireland in October 2003
AX 99 AB	LP	627174	1	2.5D RHD; use unknown
BR 12 AB	LP	126408	1	2.5D RHD; RAF, use unknown
BR 29 AB to BR 31 AB	LP	840111 to 862943	1	Series II 2.5D RHD; for BRIGNEPAL in July 2004
		Total	22	

No Discovery Series I or Series II models were ordered by the Berlin Senät.

Technical specifications, Discovery (Series I), 1989-1998

Diesel engine:
2495cc turbocharged four-cylinder with direct injection and 111bhp (200Tdi and 300Tdi)

Petrol engines:
3528cc V8-cylinder with two carburettors and 144bhp (1989-1990)
3528cc V8-cylinder with fuel injection and 164bhp, or 153bhp with catalytic converter (1990-1993)
3947cc V8-cylinder with fuel injection and 180bhp (1993-1998)

Transmission:
Permanent four-wheel drive with lockable centre differential
Five-speed manual main gearbox, or
Four-speed automatic main gearbox
Two-speed transfer gearbox
Axle ratio: 3.54:1

Suspension, steering and brakes:
Coil springs all round; some vehicles with front and rear anti-roll bars from 1993
Power-assisted worm and roller steering
Disc brakes on all four wheels with servo assistance; dual hydraulic circuits on the front wheels; separate drum-type transmission parking brake; ABS standard on top (ES) models

Electrical system:
12-volt with alternator

Dimensions:
Overall length:	178in (4521mm), 178.6in (4538mm), 1994-1998
Wheelbase:	100in (2540mm)
Overall width:	70.6in (1793mm) over door mirrors
Unladen height:	75.6in (1920mm) without roof bars
	77.5in (1968mm) with roof bars
Track:	58.5in (1486mm)

Unladen weights:
4231lb (1919kg) three-door 3.9 V8i
4359lb (1977kg) three-door V8
4363lb (1979kg) three door V8i
4432lb (2010kg) three-door Tdi
4527lb (2053kg) five-door Tdi

Performance:
(Tdi manual)
0-60mph:	17.1secs
Maximum:	92mph (148km/h)
Fuel consumption:	23mpg

(V8 manual)
0-60mph:	12.8secs
Maximum:	95mph (152km/h)
Fuel consumption:	14mpg

(3.5 V8i manual)
0-60mph:	11.7secs
Maximum:	105mph (169km/h)
Fuel consumption:	17mpg

(3.9 V8i automatic)
0-60mph:	11.8secs
Maximum:	105mph (169km/h)
Fuel consumption:	18mpg

Technical specifications, Discovery (Series II), 1998-2004

Diesel engine
2495cc turbocharged five-cylinder with direct injection by electronic unit injectors, and 136bhp (Td5)

Petrol engine
3947cc V8-cylinder with fuel injection and 182bhp

Transmission
Permanent four-wheel drive with lockable centre differential
Five-speed manual main gearbox, or
Four-speed automatic main gearbox
Two-speed transfer gearbox
Axle ratio: 3.54:1

Suspension, steering and brakes
Coil springs all round; some models with self-levelling air suspension on rear axle; front and rear anti-roll bars; some models with ACE roll control system on front axle
Power-assisted worm and roller steering
Disc brakes on all four wheels with servo assistance; dual hydraulic circuits on the front wheels; separate drum-type transmission parking brake; ABS standard

Dimensions
Overall length:	185.2in (4705mm)
Wheelbase:	100in (2540mm)
Overall width:	74.4in (1890mm) over body; 86.2in (2190mm) over door mirrors
Unladen height:	76.4in (1940mm) without roof bars
Track:	60.6in (1540mm) front, 61.4in (1560mm) rear

Unladen weights
2020kg	V8 petrol with 5 seats and all-coil suspension
2205kg	Td5 diesel with 7 seats, ACE and rear air springs

Performance
(V8 4.0-litre manual)
0-60mph:	10.9sec
Maximum:	106mph (170km/h)
Fuel consumption:	17mpg

(V8 4.0-litre automatic)
0-60mph:	11.9sec
Maximum:	106mph (170km/h)
Fuel consumption:	16.9mpg

(Td5 manual)
0-60mph:	14.2sec
Maximum:	98mph (157km/h)
Fuel consumption:	30.1mpg

(Td5 automatic)
0-60mph:	15.8sec
Maximum:	98mph (157km/h)
Fuel consumption:	27.4mpg

10

THE WOLF SAGA

Ever since the War Office ordered its first Land Rovers in 1948, the Rover Company (and, from 1978, Land Rover Ltd) had been able to rely on further orders for new vehicles. The company certainly did go to great lengths to make its Land Rovers suitable for military requirements, as our previous book, *Leaf-sprung Land Rovers in British Military Service*, makes clear, but there was rarely any serious competition for a UK military contract. Even when the 101-inch, one tonne Forward Control was competing in trials with the Volvo 4141 in the 1960s, Land Rover had an edge, because its vehicle was essentially a production version of ideas put forward by the MoD.

Things began to change in the mid-1980s. Land Rover came up against stiff competition from Reynolds-Boughton and Stonefield when the MoD wanted to replace its 101 One-Tonne models, and Chapter 5 explains how its Llama contender for the contract was unsuccessful. Around the same time, major problems arose with early deliveries of diesel Land Rovers (see Chapter 2), and Land Rover did its best to calm the waters by providing an 'interim buy' of petrol V8 Land Rovers, allegedly at an advantageous price to the MoD. Nevertheless, there was a distinctly negative attitude towards Land Rover within MoD procurement by the end of the 1980s.

It was about this time that the MoD began to think seriously about its next generation of light 4x4 vehicles. New terminology was now in use – TUL (Truck, Utility, Light) indicated the class of vehicles that the Ninety represented, and TUM (Truck, Utility, Medium) was the class in which the One Ten was then meeting the military requirement. Both were going to need replacement in the second half of the 1990s.

At the same time, the MoD began to look at its ambulance requirement. Its aim was to procure a single replacement for the three existing Battlefield Ambulances (BFA). These were the Marshall ambulance, based on the Land Rover Series III 109-inch chassis, the very different Marshall ambulance based on the Land Rover 101-inch One Tonne chassis; and the two types based on the Land Rover One Two Seven chassis, one again bodied by Marshall and the other by Locomotors.

A specification was prepared in 1988, and the MoD contacted a range of manufacturers to find suitable vehicles to test against it. The formal invitation to tender was still some way off, but Land Rover was determined to ensure that it would be on the list of invitees.

Challenger

The company was, of course, painfully aware of MoD discontent with recent Land Rover products, and there was a real fear that it might not buy any more Land Rovers at all. So, the company's Government and Military Operations division decided to whet the MoD buyers' appetites by showing them an early prototype of a new and more modern vehicle. Their thinking was that an entirely new design might help overcome the negative attitudes towards Land Rover within UK military procurement.

Two things now happened. First, the company head-hunted an MoD vehicle engineer to run the project to develop a new vehicle for the MoD. The man it recruited was Major Peter Marks, the MoD project leader on the 127 Rapier programme, and then again, the MoD's lead on the project that eventually became the Snatch 110. It had worked closely with him on both projects, and it believed that he was very well placed to understand the details of the requirement, and that his experience within MoD would prove useful.

The second thing was that Military Engineering took an interest in Project Challenger, a new Land Rover vehicle that was under development for the civilian market. The Discovery (see Chapter 9) had been introduced in 1989, and Challenger was an attempt to move into a new market sector through a utility vehicle based on the Discovery. Market research had shown that few customers actually used the heavy-duty capability of the traditional Land Rover utilities, and that there was an opportunity to sell a lighter-duty vehicle that would compete with products such as the Toyota Hi-Lux and Daihatsu Fourtrak.

The Challenger chassis was essentially that of the Discovery, shortened to provide a short-wheelbase model and lengthened to produce a 114-inch wheelbase for the long version. The front panels were to be those of the Discovery, with some differentiating changes, and there would be the usual variety of back body options. The vehicle promised to look new and modern, and was talked about as "Defender II," although it was not intended as a Defender replacement; the older model was expected to remain in low-volume production alongside it.

Right: The first Challenger military mock-up had a Land Rover High-Capacity Pick-Up body mounted on a stretched Discovery chassis with standard Discovery front panels. As the body was not long enough and the job was done quickly, there was a gap between body and cab. (LR)

Left: The front wings had to be modified to carry aerial tuner boxes, and the bonnet required a blister to cover the 90-amp alternator. This is the Challenger prototype that was shown to MoD representatives. It now survives in the Dunsfold Collection. (DLR)

Military Engineering now set up a standalone project to develop a military version of Challenger. It was known as Project Juno, and Peter Marks was put in charge. Unfortunately, some problems became apparent quite quickly. First of all, the Tdi engine's front end had not been designed to accommodate a 90-amp military alternator, and when one was fitted, a bonnet blister was needed to clear it. Nor was there anywhere to mount aerial tuners on the vehicle's front end, so redesigned wings became necessary. The windscreen then had to be made to fold onto the bonnet – which proved difficult, because the Discovery screen is curved.

Worst of all, though, was that the stretched Discovery chassis had never been intended to meet the weight requirements of a military vehicle. The only way to make it do so was to redesign it, which would mean that the cost savings associated with the shared chassis design in the original plan would disappear.

Nevertheless, the military Challenger prototype was shown to MoD officials as a flag-waving exercise in anticipation of the forthcoming call for new TUL/TUM vehicles to replace the existing Ninety and One Ten Fleet. Sadly, Challenger went no further: the whole project ground to a halt during the first half of 1991, not least because the civilian versions had run into customer acceptance problems at market research clinics, which made British Aerospace (who then owned Land Rover) reluctant to invest in the development programme.

Just one military prototype was built, and this still survives at the time of writing in the Dunsfold Collection of Land Rovers.

19 KL 11 was one of the Wolf TUM (HD) trials prototypes. The tall tilt is immediately apparent, as is the wide back body. This one had the spare wheel carried inside the side-hinged tailgate. (JT)

Wolf 1

The MoD had invited 19 motor manufacturers worldwide to tender for evaluation trials, adding that the prize would be a contract for well over 6000 vehicles. Land Rover was probably relieved to discover it had at least been invited to the party: the Challenger prototype had done its job. Of those 19 manufacturers, only three showed interest, and in November 1991, the MoD issued a contract (LV2A/088) to Land Rover for evaluation and trials vehicles. The other two contenders were Iveco-Ford (from Italy) and Steyr-Daimler-Puch (from Austria).

Above: This rear view shows the widened rear body of the TUM (HD) prototype. Note the hinged rear door and the spare wheel mount on it. Civilian-registered K253 PGK was photographed whilst in use by Qinetiq in 2002, having been retained after the trials programme. Note the external spare wheel carrier on the tailgate of this vehicle. The wheels themselves are the production heavy-duty type, identified by a ring of perforations. (GF)

Below: This was the alternator installation on 19 KL 11, showing why that bonnet blister was needed. The engine is a militarised 200Tdi type, known to Land Rover as a Gemini 2. This version of the engine did not enter volume production. (JT)

Above: The large military-pattern alternator would not fit under the standard bonnet, which was given a blister to provide clearance. This is 19 KL 11. (JT)

Below: Wing-mounted air intake boxes were fitted to the first batch of Wolf prototypes and remained part of the eventual production specification. This one is on 19 KL 11. (JT)

The formal requirement called for three new types of vehicle – TUL, TUM and TUM (HD). This third one – the letters stood for Truck, Utility, Medium (Heavy Duty) – was aimed at providing a lightweight vehicle but with higher capacity and one-ton towing capability for the specialised brigades. Later on, there would be a fourth vehicle category, defined as a Battlefield Ambulance (BFA), and initial thinking saw this as a derivative of the TUM (HD) specification. All vehicles would have to be diesel-powered, in line with the latest MoD policy.

All these new types were to be Improved Medium Mobility vehicles, that could operate close to the front line of a

Right: 19 KL 05 was one of the TUL prototypes submitted for trials in 1993. It was pictured back at Land Rover's Solihull factory in August 1995. (JT)

conventional Cold War battle, not necessarily up with the armoured battlegroup vehicles, but certainly among the gun lines of the Royal Artillery and the battlegroup's rear echelons. This was reflected in their description, which included the wording 'High Specification' – normally abbreviated to HS.

With Challenger now gone, Land Rover had to fall back

Left: 19 KL 07 was another of the early TUL trials prototypes, and was pictured in service in 2002, by which time it was nearly ten years old. The brackets on each side of the screen are for some form of anti-riot protection and are a later modification. (GF)

on the Defender. Although MoD representatives were somewhat surprised to learn that Land Rover was not now going to let them have an all-new vehicle, there was no major concern. Their real interest was not whether the vehicle was new or old, but whether it would be strong and reliable enough for the tasks they had in mind.

A new project, called Wolf within Land Rover, was set up under Peter Marks to develop versions of the Defender to meet the military requirement. A time frame of 18 months provided the opportunity to make some quite significant changes to the current production specification. For the TUL contract, the company focussed on upgraded Defender 90s, and for the TUM and TUM (HD) contracts, it supplied Defender 110s in two versions. For the Battlefield Ambulance, the plan was to develop a special-bodied Defender 130 in conjunction with Marshall of Cambridge.

At this stage there was no proper militarised version of Land Rover's latest Tdi turbocharged engine, so the engineers had to use the interim design prepared for Challenger. As on that vehicle, the Wolf bonnet needed a blister to provide clearance for the military alternator. This interim design was known as the Gemini 2 engine, as the original civilian-pattern Tdi had been developed as the Gemini type. A development project was under way to produce an engine that combined additional refinement for the civilian market with a redesigned front end that would accommodate the 90-amp alternator, but Gemini 3 (brought to market as the 300Tdi) was not ready in time for the first Wolf prototypes.

On Wolf, the engines breathed through dust-extractor filters mounted on the front wings, behind the wheelarches. The prototype vehicles had heavy-duty clutches and the R380 gearbox – which would not enter production for showroom models until early 1994 – had an oil cooler. They also had the all-round disc brakes which were just about to be released on standard production models, plus power-assisted steering. At least some of them also had new heavy-duty wheel rims designed specially for the purpose by GKN which, for production, would be distinguished from the standard wheels by a ring of holes around the circumference.

Some had 24-volt electrical systems, and were configured as FFR types. When the blister over the big alternator made it impossible to mount the spare wheel on the bonnet, it was mounted on the tailgate instead, and the tailgate was made side-hinged to suit. The TUM (HD) contenders also had a special wide body designed to accommodate a standard NATO pallet, and a taller rear roof.

Land Rover delivered a total of 18 vehicles to DRA in May 1993 for the military trials. Five were TUL prototypes, eight were TUM

types, and five more were TUM (HD) variants. The company also retained some for its own development work, giving them civilian registrations.

However, the MoD trials quickly showed up deficiencies in the Wolf prototypes. The DRA trials team found weaknesses in the structure of the vehicles and in their axles, springs and dampers. In addition, the steering proved vulnerable to damage in rough terrain, and the gearbox overheated in extreme conditions. The trials team also highlighted deficiencies in meeting the specification. So, less than five months into those trials, in September 1993, DRA brought proceedings to a halt and it was not immediately clear what the outcome would be. After a hiatus, Land Rover was invited to rectify the vehicles' failings, and the deadline for resumption of trials was set as September 1994.

Wolf 2

The failure of that first batch of Wolf prototypes was so major that the only solution was a fundamental redesign of the vehicle. However, there was no chance of developing an all-new vehicle to suit three different categories in 12 months, even with a dedicated project team of 45 people.

It was probably at this stage that Land Rover decided not to pursue its interest in the TUM (HD) contract, which was for a relatively small number of vehicles – expected to be 400. Instead, it focussed efforts on a series of major improvements to the TUM vehicles. It appears to have been agreed that if the TUM vehicles met military requirements, a similar specification would also allow the TUL models to be accepted for service. There was little risk involved here: the requirement for TUL vehicles was relatively small and, in fact, there was a period when the MoD seriously considered abandoning the TUL variant altogether. It only survived because of its use by units such as 16 Air Assault Brigade.

The second-generation Wolf prototypes – in practice, completely new vehicles – became known to Land Rover as Wolf 2 models, with the result that the earlier Wolf prototypes became known as Wolf 1 types. The development project was managed by Land Rover engineer Paul Markwick, and delivered four TUM prototypes to DRA for trials in September 1994.

Although recognisably Defender models, the Wolf 2 vehicles had been reinforced in almost every possible area compared with the civilian-specification Defender. Their chassis had stronger cross-members and massive longitudinal reinforcement under the load bed. Their axles now incorporated stronger half-shafts, four-pinion differentials and thicker casings. Springs and dampers had

(continued page 133)

This cutaway diagram shows the areas in which the standard Defender chassis was reinforced for the Wolf 2 vehicles (in blue), and the uprated axles (in red). (LR)

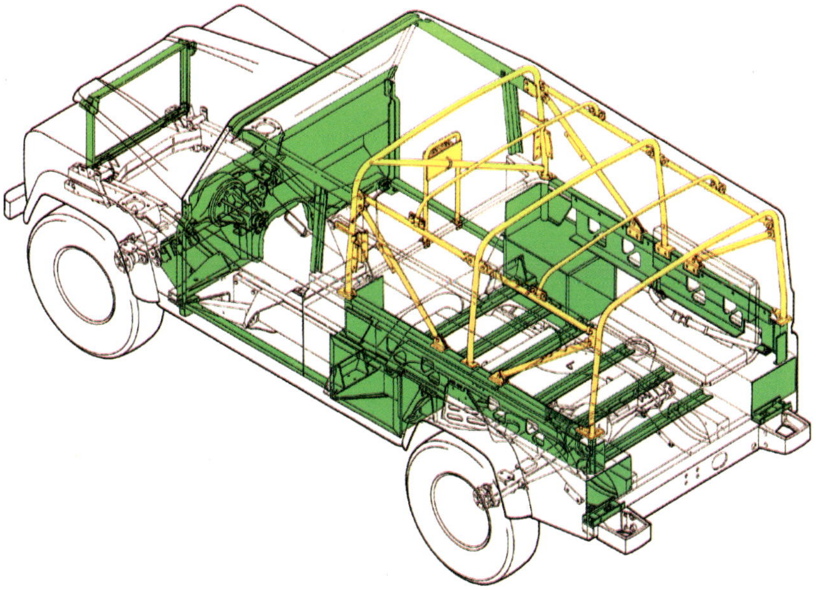

The body structure was also extensively reinforced. The green areas on this diagram show the areas of reinforcement; the demountable roll-cage is indicated in yellow. (LR)

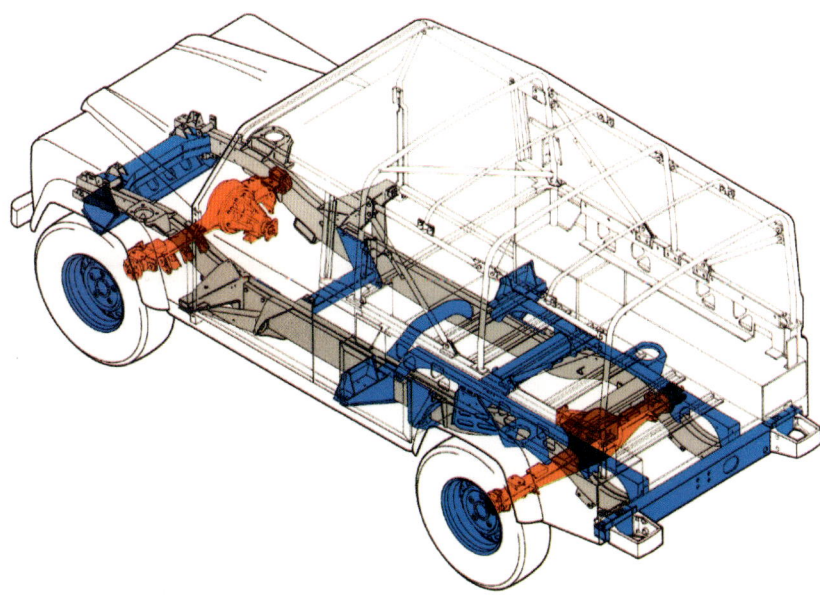

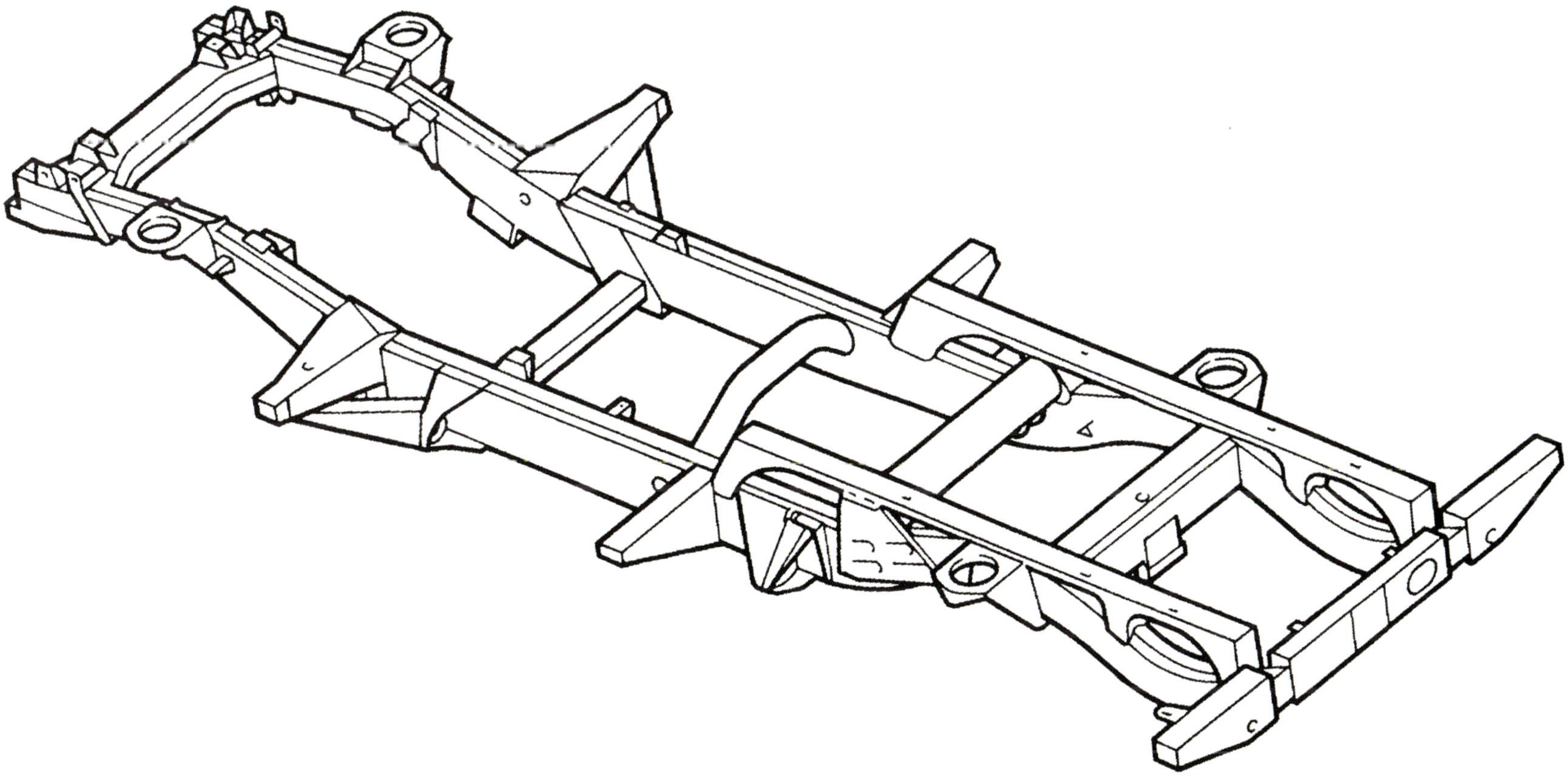

The Wolf 2 chassis looked like this when seen independently of the vehicle. (LR)

Below: This is the reinforced rear axle developed for Wolf 2, readily distinguishable by the bowed shape below the main axle casing. (LR)

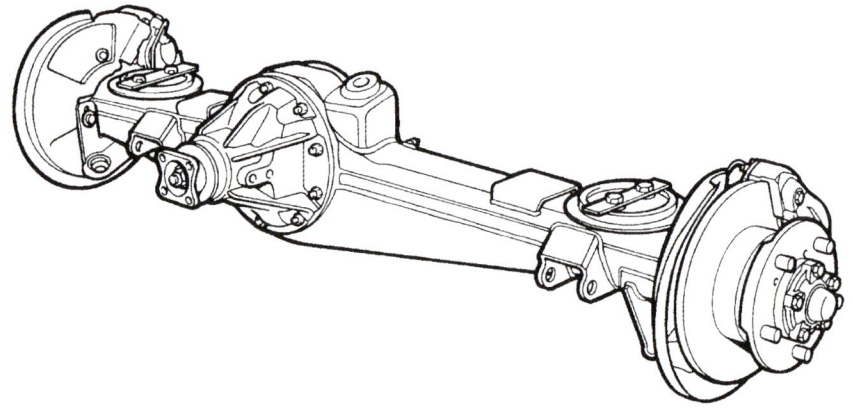

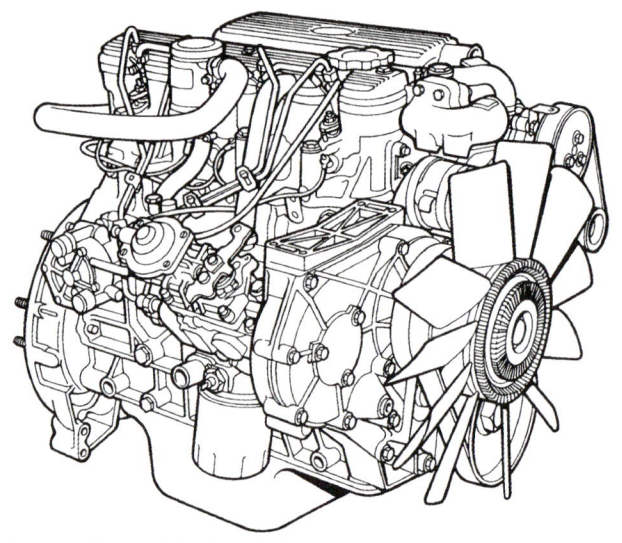

Above: The 300Tdi, or Gemini 3 engine, was a further development of the earlier 200Tdi type. It is seen here without the military 90-amp alternator that was one reason for the redesign. (LR)

This is a pre-production prototype, built in 1995, and now held in the Dunsfold Collection. It has a type of extended Hard Top to cover the roll-cage that did not appear on production vehicles but otherwise shows many of the other features that typify Wolf vehicles. (GF)

been upgraded, and the vulnerable steering components were protected by a guard plate.

The body had undergone perhaps the most radical changes of all. The less visible ones included a reinforced bulkhead, stronger sills, stronger top rails for the cab area, and a beefed-up radiator surround frame. Under the load floor, lateral reinforcement allowed a payload up to 20% greater than that of the standard Defender. More visible were the reinforcements in the sides of the load bed, fore and aft of the wheelarches.

In place of the familiar flimsy hood sticks, there was a demountable roll-cage, and troops sitting in the back were provided with seat-belt anchorage points. On Soft-Top variants, the tilt cover concealed the extra height which these brought to the body, but there was a requirement for a demountable Hard Top too, and a special one had to be developed to suit. Some prototypes had a metal hardtop, but, in the end, Land Rover developed a custom-made Hard Top made of reinforced

plastic resin that incorporated a vision hatch in the cab roof.

The tailgate had reverted to a traditional drop-down type, and although the traditional provision for mounting a spare on the bonnet was present, this was for use in emergencies only. Tests had shown that the weight of a spare could crack the bonnet at the higher speeds these Tdi-powered Wolfs could achieve over rough terrain. Reinforcement was not an option, as it would have made the whole wheel-and-bonnet assembly too heavy for practical use. So the spare wheel was now carried on a special mounting on the roll-cage, behind the door window on the passenger's side. Normally, there would be just one, but there was provision for carrying a spare on each side when necessary. To prevent the spare from blocking vision, there was a longer arm for the door mirror on the side where it was mounted.

There were no bonnet blisters on the Wolf 2 prototypes. All had militarised versions of the recently-announced 300Tdi engine, whose redesigned front end allowed a 90-amp military

CP 44 AA was one of the Wolf 2 trials vehicles, and was pictured here on the setts that formed part of the DRA trials course. (LR)

alternator to fit comfortably under the standard Defender bonnet. The big alternator would be standardised on all models, giving a 24-volt capability even to those not specially designated as FFR types. Wolf 2 retained the R380 gearbox, which was also now in production, and had the same wing-mounted engine intake filters as the Wolf 1 types. The Wolf 2 trials went well. Goodyear had to modify the design of its G90 tyre that Land Rover had fitted to all the trials vehicles, because early examples suffered an unacceptably high number of punctures. Michelin XZL types were later made available as an alternative. However, by May 1995 – around nine months into the trials – the MoD pronounced itself satisfied with the TUL and TUM vehicles. Land Rover proudly displayed its latest Wolf 2 at the British Army Equipment Exhibition in September 1995, and at the same time announced that it had been christened the Defender XD for production purposes. To anybody who thought about it, the news that the model was scheduled for production could only mean that it had won the contract.

However, the official announcement of that win was delayed for a few more months and, in the meantime, there was a third stage of trials. The MoD's plans for its new Battlefield Ambulance had changed: although the contract for TUM (HD) had been awarded to Steyr-Daimler-Puch in June 1994, that contract had not included the BFA vehicles. This now gave Land Rover a second chance to bid for that part of the contract.

The company submitted five vehicles, all based on the Defender 130 chassis upgraded with elements of the Wolf 2 specification, and with bodies to a special design by Marshall. As in the earlier TUL/TUM trials, these were up against contenders from Iveco-Ford and Steyr-Daimler-Puch, each of whom initially submitted two trials vehicles. SDP then submitted eight more in February 1994. There followed media speculation that SDP would also win the BFA contract.

Intense lobbying followed, both by Land Rover itself and by Members of Parliament representing the various Birmingham constituencies around Land Rover's Solihull plant. In the end, Land Rover was awarded the BFA contract and this was announced in Parliament on 18 January 1996, along with the news that Land Rover was the successful bidder for the TUL/TUM contract.

Land Rover, by this stage, had prepared a new marketing name for the Wolf versions of Defender. They became known as Defender XD types, and the letters in that new name of Defender XD were now revealed to stand for eXtra Duty. In full, the new models were known as Defender XD 90, Defender XD 110, and Defender XD 130, and all would become available to overseas armed forces after MoD deliveries had been completed.

As finally signed, the MoD contract called for 1411 XD 90 models to meet the TUL requirement, 6514 XD 110 models to meet the TUM requirement, and for about 800 XD 130 models configured as Battlefield Ambulances. That figure of "about 800" seems to have been 797 in practice (see Chapter 13). The two contracts together were said at the time to be worth in excess of

The Steyr-Daimler-Puch Pinzgauer was one of the competitors for the TUM contract. (GF)

This Iveco vehicle was also a contender for the TUM contract. Pictured is an example in service with the Italian Artillery – an M109 regiment. (GF)

£200 million. Deliveries were to start as soon as practicable, and were to be completed by October 1998. The first examples of the Wolf actually arrived at Vehicle Depot, Ashchurch in March 1997, and the first examples entered service on 1 April.

Deliveries were to consist of more than 20 different types of Wolf vehicles, in both RHD and LHD form, including GS and FFR types. Unit conversions and changing requirements later

ensured that there would be an even larger number of variants in service. The contract also called for Land Rover to develop special Winterised and Waterproofed variants of the main models, and the development work for this was done concurrently with early deliveries of the Wolf vehicles. These versions were predominantly destined for the units of 3 Commando Brigade, although 17 Port & Maritime Regiment, Royal Logistic Corps also required waterproofed versions.

During the first 12 months of production, between September 1996 and September 1997, vehicles were randomly taken from the production line for what were known as 'production confirmatory trials.' These trials were intended to confirm that the performance reliability of the trials vehicles was representative of those coming off the production line, and they identified just one problem – with a front wheel bearing, which was subsequently redesigned.

All the Defender XD vehicles were delivered to the MoD with a five-year, or 75,000km parts and labour warranty that included three-year cover on batteries, and one-year cover on tyres and exhausts. There was also a one-year Land Rover Assist package (essentially a breakdown scheme, operated through dealers) that was valid in the UK and in Germany.

Left: This XD 130 ambulance is one of the eight trials vehicles and was shown at Larkhill in May 1995 by Land Rover. Note the large blue light on the roof and the plastic surrounds to the headlamps which did not appear on production vehicles. The siren was later mounted on the bodywork above the cab. (GF)

This is a Wolf 2 TUM in 24-volt GS Soft Top form. It was displayed at Royal Navy and British Army Exhibition (RN&BAEE) at Aldershot in September 1995. (GF)

The Wolf 1 prototypes

Serials	Contract	Chassis nos	Total	Remarks
18 KL 96 to 19 KL 03	LV2A/088	928046 to 928463	8	Trials Vehicles Cargo, FFR and FFR w/Winch RHD (TUM); see Note below
19 KL 04 to 19 KL 08	LV2A/088	927717 to 927920	5	GS Soft Top RHD; delivered 16 April 1993 (TUL); see Note below
19 KL 09 to 19 KL 13	LV2A/088	928655 to 928849	5	Trials Vehicles for Cargo and FFR RHD (TUM (HD)); see Note below

There were also two FFR TUM (HD) models which carried civilian registrations. These were K754 GKV (which was later sold into private ownership) and K253 PGK.

The following details of trials vehicles are available:

18 KL 98	GS Soft Top
19 KL 01	FFR Soft Top, with winch
19 KL 02	with winch
19 KL 03	GS Soft Top
19 KL 07	GS Soft Top with side-mounted spare wheel
19 KL 08	GS Soft Top, RHD
19 KL 09	FFR Soft Top, RHD
19 KL 11	FFR Soft Top, RHD

The Wolf 2 and BFA prototypes

Serials	Contract	Chassis Nos	Total	Remarks
CP 42 AA to CP 45 AA	Loan	N/K to 951418	4	TUM Trials Vehicles
AH 80 AA to AH 87 AA	Loan	936702 and 937171	8	BFA Trials Vehicles; 31 October 1994

Among the vehicles retained by Land Rover on civilian plates for engineering development work was M461 KAC (SALLDHAF7MA-960411), a TUM model which at the time of writing survived in the Dunsfold Collection. It has a prototype metal hardtop which incorporates an awkward "step" between the standard hardtop-style cab roof and the raised rear section over the Roll-cage.

Wolf XD 110, 1997-1999

The production contract for TUM – the 110-inch wheelbase version of the Defender XD – was to amount to over 6000 vehicles in more than 20 types. There would be both LHD and RHD vehicles, General Service (GS) and Fitted for Radio (FFR) types, Hard Tops and Soft Tops, plus Waterproofed and Winterised versions.

It is reasonable to ask why there were so many types – there have always been GS and FFR versions of the 'Utility' vehicle, with the GS being used to carry cargo and personnel, and the FFR in command roles where communications equipment is vital. At the time the Wolf vehicles were entering service, 'communications' meant Clansman.

LHD versions were acquired for use in BAOR, although this requirement would gradually reduce and, in consequence, these versions were increasingly seen in the UK. Hard Tops are often used on the FFR versions to protect valuable communications equipment from the elements, but also from theft, and on Winterised vehicles to give weather protection. The fibreglass Hard Top on the Wolf XD 110 is unique to military vehicles, and is also much taller than equivalent civilian items in order to cover the roll-cage. Some FFR versions were built with Soft Tops to equip units that might need to deploy in the Chinook helicopter, as height through the rear door is limited. The Winterised and Waterproofed versions were predominantly for the units of 3 Commando Brigade, although 17 Port & Maritime Regiment, Royal Logistic Corps also required Waterproofed versions.

The MoD originally intended that the Wolf vehicles would be replaced by the Operational Utility Vehicle System (OUVS) that was announced in 2003. In 2011, after several years of uncertainty, it became clear that OUVS had been cancelled. It is currently expected that the new Multi-Role Vehicle – Protected (MRV-P) will take over some roles from the TUM.

As a medium-term measure in 2010, the MoD embarked on a three-year programme (called REMUS, see below) to extend the lives of Wolf Land Rovers then in service. There are expectations that a further re-work programme will be necessary to extend the life of the Wolf fleet through to 2025 or 2030. It is unlikely that the Wolf fleet will be replaced before then: money appears to be in such short supply that it is difficult to see an acquisition of several thousand vehicles being funded, even if the MoD could decide on what was needed to meet the requirement!

The major special variants of the Wolf XD 110 and the multiple upgrade programmes for the type are described below. Also worth noting is that, in 2017, the MoD introduced a modification ('MoD 42') which provided for the rear wheel to be carried on a swingaway carrier at the tail of TUL (HS) and TUM (HS) vehicles. This modification was found to be likely to cause a road traffic accident when the vehicles were towing a trailer, and a safety notice issued in April 2017 drew attention to the problem. However, units were not instructed to remove these carriers, which remained safe to use when the vehicles were not towing. A minor modification ('MoD 46') in 2017, introduced wheel nut indicators (WNIs), that were to be

HL 96 AA is a RHD version of the GS Soft Top. Note the spare wheel mounted on the bonnet, which is fairly unusual for a Wolf. The vehicle was on display at the Royal Navy and British Army Exhibition (RN&BAEE) at Aldershot in August 1997. (GF)

Another RHD GS Soft Top, again with the spare wheel on its bonnet. The other mount for the spare wheel on the Roll-cage can be seen emerging through the tilt. It was not easy to lift the wheel from the side mount, and a canvas strap was provided to assist. (GF)

This is the FFR Hard Top RHD version of the Wolf XD 110. It is seen here serving with 4626 Aeromedical Evacuation Squadron of the RAF. Almost all tactical units had FFR versions to provide communications and headquarters vehicles. (GF)

installed with a trailing pattern. None of these was photographed in time to be pictured in this book.

Bowman Harnesses and Local Area System (LAS)

There are five levels of Bowman preparation, which are: No Harness (NH), Reduced Functional LAS, Simple Harness (SH), Full Functional LAS (FFL) and Basic Functional LAS.

The local area system (LAS) provides IP-based tactical Internet connectivity. WMIKs are fitted with NH or SH, so will have one or two radios respectively. Functionality rises through the various "fits" to FFL, which is used for command vehicles. These are mainly attached to a headquarters offering VHF, HF, UHF High Capacity Data Radio, User Display Terminals, telephone exchange and the Vehicle External Distribution System (VEDS). VEDS allows other vehicles and systems (e.g. SATCOM, trunking, LAN, etc) to be linked to one another.

Helicopter support

A special version of the TUM was purchased in small numbers for units operating with helicopters. It was designed to enable field servicing to be carried out using a roof-mounted platform and rear access ladder. These Helicopter Support vehicles equipped RAF units that operated helicopters.

JDFC

JDFC is a vehicle-mounted system developed by RACAL for jamming enemy radio communications, and it has been deployed in both

Defenders and Wolf XD. The installation kit was applied to a FFR Hard Top and involved fitting various racks, wiring and control panels, cooling vents and electrical outlets to the basic vehicle. JDFC was for use by 14 Signal Regiment, Royal Corps of Signals.

Odette

This is a tactical communications electronic support measures system, mounted on mobile platforms. The system offers a persistent monitoring capability which contributes to the UK's overall battlefield intelligence picture. It enjoyed a distinguished career of more than a decade, providing vital support to operations, initially in Bosnia and Kosovo, as well as Iraq and Afghanistan. Odette was still in service at the time of writing in 2017, because of the cancellation of its proposed successor (Soothsayer) and it is likely to remain in service until the new successor (Landseeker) arrives. The system is used by 14 Signals Regiment, Royal Corps of Signals at Brawdy.

Remus

The Wolf vehicles entered service at the start of a busy period for the British army, and over the next few years saw service in Bosnia, Sierra Leone, Iraq and Afghanistan. One result of this has been that few of the vehicles have been sold, and those that have gone for auction have generally been in poor condition – usually as a result of road traffic accidents.

Announced in 2010, Project Remus involved about 6000 of the TUM Wolf fleet being reworked by Defence Support Group (DSG).

The project improved the vehicle and brought it up to the latest standards in terms of noise and passenger protection. It involved fitting each vehicle with front and rear anti-vibration acoustic matting and a Front Roll-Over Protection System (FROPS). Fitted internally, this consisted of two bars extending from the existing Roll-cage to the scuttle behind the A-pillars. Rear seat belts were removed and replaced with retractable seat belts on Cargo variants, but FFR variants were left with no facility for carrying passengers in the rear. The chassis and bulkhead were both wax-injected and the chassis was also undersealed.

DSG announced the end of the project in April 2013, at which stage, 5477 vehicles had been upgraded. Vehicles which at that stage were deployed on Operation Herrick in Afghanistan, were to be modified on return to the UK in a follow-on programme that started at the end of 2015, although no associated Asset Code change had been reported at the time of writing.

Scout

This is a variant where the windscreen, sidescreens and frames are removed to provide a reconnaissance vehicle. In addition, the front bulkhead vents are covered with a waterproof cover, and the Scout appears to operate without a tailgate. These vehicles are used by the Royal Wessex Yeomanry and also are held by Warminster Support Unit. More than 17 are known.

Below: KG 93 AA is a LHD GS Soft Top, pictured in service with 19 Regiment, Royal Artillery. Note the snorkel that has been added for deep wading, and the clean paintwork where the air intake box has been removed! It was photographed on Salisbury Plain in July 2006. (GF)

Above: KF 41 AA is seen in July 1997, a month after delivery. It is a LHD GS Soft Top and went on to serve with 35 Engineer Regiment, Royal Engineers in BAOR. (GF)

Left: LV 94 AA is fitted with a Bowman aerial even though it is a GS version serving with 17 Port & Maritime Regiment, Royal Logistic Corps. (GF)

Right: This well-worn FFR Hard Top example belonged to 23 Pioneer Regiment, Royal Logistic Corps and is in overall sand. The hose on the bonnet is fitted to the exhaust to keep exhaust gases away from the crew. This allows the engine to be run to keep the batteries charged if radios are operated when the vehicle is static. (GF)

Left: This RAF example of an FFR Hard Top is still equipped with Clansman and is towing the ¾-Tonne Cargo Trailer. This combination was found to be dangerous at higher speeds, and the trailer was replaced by the Universal Engineering Lightweight trailer. (GF)

Shoehorn

Following the introduction of the Bowman communication system to the Land Rover fleet, it was found that some TUM (HS) variants were overweight. To address this issue, Specialist & Utility Vehicles Integrated Project Team (SUV IPT) tasked ABRO to modify specific vehicles by fitting a rear anti-roll bar. This programme was known to the military as Project Shoehorn, and the modification increased the GVW of converted vehicles from 3350kg to 3500kg.

Spice – Electronic Warfare Countermeasures

Spice is known to have been an Electronic Countermeasures system, and an installation kit was developed, to mount it in a Land Rover. It was for use on Wolf Defenders by 14 Signal Regiment, Royal Corps of Signals.

Tactical Command and Analysis Detachment (TCAD)

The Detachment is attached to an Odette unit (see previous) and is responsible for determining the way Odette is deployed, then analysing the material produced. An installation kit was provided for certain TUM vehicles, and these were used by 14 Signals Regiment, Royal Corps of Signals at Brawdy. Further details were unavailable at the time of writing.

Talon support vehicle

Talon is a lightweight, deployable satellite ground terminal which uses commercial off-the-shelf technology (COTS) packaged to provide a terminal suitable for military use. The terminal is controlled from a ruggedised laptop, and can be set up by a crew of two trained operators within 30 minutes. Talon has been employed

(continued page 144)

This Land Rover Scout was photographed on Salisbury Plain Training Area in early 2017. Note the lack of windscreen or side screens and the use of a nylon camouflage fly-sheet to provide some overhead cover. (AB)

The Land Rover Scout has minimal crew protection – hence the use of goggles to protect the crew's eyes. The air vents on the bulkhead are covered. This vehicle was in use by the Royal Wessex Yeomanry in August 2014. (AB)

by the ARRC (Allied Rapid Reaction Corps) in Germany, and was used extensively in Operation Telic in Iraq. Talon terminals were brought into service in July 2002, and incorporated into the Skynet 5 contract in October 2003. Each terminal can be carried in a single vehicle, towing the generator mounted on a trailer.

VPK

The Vehicle Protection Kit (VPK) vehicles were Snatch vehicles, originally pre-Wolf Defender 110s (see Chapter 6) but subsequently upgraded to Wolf standard by Ricardo to meet the needs of Iraq and later Afghanistan. Some of these were subsequently referred to as Vixen. They were withdrawn as the Foxhound Light Protected Patrol Vehicle (LPPV) entered service.

Winter/Water

Among the specifications required in the original Wolf contract, was one known as Winter/Water. This was for a Royal Marines vehicle capable of both winter deployment in temperatures down to -46°C, and fording through water up to 1.5 metres deep. The vehicle had to be capable of preparation for either role within two hours. The original contract required 686 such vehicles.

The technical content of the Winter specification had already been established for an earlier contract of Defender 90s and 110s supplied in the 1990s. The waterproofing specification had to be newly developed. Earlier waterproofed Land Rovers had used a kit developed by ATTURM, and fitted in MoD workshops; this was known as 'Stage A'. The Marines then fitted an additional kit before use. For the Wolf vehicles, the Stage A level of preparation had to be built into the vehicles on the assembly line.

The new specification was developed by Land Rover in conjunction with ATTURM. Major elements of the design focussed on the electrical system, and a system of sealed housings was developed; all major electrical items were routed through a sealed centre console, which allowed normal use of the vehicle before final preparation for wading. Wax coating of the body, chassis and all cavities was used to control corrosion.

For the Winterised role, vehicles had a fuel-burning heater that supplied heat to the engine for a cold start and heat to the inside through radiators along the back body sides. This heater was also resistant to deep-fording.

There was an entry-into-service deadline of 1st October, 1998 – set because of forthcoming changes in European exhaust emissions regulations – and the basic Winter/Water specification was adapted to suit all three sizes of Defender XD. Most of the Winter/Water vehicles

This is a GS Soft Top Winterised and Waterproofed version for the Royal Marines. Note the screen-mounted snorkel emerging from the wing top, and the roof rack bars for carrying inflatable boats and the like. The vehicle is marked for 29 Commando Regiment Royal Artillery, and "23 BFS" indicates 23 Battery Fitter Section REME. (GF)

This RHD Winterised and Waterproofed GS Soft Top has an unusual camouflage scheme. Note the air intake is omitted on the wing and replaced by the snorkel. This vehicle belonged to the Commando Logistic Regiment. (GF)

were delivered to equip units involved in littoral operations, which were those of 3 Commando Brigade and 17 Port & Maritime Regiment, Royal Logistic Corps. In addition, many otherwise standard Wolf GS and FFR vehicles were fitted by their operating units with snorkels to give them a wading capability.

WMIK

The name WMIK (pronounced 'wimmik') stands for Weapons Mount Installation Kit, and was first used in 1999 when the MoD ordered 58 such kits for fitting to Land Rovers. These kits were developed jointly between Ricardo Special Vehicles and Land Rover, and consisted of a modular roll-cage and weapon mounts which could be fitted to existing stripped-down, or mechanically-enhanced Land Rover vehicles. WMIK kits, and further developments of them, were only ever fitted to Wolf Land Rovers or others that had been enhanced to Wolf standard.

The effect of the WMIK kit was to turn a utility vehicle into an aggressive patrol, reconnaissance or close fire support vehicle, armed with a 7.62mm GPMG and either a 0.50 cal (12.7mm) L1A1 Heavy Machine Gun or a Milan ATGM launcher. The original WMIK vehicles had an unladen weight of 2089kg and gross vehicle weight (GVW) of 3350kg. They were quickly issued to a succession

The Original-WMIK – as it became known – provided a means of providing Light Forces with a mobile weapons support platform. Visible here are the roll-cage over the cargo area that provides a weapons mounting ring for a heavy machine gun or missile launcher, and a pintle mount on the scuttle for a machine gun. The special grille is black here, and not very conspicuous. (GF)

This is a Winterised and Waterproofed GS Hard Top. Note the large escape hatch over the crew compartment and that the mounting bracket for the pick-axe head has been relocated to the front bumper from the wing. (GF)

17 Port & Maritime Regiment, Royal Logistic Corps are also users of Winterised and Waterproofed versions. This one is RHD GS Hard Top and bears a marking "CSSB/42/67" on the bumper, which is believed to be the marking for a previous unit. On Wolf vehicles built with the Winterised and Waterproofed specification, no air intake boxes were fitted to the wings. (GF)

of Army, Royal Marine and RAF units, and saw active service in Macedonia in 1999 and in a series of operations in Sierra Leone in 2000.

In mid-2006 the MoD issued an Urgent Operational Requirement (UOR) for a total of 80 WMIK equipped Land Rovers with an increased payload for use in Operation Herrick in Afghanistan. These were initially called HP WMIK (High Payload WMIK) but soon became known as E-WMIK (Enhanced WMIK) and the previous vehicles were retrospectively referred to as O-WMIK(original WMIK). The 80 E-WMIK vehicles were created by rebuilding 58 O-WMIK vehicles to E-WMIK standard, and building 22 from new.

These first E-WMIKs were followed later by a further order for approximately 170 vehicles. The base vehicles for this batch came from new and existing Land Rover stocks, including some former CAV Snatch vehicles that had been re-engined, and rebuilt to Land Rover XD standard.

The O-WMIK as normally rigged offered little weather protection, and a kit of canvas panels was included to provide a little crew comfort. Note the basket on the bonnet and the canvas strap arrangement on the spare wheel mount for lowering and raising it. The special grille is clearly visible here. (GF)

The E-WMIK had an unladen weight of 2960kg, a GVW of 3500kg, and was capable of mounting the newly acquired Heckler & Koch L134A1 40mm Automatic Light Grenade Launcher (ALGL), Manroy L1A1 (later L111A1) 0.50 cal (12.7mm) Heavy Machine Gun (HMG), or Javelin ATGM launcher, ammunition, Bowman radio equipment (with capacity for two HF and one VHF radios per vehicle), and electronic counter measure (ECM) equipment. They also had alloy wheels with tyres from Land Rover Snatch vehicles and run-flat inserts, MAPIK ballistic protection mats, under-floor mine protection and increased storage. To enable the payload to be increased, these vehicles had up-rated chassis, suspension and brakes.

This is a RAF TUM converted to O-WMIK and painted in the RAF sand camouflage which has a distinctly pink tinge. The vehicle mounts two General Purpose Machine Guns and carries sand channels. (GF)

O-WMIK with foul weather canopy – but not the doors – fitted. The vehicle was pictured on exercise in 2006 on Salisbury Plain. (GF)

In November 2007, it was announced that 22 new WMIK kits were to be purchased, and approximately 250 existing WMIK Land Rovers were to be upgraded. This new version was referred to as R-WMIK (Re-Life WMIK), and had a GVW of 4100kg.

In late 2009, the final version was announced. This was the R-WMIK+, which had an additional crew station, enhancements to vehicle ergonomics and electrics, more enhancements to protection, chassis and suspension, a new 300Tdi engine (enlarged to 2.8 litres by Ricardo), and new ZF automatic gearbox. The GVW of this version is a massive 4700kg.

Altogether, 68 R-WMIK+ examples were built in 2009, and a further 64 in 2010. As at 2013, the MoD still had a total of 375 WMIKs; 25 having left service.

Left: R-WMIK was distinguished by alloy wheels, a revised roll-cage with a bar running to the front scuttle, and a snorkel. Note the panels of slab armour to protect the crew, Bowman fittings and the IED detectors on top of each wing. The Wolf air intakes on the wings have been removed, and the engine breathes through the snorkel. (GF)

Right: The serial number in KK gives away that this R-WMIK is a rebuilt Snatch. Note the sheet covering the air vents on the scuttle, the wing-mounted detectors, Bowman aerial base, and the jerrycan holder at the rear. (GF)

R-WMIK+ was the final version of the Land Rover-based WMIK to be deployed in Afghanistan. This example clearly shows the roll-cage around the driver, and the platforms on the wings and the cab for counter-IED electronic detection systems. (GF)

Right: Pictured in July 2008, "Copeman" is an R-WMIK on patrol around Basrah International Aiport in Iraq. The main weapon is a grenade launcher and the vehicle was serving with 2 Squadron, Royal Air Force Regiment. (RS)

This R-WMIK has been based on a Winterised Hard Top version of TUM. It is fitted with a foul weather cover. The 'doors' are rolled back and the mount on the nearside of the front bumper from its days as a Winterised vehicle remains! (GF)

ASSET CODES

The Asset Codes are:

NB5005-8100	Truck, Utility, Medium, (HS), Hard Top, w/VPK, LHD, 12-volt, (With ACU), refurbished 2005
NB5006-3100	Truck, Utility, Medium, (HS), GS (Hard Top), RHD, 4x4, Land Rover 2.5 Tdi (EEGR) Heli Support
NB5007-3100	Truck, Utility, Medium, (HS), GS (Hard Top), RHD, 4x4, Land Rover 2.5 Tdi (EEGR) Talon Support Vehicle
NB5008-3100	Truck, Utility, Medium, (HS), 4x4, GS, Hard Top, Winter/Water, Land Rover 2.5-Ltr Turbo Diesel, (with EEGR)
NB5008-3160	Truck, Utility, Medium, (HS), 4x4, GS, Hard Top, Winter/Water, Land Rover 2.5-Ltr Turbo Diesel, (with EEGR) with Bowman NH
NB5009-3100	Truck, Utility, Medium, (HS), 4x4, GS, Soft Top, Winter/Water, Land Rover 2.5-Ltr Tbo Dsl, (w/ EEGR)
NB5009-3160	Truck, Utility, Medium, (HS), 4x4, GS, Soft Top, Winter/Water, Land Rover 2.5-Ltr Tbo Dsl, (w/ EEGR) with Bowman NH
NB5009-3170	Truck, Utility, Medium, (HS), 4x4, GS, Soft Top, Winter/Water, Land Rover 2.5-Ltr Tbo Dsl, (w/ EEGR) with Bowman SH
NB5010-3100	Truck, Utility, Medium, (HS), 4x4, GS, Soft Top, Land Rover 2.5-Ltr Turbo Diesel, (Non-EEGR)
NB5010-3101	Truck, Utility, Medium, (HS), 4x4, GS, Soft Top, Land Rover 2.5-Ltr Turbo Diesel, (with EEGR)
NB5010-3160	Truck, Utility, Medium, (HS), 4x4, GS, Soft Top, Land Rover 2.5-Ltr Turbo Diesel, (with EEGR) with Bowman NH
NB5010-3161	Truck, Utility, Medium, (HS), 4x4, GS, Soft Top, Land Rover 2.5-Ltr Turbo Diesel, (with EEGR) with Bowman NH
NB5010-3170	Truck, Utility, Medium, (HS), 4x4, GS, Soft Top, Land Rover 2.5-Ltr Turbo Diesel, (non-EEGR) with Bowman SH
NB5010-3171	Truck, Utility, Medium, (HS), 4x4, GS, Soft Top, Land Rover 2.5-Ltr Turbo Diesel, (with EEGR) with Bowman SH
NB5010-3199	Truck, Utility, Medium, (HS), 4x4, GS, Soft Top, Land Rover 2.5-Ltr Turbo Diesel, (Non-EEGR) Trials Vehicle

NB5010-8100	Truck, Utility, Medium, (TUM HS), 4x4, GS, Soft Top, LHD, Land Rover 2.5-Ltr Turbo Diesel, (with EEGR)
NB5010-8160	Truck, Utility, Medium, (HS), 4x4, GS, Soft Top, LHD, Land Rover 2.5-Ltr Turbo Diesel, (with EEGR) with Bowman NH
NB5010-8170	Truck, Utility, Medium, (HS), 4x4, GS, Soft Top, LHD, Land Rover 2.5-Ltr Turbo Diesel, (with EEGR) with Bowman SH
NB5011-3100	Truck, Utility, Medium, (HS), 4x4, GS, Soft Top, RHD, Land Rover 2.5-Ltr Turbo Diesel, (with EEGR) Winter/Water WMIK
NB5011-3160	Truck, Utility, Medium, (HS), 4x4, GS, Soft Top, RHD, Land Rover 2.5-Ltr Turbo Diesel, (with EEGR) Winter/Water R-WMIK with Bowman NH
NB5012-3100	Truck, Utility, Medium, (HS), GS, Soft Top, Land Rover 2.5-Ltr Turbo Diesel, (with EEGR) WMIK
NB5012-3101	Truck, Utility, Medium, (HS), GS, Soft Top, Land Rover 2.5-Ltr Turbo Diesel, (with EEGR) Phase 1 WMIK
NB5013-8100	Truck, Utility, Medium, (HS), GS, LHD, Land Rover 2.5-Ltr Turbo Diesel, (with EEGR) Scout
NB5014-3100	Truck, Utility, Medium, (HS), GS, Land Rover, Special Role
NB5017-3100	Truck, Utility, Medium, (HS), 4x4, GS, Hard Top, Land Rover 2.5-Ltr Turbo Diesel, (with EEGR)
NB5017-3160	Truck, Utility, Medium, (HS), 4x4, GS, Hard Top, Land Rover 2.5-Ltr Turbo Diesel, (with EEGR) with Bowman NH
NB5017-3190	Truck, Utility, Medium, (HS), 4x4, GS, Hard Top, Land Rover 2.5-Ltr Turbo Diesel, (with EEGR) with Bowman FF LAS
NB5017-8100	Truck, Utility, Medium, (HS), 4x4, GS, Hard Top, LHD, Land Rover 2.5-Ltr Turbo Diesel, (with EEGR)
NB5020-3100	Truck, Utility, Medium, (HS), 4x4, FFR, Hard Top, Land Rover 2.5-Ltr Turbo Diesel, (with EEGR)
NB5020-3101	Truck, Utility, Medium, (HS), 4x4, FFR, Hard Top, Land Rover 2.5-Ltr Turbo Diesel, (with EEGR) with Odette DF IK
NB5020-3102	Truck, Utility, Medium, (HS), 4x4, FFR, Hard Top, Land Rover 2.5-Ltr Turbo Diesel, (with EEGR) with Odette IC IK
NB5020-3103	Truck, Utility, Medium, (HS), 4x4, FFR, Hard Top, Land Rover 2.5-Ltr Turbo Diesel, (with EEGR) with Odette DF IK
NB5020-3104	Truck, Utility, Medium, (HS), 4x4, FFR, Hard Top, Land Rover 2.5-Ltr Turbo Diesel, (with EEGR) with Odette TCAD IK
NB5020-3105	Truck, Utility, Medium, (HS), 4x4, FFR, Hard Top, Land Rover 2.5-Ltr Turbo Diesel, (with EEGR) with WILDCAT IK
NB5020-3106	Truck, Utility, Medium, (HS), 4x4, FFR, Hard Top, Land Rover 2.5-Ltr Turbo Diesel, (with EEGR) with DSL PILOT IK
NB5020-3107	Truck, Utility, Medium, (HS), 4x4, FFR, Hard Top, Land Rover 2.5-Ltr Turbo Diesel, (with EEGR) with Spice IK
NB5020-3160	Truck, Utility, Medium, (HS), 4x4, FFR, Hard Top, Land Rover 2.5ltr Turbo Dsl w/EEGR with Bowman NH
NB5020-3161	Truck, Utility, Medium, (HS), 4x4, FFR, Hard Top, Land Rover 2.5ltr Turbo Dsl w/EEGR with Odette DF IK and Bowman NH

NB5020-3170	Truck, Utility, Medium, (HS), 4x4, FFR, Hard Top, Land Rover 2.5ltr Turbo Dsl w/EEGR with Bowman SH
NB5020-3190	Truck, Utility, Medium, (HS), 4x4, FFR, Hard Top, Land Rover 2.5ltr Turbo Dsl w/EEGR with Bowman FF LAS
NB5020-8100	Truck, Utility, Medium, (HS), 4x4, FFR, Hard Top, LHD, Land Rover 2.5-Ltr Turbo Diesel, (with EEGR)
NB5020-8101	Truck, Utility, Medium, (HS), 4x4, FFR, Hard Top, LHD, Land Rover 2.5-Ltr Turbo Diesel, (with EEGR) with Odette DF IK
NB5020-8102	Truck, Utility, Medium, (HS), 4x4, FFR, Hard Top, LHD, Land Rover 2.5-Ltr Turbo Diesel, (with EEGR) with Odette IC IK
NB5020-8103	Truck, Utility, Medium, (HS), 4x4, FFR, Hard Top, LHD, Land Rover 2.5-Ltr Turbo Diesel, (with EEGR) with Odette TCAD IK
NB5020-8104	Truck, Utility, Medium, (HS), 4x4, FFR, Hard Top, LHD, Land Rover 2.5-Ltr Turbo Diesel, (with EEGR) with NBC Support
NB5020-8160	Truck, Utility, Medium, (HS), 4x4, FFR, Hard Top, LHD, Land Rover 2.5-Ltr Turbo Diesel, (with EEGR) Bowman NH
NB5020-8170	Truck, Utility, Medium, (HS), 4x4, FFR, Hard Top, LHD, Land Rover 2.5-Ltr Turbo Diesel, (with EEGR) Bowman SH
NB5020-8180	Truck, Utility, Medium, (HS), 4x4, FFR, Hard Top, LHD, Land Rover 2.5-Ltr Turbo Diesel, (with EEGR) Bowman BF LAS
NB5020-8190	Truck, Utility, Medium, (HS), 4x4, FFR, Hard Top, LHD,Land Rover 2.5-Ltr Turbo Diesel, (with EEGR) with Bowman FF LAS
NB5021-3100	Truck, Utility, Medium, (HS), 4x4, FFR, Hard Top, Winter/Water, Land Rover 2.5-L Tbo Dsl, (w/ EEGR)
NB5021-3160	Truck, Utility, Medium, (HS), 4x4, FFR, Hard Top, Winter/Water, Land Rover 2.5-L Tbo Dsl, (w/ EEGR) with Bowman NH
NB5021-3170	Truck, Utility, Medium, (HS), 4x4, FFR, Hard Top, Winter/Water, Land Rover 2.5-L Tbo Dsl, (w/ EEGR) with Bowman SH
NB5021-3180	Truck, Utility, Medium, (HS), 4x4, FFR, Hard Top, Winter/Water, Land Rover 2.5-L Tbo Dsl, (w/ EEGR) with Bowman BF LAS
NB5021-3190	Truck, Utility, Medium, (HS), 4x4, FFR, Hard Top, Winter/Water, Land Rover 2.5-L Tbo Dsl, (w/ EEGR) with Bowman FF LAS
NB5022-3100	Truck, Utility, Medium, (HS), 4x4, FFR, Hard Top, Winter/Water, Land Rover 2.5-L Tbo Dsl, (w/ EEGR) with Commander's IK
NB5030-3100	Truck, Utility, Medium, (HS), 4x4, FFR, Soft Top, Land Rover 2.5ltr Turbo Dsl w/EEGR, WMIK
NB5030-3101	Truck, Utility, Medium, (HS), 4x4, FFR, Soft Top, Land Rover 2.5ltr Turbo Dsl w/EEGR, Phase 1 WMIK
NB5030-3102	Truck, Utility, Medium, (HS), 4x4, FFR, Hard Top, Land Rover 2.5ltr Turbo Dsl w/EEGR, Phase 1 WMIK
NB5031-3100	Truck, Utility, Medium, (HS), 4x4, FFR, Soft Top, Land Rover 2.5-Ltr Turbo Diesel, (with EEGR)
NB5031-3160	Truck, Utility, Medium, (HS), 4x4, FFR, Soft Top, Land Rover 2.5-Ltr Turbo Diesel, (with EEGR) with Bowman NH

NB5031-3170	Truck, Utility, Medium, (HS), 4x4, FFR, Soft Top, Land Rover 2.5-Ltr Turbo Diesel, (with EEGR) with Bowman SH
NB5031-3180	Truck, Utility, Medium, (HS), 4x4, FFR, Soft Top, Land Rover 2.5-Ltr Turbo Diesel, (with EEGR) with Bowman BF LAS
NB5031-8100	Truck, Utility, Medium, (HS), 4x4, FFR, Soft Top, LHD, Land Rover 2.5-Ltr Turbo Diesel, (with EEGR)
NB5031-8160	Truck, Utility, Medium, (HS), 4x4, FFR, Soft Top, LHD, Land Rover 2.5-Ltr Turbo Diesel, (with EEGR) with Bowman NH
NB5032-3100	Truck, Utility, Medium, (HS), FFR, HP, 4x4, Land Rover 2.5-Ltr Turbo Diesel, (with EEGR), WMIK (Higher Payload)
NB5032-3160	Truck, Utility, Medium, (HS), FFR, HP, 4x4, Land Rover 2.5-Ltr Turbo Diesel, (with EEGR), WMIK with Bowman NH
NB5032-3161	Truck, Utility, Medium, (HS), FFR, HP, 4x4, Land Rover 2.5-Ltr Turbo Diesel, (with EEGR) WMIK with Bowman NH (Refurbished)
NB5032-3162	Truck, Utility, Medium, (HS), FFR, HP, 4x4, Land Rover 2.5-Ltr Turbo Diesel, (with EEGR) WMIK with Bowman NH (Refurbished) Training Vehicle
NB5032-3170	Truck, Utility, Medium, (HS), FFR, HP, 4x4, Land Rover 2.8-Ltr Turbo Diesel, Auto Transmission, R-WMIK with Bowman SH
NB5032-3171	Truck, Utility, Medium, (HS), FFR, HP, 4x4, Land Rover 2.8-Ltr Turbo Diesel, Auto Transmission, R-WMIK with Bowman SH
NB5032-3180	Truck, Utility, Medium, (HS), FFR, HP, 4x4, Land Rover 2.8-Ltr Turbo Diesel, Auto Transmission, R-WMIK with Bowman BF LAS
NB5033-3100	Truck, Utility, Medium, (HS), FFR, 4x4, Land Rover 2.5 Ltr Dsl with EEGR, Scout
NB5033-3160	Truck, Utility, Medium, (HS), FFR, 4x4, Land Rover 2.5 Ltr Turbo Dsl with EEGR, Scout, Bowman NH
NB5033-3170	Truck, Utility, Medium, (HS), FFR, 4x4, Land Rover 2.5 Ltr Turbo Dsl with EEGR, Scout, Bowman SH
NB5033-8100	Truck, Utility, Medium, (HS), FFR, 4x4, LHD, Land Rover 2.5 Ltr Dsl with EEGR, Scout
NB5034-3100	Truck, Utility, Medium, (HS), 4x4, Land Rover WMIK Trainer (TWMIK)
NB5035-3100	Truck, Utility, Medium, (HS), 4x4, FFR, Hard Top, Land Rover 2.5-Ltr Turbo Diesel, (with EEGR) (Signals)
NB5037-3100	Truck, Utility, Medium, (HS), 4x4, FFR, Soft Top, Land Rover 2.5-Ltr Turbo Diesel, (with EEGR), TETHYS IK
NB5040-3100	Truck, Utility, Medium, (HS), GS (S/Wagon), RHD 4x4 Land Rover 2.5 Tdi (EEGR) 110 Media Operations Support Vehicle
RB5006-3100	Truck, Utility, Medium, (HS), 4x4, GS, Hard Top, Helicopter Support, Land Rover 2.5-Ltr Turbo Diesel, (with EEGR)
RB5010-3100	Truck, Utility, Medium, (HS), 4x4, GS, Soft Top, Land Rover 2.5-Ltr Turbo Diesel
RB5010-3101	Truck, Utility, Medium, (HS), 4x4, GS, Soft Top, Land Rover 2.5-Ltr Turbo Diesel, (with EEGR)
RB5020-3100	Truck, Utility, Medium, (HS), 4x4, FFR, Hard Top, Land Rover 2.5-Ltr Turbo Dsl, (with EEGR)
RB5030-3100	Truck, Utility, Medium, (HS), 4x4, FFR, Soft Top, Land Rover 2.5ltr Turbo Dsl w/EEGR, WMIK
RB5031-3100	Truck, Utility, Medium, (HS), 4x4, FFR, Soft Top, Land Rover 2.5-Ltr Turbo Diesel, (with EEGR)

RB5042-3100	Truck, Utility, Medium, (HS), 4x4, GS, Hard Top, Winterised, Helicopter Support, Land Rover 2.5-Ltr Turbo Diesel, (with EEGR)	
TB5009-3100	Truck, Utility, Medium, (HS), 4x4, GS (Soft Top), Winterised Waterproofed, Land Rover 2.5-Ltr Turbo Diesel, (with EEGR)	
TB5021-3100	Truck, Utility, Medium, (HS), 4x4, FFR (Hard Top), Winterised Waterproofed, Land Rover 2.5-Ltr Turbo Diesel, (with EEGR)	

SUMMARY OF DELIVERIES

Serials	Contract	Chassis nos	Total	Remarks
HH 06 AA to HM 08 AA	LV2A/088	991948 to 100624	403	GS Soft Top RHD
HM 09 AA to HM 55 AA	LV2A/088	100608 to N/K	47	GS Soft Top RHD; for RAF
HM 56 AA to HR 32 AA	LV2A/088	102829 to 107936	277	FFR Hard Top RHD
HR 33 AA to HS 05 AA	LV2A/088	107619 to N/K	73	FFR Hard Top RHD; for RAF
HS 06 AA to HS 85 AA	LV2A/088	103048 to 103286	80	FFR Soft Top RHD
KC 36 AA to KE 98 AA	LV2A/088	105327 to 112337	63	GS Soft Top RHD
KE 99 AA to KH 36 AA	LV2A/088	117658 to 119761	238	GS Soft Top LHD
KH 37 AA to KJ 25 AA	LV2A/088	114667 to 127093	89	GS Hard Top RHD
KJ 26 AA to KJ 36 AA	LV2A/088	128823 to 130604	11	GS Hard Top LHD
KJ 37 AA to KR 98 AA	LV2A/088	110166 to 125640	662	FFR Hard Top RHD
KR 99 AA to KX 53 AA	LV2A/088	109592 to 126328	455	FFR Hard Top LHD
KX 54 AA to KX 75 AA	LV2A/088	127050 to 127796	22	FFR Soft Top RHD
KX 76 AA to KX 78 AA	LV2A/088	127756 to 127903	3	FFR Soft Top LHD
LV 32 AA to LW 01 AA	LV2A/088	159526 to 160204	70	GS Hard Top Winterised RHD
LW 02 AA to MF 89 AA	LV2A/088	124657 to 149075	888	GS Soft Top RHD
MJ 62 AA to MK 40 AA	LV2A/088	N/K to 153860	79	GS Hard Top RHD
MK 41 AA to MU 65 AA	LV2A/088	127946 to 151773	785	FFR Hard Top RHD
MU 66 AA to MY 25 AA	LV2A/088	128383 to 147920	360	FFR Hard Top LHD
MY 26 AA to MY 76 AA	LV2A/088	154289 to 154823	51	FFR Soft Top LHD
NH 39 AA to NH 40 AA	LP	120620 to 120085	2	FFR Hard Top LHD; for NATO
NR 25 AA to NS 24 AA	MICH 02	138869 to 153229	100	FFR Hard Top RHD; for RAF
NT 73 AA to NT 86 AA	MICH 03	149270 to N/K	14	GS Soft Top RHD; for RAF
NV 46 AA to NV 48 AA	LV2A/088	127897 to N/K	3	FFR Hard Top RHD (Signals)
NV 92 AA to NV 96 AA	LV2A/088	128863 to N/K	5	FFR Hard Top RHD (Signals)
NY 73 AA to NY 77 AA	N/K	148997 to 149158	5	GS Soft Top RHD
NY 78 AA to NY 81 AA	LRFAX3/2/98	753500 to 153320	4	GS Soft Top LHD
NY 82 AA to NZ 03 AA	LRFAX3/2/98	151689 to 153041	22	FFR Hard Top RHD
NZ 04 AA to NZ 05 AA	LRFAX3/2/98	149866 to 150163	2	GS Soft Top RHD

PE 00 AA to PF 64 AA	LV2A/088	159741 to 160415	165	GS Soft Top Winterised RHD
PG 12 AA to PJ 69 AA	LV2A/088	160108 to 161368	258	FFR Hard Top Winterised RHD
PJ 70 AA to PK 79 AA	LV2A/088	153123 to 157267	115	GS Soft Top RHD
PK 89 AA to PN 65 AA	LV2A/088	153158 to 157179	77	FFR Hard Top RHD
PN 80 AA to PP 20 AA	LV2A/088	160698 to 160651	41	GS Soft Top Winterised RHD
PP 21 AA to PP 23 AA	LV2A/088	157274 to 157338	3	GS Soft Top RHD
PP 24 AA to PP 43 AA	LV2A/088	161308 to 161291	20	FFR Hard Top Winterised RHD
PP 44 AA to PR 38 AA	LV2A/088	154738 to 156728	95	FFR Soft Top RHD
PR 97 AA to PS 61 AA	MICH 04	156635 to 158098	77	FFR Soft Top RHD; for RAF
PU 36 AA to PU 37 AA	MICH 06	N/K to 158985	2	Helicopter Support RHD
PU 38 AA to PU 45 AA	MICH 07	156947 to 157067	8	Helicopter Support RHD; for RAF
PX 28 AA	LV2A/088	157572	1	GS Hard Top RHD
PX 29 AA to PX 90 AA	LV2A/088	157599 to 157655	62	FFR Hard Top RHD
		Total	5754	

Note: PK 80 AA to PK 84 – GS Soft Top RHD, and PK 85 AA to PK 88 AA – GS Soft Top RHD, are thought to have been cancelled.

Technical specifications, Defender XD 110 models

Diesel engines
2495cc turbocharged four-cylinder with direct injection and 111bhp (300Tdi)
2785cc turbocharged four-cylinder with direct injection and 135bhp approximately (R-WMIK+ only).

Transmission
Permanent four-wheel drive with lockable centre differential
Five-speed manual main gearbox (standard), or
Four-speed ZF automatic main gearbox (R-WMIK+ only)
Two-speed transfer gearbox
Axle ratio: 3.54:1

Suspension, steering and brakes
Coil springs all round
Worm and roller steering with power assistance
Disc brakes on all four wheels; servo assistance; separate drum-type transmission parking brake

Electrical system
12-volt with alternator, or 24-volt with 90-amp alternator

Dimensions
Overall length:	175in (4445mm) for truck cab and Soft Top
Wheelbase:	110in (2794mm)
Overall width:	70.5in (1791mm)
Unladen height:	80.1in (2034mm)
Track:	58.5in (1486mm)

Unladen weights
4605lb (2089kg)	WMIK
6525lb (2960kg)	E-WMIK

Performance
No official figures available.

DEFENDER XD90, 1997-1999

The XD 90 version of the Defender was procured under the same contract as the XD 110, although it was always intended for there to be far fewer of these vehicles. Known to the MoD as the Truck, Utility, Light (High Specification) or TUL (HS) type, the XD 90 shared most components with the XD 110; the major difference obviously being its shorter wheelbase.

TUL was acquired in General Service and Fitted For Radio (FFR) versions, in both RHD and LHD form, and most variants were available with Soft or Hard Top configuration. As was the case with the XD 110 (TUM), there were also Winterised and Waterproofed versions of the major types for units required to carry out Arctic and littoral operations.

The first TULs were receipted into Ashchurch Depot in March 1997, and by October that year the first issues were made to the Defence School of Transport at Leconfield, and to units of 5 Airborne Brigade (which, in 1999, was merged with 16 Air Assault Brigade). By December, other units were also being equipped.

In service, the TUL became the lightest tactical vehicle the army deployed once the last of the Harley Davidson General Service Motorcycles had been withdrawn in 2009. However, two other light vehicles – the Quadbike and the EPS Springer – were purchased as Urgent Operational Requirements and served on Operation Herrick in Afghanistan.

The TUL has attracted few specialist roles, because its small size limits the amount of equipment and personnel that can be carried.

TUM has always offered greater capacity for a small increase in cost and almost no difference in cross-country ability. Units have to work to an 'establishment,' which lists the number and types of equipment they must hold. However, these establishments change over time, and many have been amended as TUMs have replaced TULs in the roles originally allocated to the smaller vehicle. As a consequence of this, and of the reduction in the overall size of UK forces, a large number of TULs have become surplus to requirements.

At the time of going to press, the number of TULs in service

This line drawing shows the vehicle as originally delivered, with the pioneer tools mounted in the brackets on the bonnet.
(Land Rover)

is undoubtedly on the decline. A few remain in communications and liaison roles, but most seem to have been phased out. The major specialist roles remaining for TUL are with the units in 3 Commando Brigade and the units of 16 Air Assault Brigade, where its size and weight offer advantages. In particular, there is the Air Droppable version for 16 Brigade.

This TUL has a weathered appearance. The driver's door bears evidence of previous tactical markings, probably radio call signs, and there is a lack of tools on the bonnet. The bumper is showing signs of rust and the tilt is rather baggy! (GF)

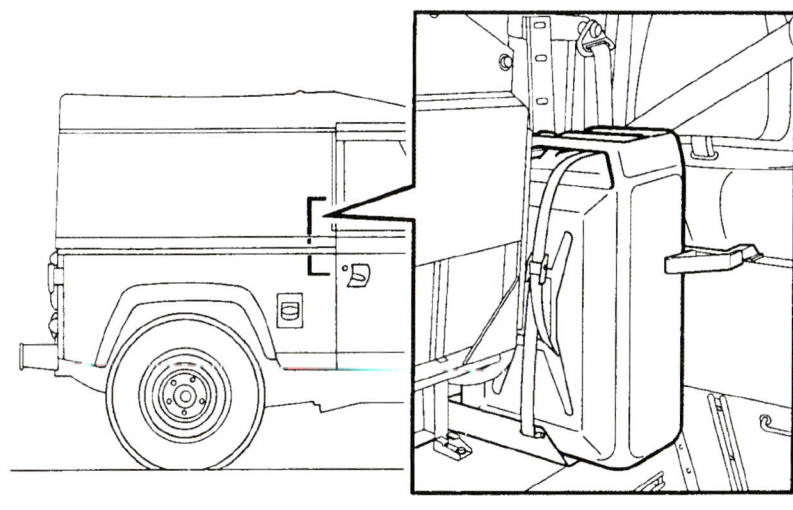

Another line drawing, showing the planned jerrycan storage on the passenger side, behind the front seats. (LR)

Above: A TUL GS Soft Top with a tent and an extension to the exhaust to take exhaust fumes away from the occupants. It was photographed during Exercise Tractable 2016. (GF)

Air Droppable

A small number of TUL FFRs was converted to Air Droppable specification, as had happened with the standard Defender 90 (see Chapter 7). This conversion was carried out by Ricardo, under contract LV2/MIL/25 issued in September 1998.

On an Air Droppable TUL, the upper part of the rear body tub can be removed to allow two vehicles to be carried on a Medium Stressed Platform. The lower vehicle on the MSP has to have the removable parts, although the upper one could be conventional. Such vehicles were intended for use with reconnaissance elements of 16 Air Assault Brigade, including the Pathfinder Platoon. The 28 examples known to have been converted are: HG 76 AA, KC 26 AA to KC 32 AA, KC 34 AA, KC 35 AA, LS 30 AA, LS 49 AA, LS 66 AA, LS 68 AA, LS 71 AA, LS 83 AA, LS 95 AA, LT 15 AA, LT 20 AA, LT 30 AA, LT 34 AA, LT 48 AA, LT 75 AA, LT 76 AA, LT 77 AA, LT 86 AA, LT 88 AA and LV 27 AA.

Above: This Air-Droppable TUL (HS) was pictured on display at Thorney Island where it was serving with 21 Air Defence Battery of 47 Regiment Royal Artillery. The battery has a role in support of 16 Air Assault Brigade. (GF)

Above: This FFR Soft Top has been converted to Air-Droppable form. Note the removable upper rear body panels, which have a label bearing the vehicle's registration number so that they can be re-fitted correctly after a drop. (GF)

Left and right: An Air-Droppable TUL rigged for dropping with the body sides removed and the tilt frame stowed. The vehicle was displayed by Headquarters 16 Air Assault Brigade at Colchester Military Festival in 2005. (DP)

Two TULs can be carried on a standard Medium Stressed Platform provided the one below is an Air Droppable version, and this picture shows why. An alternative MSP load is a TUM with Lightweight Trailer. (CE)

FFR and Bowman

Once the new Bowman tactical communications system was introduced (initial operating capability in 2004, and full roll-out by 2008), the lack of space in TUL FFR proved a further problem. When the military decided to fit forward facing seats in the rear compartment, this further reduced the TUL's usefulness. A statement from a Signals Officer in 2010 suggested that, on his unit, the two signallers normally attached to the TUL FFR were being carried by a TUM GS during exercises!

Below: A RHD TUL FFR Hard Top in as-delivered condition at Ashchurch Vehicle Depot in 1999. This vehicle was issued to 11 Field Squadron, Royal Engineers in 2004. (GF)

Left: A RHD TUL FFR Hard Top in service with O Headquarters Battery of 1 Regiment, Royal Horse Artillery. Note the Stabilisation Force (SFOR) marking on the door, the fluorescent AS90 (an armoured, self-propelled artillery weapon) on the passenger side of the windscreen, and the battery sign on the front of the wing. (RS)

This Winterised and Waterproofed FFR Hard Top belonged to 17 Port & Maritime Regiment, Royal Logistic Corps. Note the escape hatch in the roof over the crew compartment. (DP)

This TUL FFR Hard Top was photographed during Exercise Tractable 2015 with an Engineer Field Squadron. It is fitted with Bowman although this is an unusual arrangement as most Bowman configurations require the extra space of a TUM. (GF)

Above: The TUL FFR Soft Top was purchased in very small numbers – 15 in total. Its use was solely for units needing the ability to be transported inside the Chinook helicopter. (LR)

Stretch

Project Stretch, carried out by DSG Colchester in 2012, examined the feasibility of taking the front end bodywork and transmission from a TUL to create a TUM by using Asset Managed, re-manufactured parts taken from vehicles declared 'beyond economic repair' (BER). A single vehicle was converted (19 KL 07, one of the 1993 TUL trials vehicles) and was sent to the Combat Service Support Trials and Development Unit (CSS TDU) at Longmoor for testing. Nothing further is known, although it is believed that the project has not proceeded as the MoD has more than adequate stocks of TUMs to equip 'Army 2020.'

ASSET CODES

NB4219-3100	Truck, Utility, Light (HS), 4x4, GS, Soft Top, Winter/Water, Land Rover 2.5-Ltr Turbo Diesel (w/EEGR)
NB4220-3100	Truck, Utility, Light (HS), 4x4, GS, Soft Top, Land Rover 2.5-Ltr Turbo Diesel (with EEGR)
NB4220-3199	Truck, Utility, Light (HS), 4x4, GS, Soft Top, Land Rover 2.5-Ltr Turbo Diesel (with EEGR), Trials Vehicle
NB4220-8100	Truck, Utility, Light (HS), 4x4, GS, Soft Top, LHD, Land Rover 2.5-Ltr Turbo Diesel (with EEGR)
NB4223-3100	Truck, Utility, Light (HS), 4x4, GS, Hard Top, Land Rover 2.5-Ltr Turbo Diesel (with EEGR)
NB4225-3100	Truck, Utility, Light (HS), 4x4, FFR, Hard Top, Land Rover 2.5-Ltr Turbo Diesel (with EEGR)
NB4225-8100	Truck, Utility, Light (HS), 4x4, FFR, Hard Top, LHD, Land Rover 2.5-Ltr Turbo Diesel (with EEGR)
NB4226-3100	Truck, Utility, Light (HS), 4x4, FFR, Hard Top, Winter/Water, Land Rover 2.5-Ltr Turbo Diesel (w/EEGR)
NB4226-3170	Truck, Utility, Light (HS), 4x4, FFR, Hard Top, Winter/Water, Land Rover 2.5-Ltr Turbo Diesel (w/EEGR) Bowman SH
NB4228-3100	Truck, Utility, Light (TUL HS), 4x4, FFR, Soft Top, Land Rover 2.5-Ltr Turbo Diesel (with EEGR)
NB4229-3100	Truck, Utility, Light (TUL HS), 4x4, FFR, Soft Top, Winter/Water, Land Rover 2.5-Ltr Turbo Diesel (w/EEGR)
NB4232-3100	Truck, Utility, Light (TUL HS), 4x4, FFR, Soft Top, Air Droppable, Land Rover 2.5l Turbo Diesel w/EEGR
RB4224-3100	Truck, Utility, Light (TUL HS), 4x4, GS, Hard Top, Winterised, Land Rover 2.5-Ltr Turbo Diesel (w/EEGR)
TB4226-3100	Truck, Utility, Light (HS), 4x4, FFR, Hard Top, Winter/Water, Land Rover 2.5-Ltr Turbo Diesel (w/EEGR)

SUMMARY OF DELIVERIES, 1997 onwards

Tri-Service

Serials	Contract	Chassis nos	Total	Remarks
HF 64 AA to HG 38 AA	LV2A/088	106099 to 107029	75	GS Soft Top RHD
HG 39 AA to HG 83 AA	LV2A/088	108106 to 109643	45	GS Soft Top LHD
JZ 79 AA to KA 93 AA	LV2A/088	122651 to 119968	115	GS Soft Top RHD
KA 94 AA to KB 00 AA	LV2A/088	122959 to 122730	7	GS Soft Top LHD
KB 01 AA to KB 82 AA	LV2A/088	124461 to 126455	82	FFR Hard Top RHD
KB 83 AA to KC 25 AA	LV2A/088	126582 to 127153	43	FFR Hard Top LHD [Note KC 25 AA is now a TUM RHD!]
KC 26 AA to KC 35 AA	LV2A/088	124494 to 124681	10	FFR Soft Top RHD
LL 18 AA to LP 83 AA	LV2A/088	121838 to 139242	366	GS Soft Top RHD
LP 84 AA to LR 82 AA	LV2A/088	139342 to N/K	99	GS Soft Top LHD
LR 83 AA to LR 84 AA	LV2A/088	139328 to 139235	2	GS Hard Top RHD
LR 85 AA to LU 59 AA	LV2A/088	138707 to 152946	275	FFR Hard Top RHD
LU 60 AA to LV 26 AA	LV2A/088	148825 to 151304	67	FFR Hard Top LHD
LV 27 AA to LV 31 AA	LV2A/088	145956 to 142133	5	FFR Soft Top RHD
PD 33 AA to PD 99 AA	LV2A/088	161979 to 162437	67	GS Soft Top Winter/Water RHD
PR 86 AA and PR 87 AA	LV2A/088	163104 and 162831	2	FFR Hard Top Winter/Water RHD
PR 88 AA and PR 89 AA	LV2A/088	162698 and 162692	2	FFR Hard Top Winter/Water RHD; for Royal Navy
PS 62 AA to PS 71 AA	MICH05	158578 to 158632	10	GS Hard Top Winterised RHD; for RAF
		Total	1272	

Technical specifications, Defender XD 90 models

Engine

2495cc turbocharged four-cylinder diesel with direct injection and 111bhp (300Tdi)

Transmission

Permanent four-wheel drive with lockable centre differential
Five-speed manual main gearbox
Two-speed transfer gearbox
Axle ratio: 3.54:1

Suspension, steering and brakes

Coil springs all round
Worm and roller steering with power assistance
Disc brakes on all four wheels; servo assistance; separate drum-type transmission parking brake

Electrical system

12-volt with alternator, or 24-volt with 90-amp alternator

Dimensions

Overall length:	146.5in (3720mm)
Wheelbase:	92.9in (2360mm)
Overall width:	70.5in (1791mm)
Unladen height:	77.4in (1966mm) for Soft Top
	77.6in (1971mm) for Hard Top
Track:	58.5in (1486mm)

Unladen weights

3800lb (1724kg) approximately (typical figure)

Performance

No official figures available

13

DEFENDER XD130, 1996–99

When the MoD initiated Project Pulse in 1988, its aim was to procure a single replacement for the three existing Battlefield Ambulances (BFA). These were the Marshall ambulance based on the Land Rover Series III 109-inch chassis; the very different Marshall ambulance based on the Land Rover 101-inch, One-Tonne chassis, and the two types based on the Land Rover One Two Seven chassis: one bodied by Marshall and the other by Locomotors.

The original plan was to mount the new BFA on what would become the Truck, Utility, Medium (Heavy Duty) or TUM (HD) chassis, which had been proposed in 1988. In due course, Land Rover put forward five 110-inch wheelbase prototypes to meet the General Service and FFR roles in this category, but the plan fell apart when, in late 1994, the TUM (HD) contract did not go to Land Rover but to Steyr-Daimler-Puch for its Pinzgauer.

Nevertheless, the BFA requirement, known to the MoD as Project Pulse, was by this stage, being treated separately. Around late 1993, Land Rover was one of three manufacturers invited to submit prototypes for the BFA: the other two were Steyr-Daimler-Puch (SDP) and Iveco-Ford. Prototypes were submitted: five from Land Rover and two each from SDP and Iveco. In February 1994, SDP submitted a further eight vehicles.

In view of SDP's success with TUM (HD), there was media speculation in advance

One of the first production batch of BFAs in service with 4 GS Medical Regiment, Royal Army Medical Corps, in 2004. This example has its Red Cross marking pinned up, as is common when the ambulance is not on duty. The word 'Ambulance' is, nevertheless, still visible in blue. (GF)

This view clearly shows the rear of the body with its asymmetric window and full-width double doors. Note how the standard Defender filler cap is fitted in to the rear body. This vehicle is one of those fitted with reflective plates. (GF)

A pair of ambulances stand and wait for a call during an Air Display, at Middle Wallop in September 2000. It is believed they equipped the School of Army Aviation but were being operated by 202 Field Hospital RAMC (V). (GF)

of the announcement that the SDP version of BFA would be purchased for the PULSE requirement. Intense lobbying followed, by Land Rover itself, and by Members of Parliament representing the various Birmingham constituencies around Land Rover's Solihull plant. In the end, Land Rover was awarded the BFA contract, and this was announced in Parliament on 18 January 1996. The vehicle was to be based on a Defender 130 chassis, but with the mechanicals and cab from the Wolf 2 vehicle; it was, therefore, known to Land Rover as a Defender XD 130. The ambulance bodywork would be provided by Marshall of Cambridge. These became the MoD's first diesel-powered Land Rover Battlefield Ambulances.

Above: This is a LHD example in use in the UK. Note that despite its left-hand drive, the Bowman aerial and the siren are fitted on the nearside. (AB)

The first production batch of the new BFA entered service in November 1996, and the vehicles were delivered without the engine exhaust gas recycling (EEGR) system that was fitted to all subsequent batches. This first batch also had reflective number plates, even though 'tactical' vehicles normally had black and grey plates. BFA deliveries continued until December 1999 and, as usual, there were several variants.

Bowman

From around 2005, some vehicles were

An ambulance of 1 Royal Tank Regiment. Note the grille extension and Bowman aerial, confirming the upgrades to 'desertised' and Bowman radio. (AB)

given a Bowman installation that did not involve fitting a harness. This was known as Bowman NH (see Chapter 11). Such vehicles can be identified by the standard Bowman aerial mount fitted to the ambulance body above the cab on the driver's side.

Desertised versions

As the number of units operating in Iraq and later Afghanistan increased, so the supply of the dedicated 'Tropical' BFA (see below) became insufficient to meet the need. A number of vehicles were therefore 'desertised' (which included the addition of air conditioning). However, when the Ridgback Medium Protected Patrol Vehicle became available in Ambulance form, this took over all the BFA roles in Afghanistan, except within the confines of Camp Bastion.

Hebe conversions

By around 2009, the MoD considered that several hundred of its BFAs were surplus to requirements; as of 2015, that surplus was in the order of 300 vehicles. Project Hebe was initiated in 2010 to create new and more useful vehicles on the basis of these surplus chassis.

As a first stage, two prototype Crew Cab Pick-ups (LB 49 AA and LA 77 AA) were built in 2010 from the chassis and cabs of surplus pulse ambulances, using Land Rover standard parts. The Hebe vehicle was exhibited at the Defence Vehicle Dynamics Show later that year as a potential fire support vehicle for Mortar Platoons. It was a double-cab pick-up truck with accommodation for four people. The conversion included fitment of an internal roll-over protection system, rear hood and Wolf-pattern raised Hard Top.

DSG Colchester completed an additional six Hebe vehicles

Left: This Ambulance has been 'desertised' and fitted with Bowman. It was pictured during exercise kush dragon in 2007. Note the panels where previous markings have been painted out and the new front wing. (GF)

Below: This example has been 'desertised' with extra engine cooling and air-conditioning. This can be seen by the extension to the radiator grille. The vehicle was photographed in 2005. (GF)

for the British Army Training Unit Kenya (BATUK) in 2011, using donor vehicles to provide obsolete parts and other fixtures and fittings. This asset recovery method of creating new vehicles from unwanted older ones led to considerable cost savings because there was no need to procure or manufacture replacement parts. Minor adjustments to the prototype Hebe design were necessary to meet the BATUK requirement, and notably custom-made soft tops with added protective padding were fitted. Known examples are: KY 57 AA, KZ 53 AA, KZ 66 AA, LA 40 AA, LA 74 AA and LA 96 AA. It appears that at least one further batch of six was subsequently completed, and at the time of writing it appears these conversions are a continuing process.

MMIK

A number of BFA vehicles was fitted with a Medical Monitoring Improvement Kit (MMIK) from around 2004. This allowed the medical attendant to monitor the patients' vital signs – blood pressure, body temperature and heart rate. The MMIK versions can be distinguished by a rack providing stowage for the additional equipment, on the forward underside of the offside stretcher.

Tropical versions

Tropicalised versions of the BFA were purchased to meet the needs of units operating in warmer climates. Deliveries began quite late on, around spring 1999. The Tropical version can be distinguished by the extended grille that conceals a condenser radiator for the air conditioning. This extended grille has an indent to allow the front pintle pin to be extracted.

Winter/Water versions

Some units involved in littoral operations (mainly the Royal Marine Commandos) had a need for a Winter/Water version of the BFA. Like the Tropicalised versions, these were not delivered until the spring of 1999. They can easily be recognised by the large snorkel on the right-hand side of the windscreen frame.

Media Operations conversions

A rebuilt version of the ambulance was developed for Media Operations. Eight are known to have been built on surplus ambulance chassis cabs: HF 57 AA, KX 92 AA, KY 50 AA, KZ 18 AA, KZ 23 AA, LA 01 AA, LB 16 AA and LB 53 AA. Media Operations also uses a further modification of this vehicle, known as the Defence Monitoring System. This is assumed to be for monitoring broadcasts in areas of operation.

Above: The Project Hebe conversion was said at the time of its launch to offer a vehicle that could be used to carry a Mortar Section or be used for Convoy Escort. It is known that a number of examples have been used by the British Army Training and Liaison Staff Kenya (BATLSK). (GF)

Left: A number of Crew Cab versions with High Capacity Pick-Up (HCPU) bodies has been created by Defence Support Group (DSG) from surplus Ambulances. They provide a vehicle that offers increased carrying capacity over the TUM (XD), yet shares many parts. (GF)

Left: This is a Winterised and Waterproofed version of the BFA. Note the high snorkel mounted on the 'head' of the ambulance body. This example was already in preservation by 2010. (GF)

ASSET CODES

The Asset Codes for Defender XD 130 Pulse and Hebe vehicles are as follows.

NB1047-3100	Ambulance, Battlefield, (HS), 4-Stretcher, 4x4, Land Rover 2.5-Ltr Turbo Diesel (non EEGR)
NB1047-3101	Ambulance, Battlefield, (HS), 4-Stretcher, 4x4, Land Rover 2.5-Ltr Turbo Diesel (EEGR)
NB1047-3102	Ambulance, Battlefield, (HS), 4-Stretcher, 4x4, Land Rover 2.5-Ltr Turbo Diesel with Medical Monitoring IK
NB1047-3160	Ambulance, Battlefield, (HS), 4-Stretcher, 4x4, Land Rover 2.5-Ltr Turbo Diesel (non-EEGR) with Bowman NH
NB1047-3161	Ambulance, Battlefield, (HS), 4-Stretcher, 4x4, Land Rover 2.5-Ltr Turbo Diesel (EEGR) with Bowman NH
NB1047-8100	Ambulance, Battlefield, (HS), 4-Stretcher, 4x4, LHD, Land Rover 2.5-Ltr Turbo Diesel, (EEGR)
NB1047-8160	Ambulance, Battlefield, (HS), 4-Stretcher, 4x4, LHD, Land Rover 2.5-Ltr Turbo Diesel, (EEGR) with Bowman NH
NB1048-3100	Ambulance, Battlefield, (HS), 4-Stretcher, 4x4, Land Rover 2.5-Ltr Turbo Diesel (EEGR) Winterised, Waterproofed for 600mm Depth
NB1049-3100	Ambulance, Battlefield, (HS), 4-Stretcher, 4x4, Tropical, Land Rover 2.5-Ltr Turbo Diesel (EEGR)
NB1049-3101	Ambulance, Battlefield, (HS), 4 Stretcher, 4x4, Tropical, Land Rover 2.5-Ltr Turbo Diesel, with Medical Monitoring Improvement Kit (EEGR)
NB1049-3102	Ambulance, Battlefield, (HS), 4 Stretcher, 4x4, Land Rover 2.5-Ltr Turbo Diesel, Desertised, with Medical Monitoring Improvement Kit (non-EEGR)
NB1049-3103	Ambulance, Battlefield, (HS), 4 Stretcher, 4x4, Land Rover 2.5-Ltr Turbo Diesel, Desertised With Medical Monitoring Improvement Kit (EEGR)
NB1047-3104	Ambulance, Battlefield, (HS), 4 Stretcher, 4x4, Land Rover 2.5-Ltr Turbo Diesel, Desertised with Medical Monitoring Improvement Kit (non-EEGR)
NB1049-3160	Ambulance, Battlefield, (HS), 4 Stretcher, 4x4, Land Rover 2.5-Ltr Turbo Diesel (EEGR), Desertised with Bowman NH
NB1049-3161	Ambulance, Battlefield, (HS), 4 Stretcher, 4x4, Land Rover 2.5-Ltr Turbo Diesel (EEGR), Desertised with Bowman NH and Medical Monitoring Improvement Kit
NB1049-3162	Ambulance, Battlefield, (HS), 4 Stretcher, 4x4, Land Rover 2.5-Ltr Turbo Diesel (non-EEGR), Desertised with Bowman NH and Medical Monitoring Improvement Kit
NB5041-3100	Truck, Utility, Medium, (HS), 4x4, GS, Land Rover 2.5-Ltr Turbo Diesel, (EEGR) 130 Media Operations Base Vehicle
NB5041-3101	Truck, Utility, Medium, (HS), 4x4, GS, Land Rover 130 2.5-Ltr Turbo Diesel, (with EEGR) Defence Monitoring System
NB5045-3100	Truck, Utility, Medium, (HS), 4x4, GS, Hard Top, Land Rover 130 2.5 Ltr Turbo Dsl, Double Cab Pick Up (DCPU)
NB5046-3100	Truck, Utility, Medium, (HS), 4x4, GS, Soft Top, Land Rover 130 2.5 Ltr Turbo Dsl, Double Cab Pick Up (DCPU)
RB1047-3101	Ambulance, Battlefield, (HS), 4-Stretcher, 4x4, Land Rover 2.5-Ltr Turbo Diesel (EEGR)

Below: A view of the interior of a Pulse ambulance, showing the off-side stretcher and the storage racks mounted on the folded second stretcher. There is a clear view through the hatch into the front cab, as the communicating door is open. (GF)

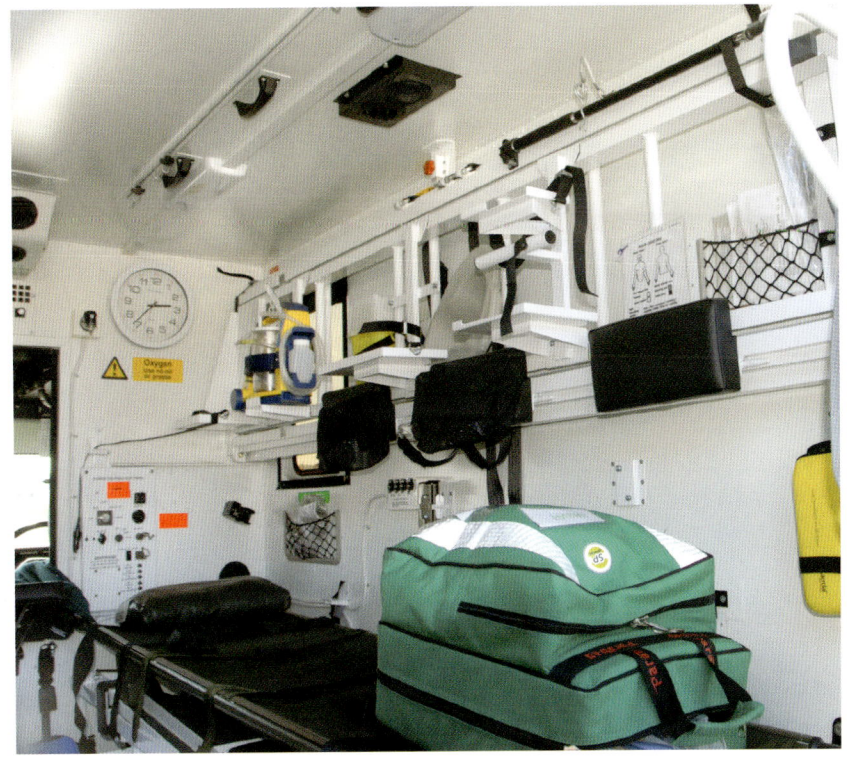

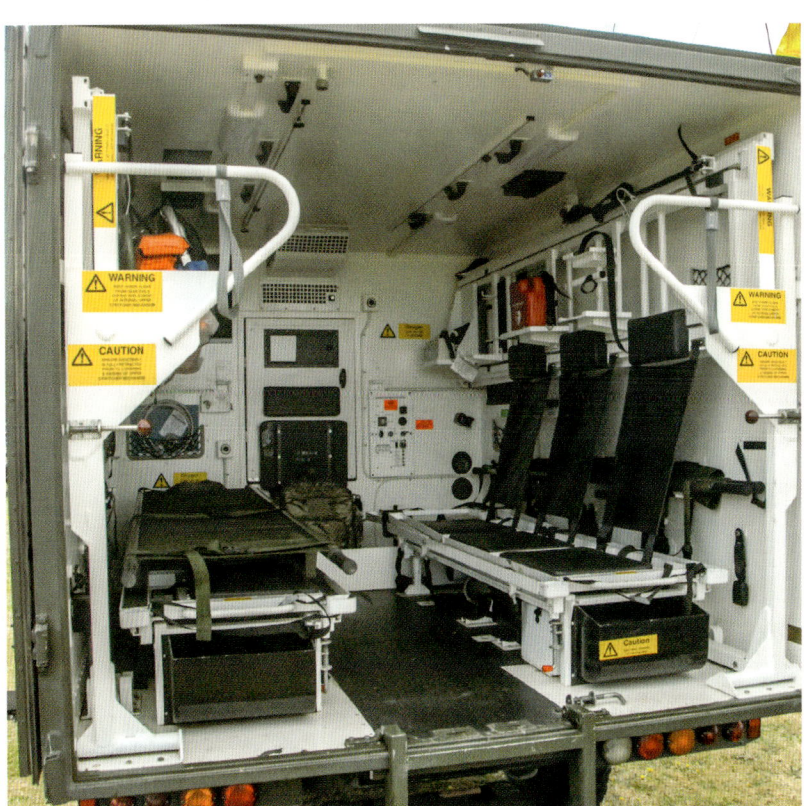

Above: This interior view shows the ambulance rigged for three sitting patients and one on a stretcher. The medical attendant's bag is stowed beneath the seat. (GF)

SUMMARY OF DELIVERIES, 1996 onwards

Tri-Service

Serials	Contract	Chassis nos	Total	Remarks
HE 09 AA to HF 58 AA	LV2B/179	100665 to 108188	150	BFA RHD non-EEGR
KX 79 AA to LB 73 AA	LV2B/179	108829 to 139010	395	BFA RHD EEGR
LB 74 AA to LC 18 AA	LV2B/179	108838 to 115075	45	BFA LHD EEGR
NF 10 AA to NF 32 AA	LV2B/179	139364 to 142637	23	BFA RHD EEGR; for RAF
NS 35 AA to NT 60 AA	LV2B/179	144279 to 148297	26	BFA RHD EEGR
NT 61 AA	LV2B/179	148204	1	BFA RHD EEGR
NT 62 AA to NT 70 AA	LV2B/179	148248 to 148240	9	BFA LHD EEGR
PR 39 AA to PR 49 AA	LV2B/179	153626 to 155886	11	BFA Tropical RHD
PR 50 AA to PR 85 AA	LV2B/179	157493 to 158783	36	BFA Winter/Water RHD
PR 90 AA and PR 91 AA	LV2B/179	154404 and 918919 *	2	BFA RHD EEGR
		Total	798	

Note: The total of 798 shown here excludes the seven BFA trials vehicles. Land Rover claimed publicly that they were to supply "around 800" BFAs. The last example delivered (PR 91 AA) has an odd serial number that suggests a July 1992 build date, although the VIN prefix indicates a 1996 model-year vehicle. It is possible that the vehicle was an updated Pulse prototype.

Below, background: An unusual view of a BFA. The Maltese Cross superimposed on the standard red cross was an exercise marking indicating an Opposing Force (OPFOR) vehicle. (DP)

Right, foreground: NF 27 AA is one of a batch purchased for the RAF. These were intended for tactical use, as the airfield role was fulfilled by a Steyr-Daimler-Puch Pinzgauer. This ambulance is in use by 4626 Aeromedical Evacuation Squadron, Royal Auxiliary Air Force. (DP)

Right: A Winterised and Waterproofed version of the BFA moves through Salisbury Plain during Exercise kush dragon in July 2008. This exercise was a Mission Rehearsal for Operation Herrick in Afghanistan. (AB)

KY 99 AA has been fitted with some anti-riot protection in the form of mesh screens and a bull bar, the latter possibly from an earlier Defender 130 Ambulance. All these are in-service modifications. (GF)

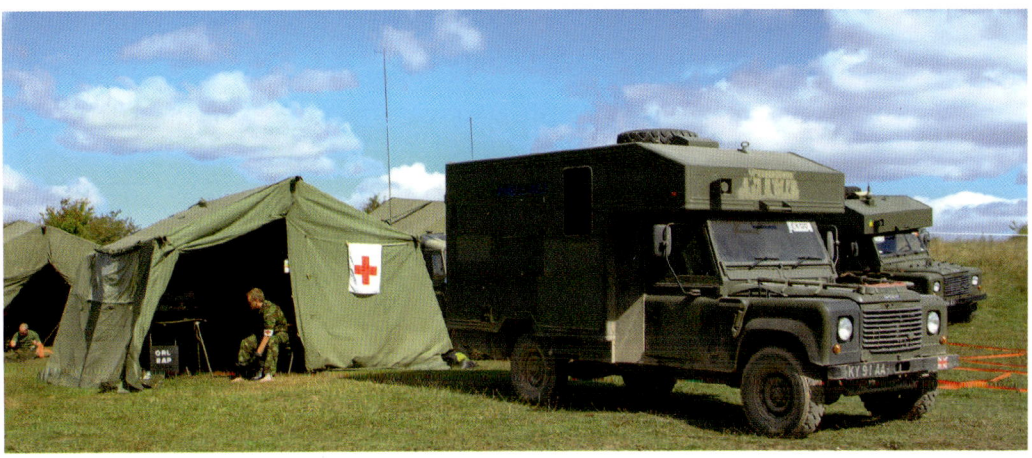

A pair of Ambulances standing awaiting the call outside the Regimental Aid Post of the Queen's Royal Lancers during Exercise Desert Dragon in 2006. Once again, there are panels where previous markings have been painted out; the one nearer the camera has a black panel around the off-side headlamp. (GF)

Technical specifications, Defender XD 130 models

Engine
2495cc turbocharged four-cylinder diesel with direct injection and 111bhp

Transmission
Permanent four-wheel drive with lockable centre differential
Five-speed manual main gearbox
Two-speed transfer gearbox
Axle ratio: 3.54:1

Suspension, steering and brakes
Coil springs all round
Worm and roller steering with power assistance
Disc brakes on all four wheels; servo assistance; separate drum-type transmission parking brake

Electrical system
12-volt with alternator

Dimensions
Overall length:	198in (5029mm)
Wheelbase:	127in (3226mm)
Overall width:	70.5in (1791mm)
Unladen height:	80.1in (2034mm)
Track:	58.5in (1486mm)

Unladen weights
TBA

Performance
No performance figures available.

Appendix A

MILITARY SERIAL NUMBERS

At first sight, the vehicle serial numbering system used by the British Armed Forces may appear impenetrable, but it is in fact very easy to understand. Three different systems were used for the vehicles covered in this book: one up to the end of 1981, the second from 1982 to 1994, and the third from 1994 to the present day.

First system to late 1981 (eg 21 FM 22)

This system uses six-digit numbers, consisting of two numbers, followed by two letters, followed by two more numbers.

The numbers are, in fact, a four-digit number that is split by the letter pair. So, for example, 00 EG 01 would be followed by 00 EG 02, and so on, up to 99 EG 99. (In practice, very few series actually used all 9999 numbers).

There was not necessarily any correlation between chassis number order and military serial number within batches. In army use, each letter pair indicated the financial year in which the vehicle was purchased (not necessarily the same as the year it entered service).

However, some letter pairs were reserved for special purposes. For example, AA to AZ were for the RAF, CC was a temporary allocation for vehicles awaiting bodywork, RN was for the Royal Navy, and the XA to XZ series were reserved for the Berlin Garrison.

In RAF use, the letter pair was not an indicator of the year in which a vehicle was purchased, or entered service. As with the Army system, there was not necessarily any correlation between chassis number order and military serial number within batches.

The Royal Navy letter pair RN was used in exactly the same way as the Army and RAF letter pairs, but this single letter pair allowed for a total of 9999 vehicles. As a result, the Royal Navy re-used the numbers from vehicles taken out of service. It is therefore obvious that Royal Navy serial numbers were not used to date either the contract or the entry into service. As with the Army and RAF systems, there was not necessarily any correlation between chassis number order and military serial number within batches.

The Berlin Garrison did not allocate serial letters in any particular sequence, but simply filled whatever gaps were available in the existing 'X' registers. To coincide with the introduction of tri-service allocation with KA for the rest of the Army (see below), XK was used. When the Berlin Garrison closed in 1994, some of its vehicles were re-serialled under the Tri-Service system then in use.

The Army letter pairs relevant to vehicles in this book (all were Range Rovers) and their issue dates were as follows:

FM	1972-1973	GT	1977-1978
GB	1973-1974	GX	1977-1978
GF	1974-1975	HF	1978-1979
GN	1976-1977	XB	(Berlin); not dated

KA	December 1981	KH	June 1988
KB	August 1982	KJ	September 1989
KC	December 1983	KK	July 1990
KD	July 1984	KL	December 1992
KF	November 1985	KM	Introduced 1996 for serials allocated "on behalf of Equipment Managers"
KG	October 1986	XK	(Berlin); introduced 1982 but not otherwise dated

Unified system, 1982-1993 (eg 31 KB 18)

At the end of 1981, all three services switched to using a common, or unified, system. This system (also known as the Tri-Service system) followed the pattern already established by army serials, and began at 00 KA 01. Once 99 KA 99 was reached, 00 KB 01 followed immediately, and so on. Each letter pair could be used to identify the approximate date when the vehicle was purchased (which was not necessarily the same as the date when it entered service), but the pairs were not tied to calendar years in the same way as before. The letters relevant to vehicles in this book are shown below with their dates of first issue.

Note that there was also one 'locally-issued' series that conformed to this pattern. This was used in Iraq, where MND (SE), the Multi-National Division (South East), used the series 00 MD 01 to 99 MD 99.

New unified system, from 1993 (eg HH 06 AA)

A new unified or Tri-Service system was introduced in September 1993. This again consisted of six digits. The six digits consisted of two letters, followed by two numbers, followed by two more letters. The serials began at AA 01 AA, which was followed by AA 02 AA and continued up to AA 99 AA, when the next serial was AA 01 AB. The first serials in the AB sequence were issued in 2004. There was also a 'locally issued' series, that conformed to this pattern. In Kosovo, serials between UK 00 ZZ and UK 999 ZZ were allocated. Some of the vehicles that attracted these were later transferred to the standard 'Census' system.

Two different chassis numbering systems were used on the vehicles covered in this book. The earlier one (which in practice only applies to Range Rovers) depended on a three-digit identifying prefix, and was used until 1979. From 1979, all Land Rovers carried standardised VINs.

The Land Rover model-year typically began in September and continued until the end of the following July, leaving August clear for the works' annual holiday and for preparing the assembly lines to take new models. A Land Rover (or Range Rover) built in the 1978 model-year could therefore have been built at any time between September 1977 and July 1978.

Three-digit identifiers

The three-digit identifying prefix in the chassis number indicated the model type, steering position and other factors. Neither the model-year nor the calendar-year of manufacture was indicated. The three-figure prefix was followed by a five-figure serial number that began at 00001 for each separate sequence, and this in turn was followed by a suffix letter. The suffix letter indicated modifications which affected the mechanical specification. So a typical code might be 355-10536D. (Note that the hyphen is not shown on the vehicle's chassis plate or documentation, but is used here to make interpretation of the numbers easier.)

355	Range Rover, home market
358	Range Rover, LHD, export

VINs

From 1 November 1979, the Land Rover chassis numbering system changed to conform to internationally-agreed VIN (Vehicle Identification Number) code standards. It is probable that some vehicles built in October 1979 also had these codes. Those used for the first year (i.e. 1980 model-year) had 14 characters and began with the letters LB. From 1 November 1980, three further characters (SAL) were added to the prefix, making 17 characters in all.

In the beginning, a single sequential serial numbering system, beginning at 100001, was used for all types. However, the system became more complex later when individual types were given their own number sequences. This enabled sequences to be re-used for different models; so, for example, the 900000 series that was used for Discovery II models from 1998 had been used for Defenders between 1991 and 1996. Although it is therefore possible for two vehicles to have the same serial number, the full VIN will be different because of the different prefix codes.

A theoretical example of the 17-digit VIN is SALLDAAA1AA-123456. This breaks down as follows:

SAL	Manufacturer code (ie Land Rover)
LD	Land Rover Ninety, One Ten or One Two Seven
	LH - Range Rover (first generation)
	LJ - Discovery (first generation)
	LK - Llama (prototypes only)
A	100-inch wheelbase (Range Rover), or Defender 90 XD, or Standard (from approximately 2000)

B - One Ten heavy-duty, or Defender 110 XD
C - Defender 130 XD
G - Discovery (first or second generation)
H - Defender 110, or Defender 110 XD, or Llama
K - Defender 130
R - One Ten or Defender 110 with military specification
S - One Ten V8 with military specification
V - Ninety or Defender 90

A Utility body (Soft Top, truck cab or Hard Top), or Two-door Range Rover (diesel), or Three-door Discovery, or Standard (from approximately 2000)
B - Two-door Range Rover, or Short-wheelbase (90) Station Wagon, or Three-door Discovery
F - Four-door Crew Cab (not HCPU)
H - HCPU on 110 or 130
M - Long-wheelbase (110) Station Wagon, or Four-door Range Rover, or Five-door Discovery
W - Truck cab (Defender 130 only)

A 2.5-litre diesel engine
B - 2.5-litre Diesel Turbo
C - 2.5-litre naturally aspirated diesel
D - 2.25-litre petrol, or 2.5-litre petrol
E - 2.4-litre VM diesel
F - 2.5-litre 200Tdi diesel, no EGR or catalyst
G - 2.25-litre diesel
H - 2.25-litre petrol
K - 2.5-litre Tdi diesel, with EGR and/or catalyst
L - 3.5-litre V8 with injection
M - 3.9-litre V8
N - 2.5-litre VM diesel
V - 3.5-litre V8 carburettor
5 - 2.5-litre Td5 diesel
6 - 2.5-litre 300Tdi diesel with EGR and/or catalyst
7 - 2.5-litre Td5 diesel with EGR but no catalyst (Defender)

8 - 2.5-litre Td5 diesel with EGR and catalyst
9 - 2.5-litre Td5 with EGR but no catalyst (Discovery II)

1 RHD with 4-speed manual gearbox
2 - LHD with 4-speed manual gearbox
3 - RHD automatic
4 - LHD automatic
7 - RHD with 5-speed manual gearbox
8 - LHD with 5-speed manual gearbox

A Used for all models up to 1985
B - 1985-1987 One Ten and Ninety, or 1985-model Range Rover
C - 1986-model Range Rover
D - 1987-model Range Rover
E - 1988 model-year
F - 1989 model-year
G - 1990 model-year
H - 1991 model-year
J - 1992 model-year
K - 1993 model-year
L - 1994 model-year
M - 1995 model-year
T - 1996 model-year
V - 1997 model-year
W - 1998 model-year
X - 1999 model-year
Y - 2000 model-year
1 - 2001 model-year
2 - 2002 model-year
3 - 2003 model-year
4 - 2004 model-year
5 - 2005 model-year
6 - 2006 model-year
7 - 2007 model-year

A Assembled at Solihull, UK

Index

Glossary

ACE	Allied Commander Europe (in car specification) Active Cornering Enhancement	EW	Electronic Warfare	MAW	Mountain and Arctic Warfare
		FFR	Fitted For Radio	MERLIN	A Vehicle Asset Control Computer System
		FRY	Former Republic of Yugoslavia		
AMF (L)	ACE Mobile Force (Land) APV Armoured Patrol Vehicle	FV	Fighting Vehicle	MIJA	Mobile Interceptor/Jammer
		GPMG	General Purpose Machine Gun	MOG	Media Operations Group
ARRC	Allied Rapid Reaction Corps	Granby	Operational name given to military operations during the 1991 Gulf War.	MND(SE)	Multi-National Division (South East)
ATTURM	Amphibious Trials and Training Unit, Royal Marine			MPGS	Military Provost Guard Service
				MRS	Mountain Rescue Service
		GRP	Glass Reinforced Plastic	MRV	Mini Radar Van
BAEE	British Army Equipment Exhibition	GS	General Service	MRV-P	Multi-Role Vehicle - Protected
BAOR	British Army of the Rhine	GVW	Gross Vehicle Weight	MSP	Medium Stressed Platform
BFA	Battlefield Ambulance	HCPU	High Capacity Pickup (Body)	MVEE	Military Vehicles and Engineering Establishment
BMLO	British Military Liaison Officer	Herrick	Operational name given to military operations in Afghanistan after 2002		
CAV	Composite Armoured Vehicle			OUVS	Operational Utility Vehicle System
CL	Civilian	HS	High Specification	Pulse	Ambulance variant of Wolf
COTS	Commercial Off-The-Shelf	IED	Improvised Explosive Device	RARDE	Royal Armament Research and Development Establishment
DERA	Defence Evaluation and Research Agency	IFOR	Implementation Force (in FRY)		
		JAMES	Joint Asset Management and Engineering Solutions (Computer System)	REME	Royal Electrical and Mechanical Engineers
DRA	Defence Research Agency			Remus	Life Extension Programme for Wolf XD
DROPS	Demountable Rack and Offload and Pickup System	JEWCS	Joint Electronic Warfare Core Staff	Resolute	Operational name given to military operations in support of the Dayton Accord in FRY
		LEP	Life Extension Programme		
DSG	Defence Support Group	LP	Local Purchase		
EEGR	Engine Exhaust Gas Recycling	LPPV	Light Protected Patrol Vehicle		
EUFOR	European Force (in FRY)	NK	Not Known		

SAAS	Service Attaché and Adviser Service	
SACEUR	Supreme Allied Commander Europe	
SAS	Special Air Service	
SDP	Steyr-Daimler-Puch	
SFOR	Stabilisation Force (in FRY)	
SUV IPT	Specialist and Utility Vehicles Integrated Project Team	
Telic	Operational name given to military operations in Iraq after 2003	
Tithonus	Life Extension Programme for Defender 110s	
TUH	Truck, Utility, Heavy	
TUL	Truck, Utility, Light	
TUM	Truck, Utility, Medium	
TUM (HD)	Truck, Utility, Medium (Heavy Duty)	
UOR	Urgent Operational Requirement	
VPK	Vehicle Protection Kit	
VIN	Vehicle Identification Number	
WMIK	Weapons Mount Installation Kit	
Wolf	XD variant of basic Defender	
XD	eXtra Duty